INTERNATIONAL PERSPECTIVES ON CYBERBULLYING

INTERNATIONAL PERSPECTIVES ON CYBERBULLYING

Edited by:

Marko Nikolić

SOCIETY Publishing

www.societypublishing.com

International Perspectives on Cyberbullying

Marko Nikolić

Society Publishing
2010 Winston Park Drive,
2nd Floor
Oakville, ON L6H 5R7
Canada
www.societypublishing.com
Tel: 001-289-291-7705
001-905-616-2116
Fax: 001-289-291-7601
Email: orders@arclereducation.com

ISBN: 978-1-77361-534-9 (Hardcover)

DECLARATION

Some content or chapters in this book are open access copyright free published research work, which is published under Creative Commons License and are indicated with the citation. We are thankful to the publishers and authors of the content and chapters as without them this book wouldn't have been possible.

ABOUT THE EDITOR

Marko obtained his Master's degree from University of Belgrade - Faculty of Law in 2014. He specialized in Criminal Law, Family Law and Environmental Law. He spent his Master year studying about international child abduction. He is currently employed in Ministry of Defense's Legal Department.

TABLE OF CONTENTS

LIST OF CONTRIBUTORS

Chantal Faucher
Centre for Education, Law and Society, Simon Fraser University, 5288-13450-102 Avenue, Surrey, BC, Canada V3T 0A3

Margaret Jackson
School of Criminology, Simon Fraser University, 8888 University Drive, Burnaby, BC, Canada V5A 1S6

Wanda Cassidy
Faculty of Education, Simon Fraser University, 8888 University Drive, Burnaby, BC, Canada V5A 1S6

Lucie Corcoran
School of Arts, Dublin Business School, Dublin 2, Ireland

Conor Mc Guckin
School of Education, Trinity College Dublin, Dublin 2, Ireland

Garry Prentice
School of Arts, Dublin Business School, Dublin 2, Ireland

Li Qing
Department of Educational Technology and Literacy, College of Education, Towson, USA

Francisco Caravaca Sánchez
Department of Social and Health Sciences, University of Murcia, 30100 Campus of Espinardo, Murcia, Spain

María Falcón Romero
Department of Social and Health Sciences, University of Murcia, 30100 Campus of Espinardo, Murcia, Spain

Javier Navarro-Zaragoza
Department of Social and Health Sciences, University of Murcia, 30100 Campus of Espinardo, Murcia, Spain

Aurelio Luna Ruiz-Cabello
Department of Social and Health Sciences, University of Murcia, 30100 Campus of Espinardo, Murcia, Spain

Oriali Rodriges Frantzisko
Department of Social and Health Sciences, University of Murcia, 30100 Campus of Espinardo, Murcia, Spain

Aurelio Luna Maldonado
Department of Social and Health Sciences, University of Murcia, 30100 Campus of Espinardo, Murcia, Spain

Niels C.L. Jacobs
Faculty of Psychology and Educational Sciences, Open University The Netherlands, Valkenburgerweg 177, 6419 AT Heerlen, The Netherlands

Linda Goossens
Faculty of Psychology and Educational Sciences, Open University The Netherlands, Valkenburgerweg 177, 6419 AT Heerlen, The Netherlands

Francine Dehue
Faculty of Psychology and Educational Sciences, Open University The Netherlands, Valkenburgerweg 177, 6419 AT Heerlen, The Netherlands

Trijntje Völlink
Faculty of Psychology and Educational Sciences, Open University The Netherlands, Valkenburgerweg 177, 6419 AT Heerlen, The Netherlands

Lilian Lechner
Faculty of Psychology and Educational Sciences, Open University The Netherlands, Valkenburgerweg 177, 6419 AT Heerlen, The Netherlands

Tanrikulu
Department of Psychological Counseling and Guidance, Fatih University, Istanbul, Turkey

Taskin
Department of Psychological Counseling and Guidance, Fatih University, Istanbul, Turkey

Tom Harrison
Jubilee Centre for Character and Virtues, School of Education, University of Birmingham, Birmingham B15 2TT, UK

Tuija Muhonen
Centre for Work Life and Evaluation Studies, Malmö University, Malmö, Sweden and Department of Urban Studies, Faculty of Culture and Society, Malmö University, Malmö, Sweden

Sandra Jönsson
Centre for Work Life and Evaluation Studies, Malmö University, Malmö, Sweden and Department of Urban Studies, Faculty of Culture and Society, Malmö University, Malmö, Sweden

Martin Bäckström
Department of Psychology, Lund University, Lund, Sweden

Zsa Zsa Tajol Asanan
Faculty of Business and Management, Asia Pacific University of Technology and Innovation, Kuala Lumpur, Malaysia

Ibiwani Alisa Hussain
Faculty of Business and Management, Asia Pacific University of Technology and Innovation, Kuala Lumpur, Malaysia

Nooraneda Mutalip Laidey
Faculty of Business and Management, Asia Pacific University of Technology and Innovation, Kuala Lumpur, Malaysia

Ross King, Rebecca Moorfoot
School of Psychology, Deakin University, Victoria, Australia

Mary Kotronakis
School of Psychology, Deakin University, Victoria, Australia

Sukma Ari Ragil Putri
University of 17 Agustus 1945 Surabaya, FISIP Untag Surabaya, Jl. Semolowaru No. 45 Surabaya, Indonesia

A.A.I Prihandari Satvikadewi
University of 17 Agustus 1945 Surabaya, FISIP Untag Surabaya, Jl. Semolowaru No. 45 Surabaya, Indonesia

Ming-Shinn Lee
Department of Curriculum Design and Human Potentials Development, National Dong Hwa University, Hualien, Taiwan

Wu Zi-Pei
Department of Curriculum Design and Human Potentials Development, National Dong Hwa University, Hualien, Taiwan

Leif Svanstrom
Department of Public Health Science, Karolinska Institutet, Stockholm, Sweden

Koustuv Dalal
Centre for Injury Prevention and Safety Promotion (CIPSP), School of Health and Medical Sciences, O¨ rebro University, O¨ rebro, Sweden

Eveline A. Crone
Department of Psychology, Faculty of Social Sciences, Leiden University, Wassenaarseweg 52, 2333AK Leiden, Netherlands

Elly A. Konijn
Department of Communication Science, Media Psychology, Vrije Universiteit Amsterdam, De Boelelaan 1105, 1081 HV Amsterdam, Netherlands

Anastasia Apostolides
Department of Christian Spirituality, Church History and Missiology, University of South Africa, South Africa

Jacob Amedie
Santa Clara University

José A. Álvarez-Bermejo
Department of Informatics, Universidad de Almería, Almería, Spain

Luis J. Belmonte-Ureña
Department of Economy and Business, Universidad de Almería, Almería, Spain

Africa Martos-Martínez
Department of Psychology, Universidad de Almería, Almería, Spain

Ana B. Barragán-Martín
Department of Psychology, Universidad de Almería, Almería, Spain

María del Mar Simón-Marquez
Department of Psychology, Universidad de Almería, Almería, Spain

César Arroyo López
Asociación Socioeducativa Llere, Toledo, Spain

Roberto Moreno López
University of Castilla—La Mancha, Talavera de la Reina, Spain

Francine Dehue
Faculty of Psychology, Open University, Valkenburgerweg 177, 6419 AT Heerlen, The Netherlands

Lola F. Tatarinova
"Turan" University, Kazakhstan

Karimzhan N. Shakirov
Al-Farabi Kazakh National University, Kazakhstan

Danila V. Tatarinov
Al-Farabi Kazakh National University, Kazakhstan

LIST OF ABBREVIATIONS

IM	Intervention Mapping
POs	Performance objectives
PaS	Pleasure at school
RE(B)T	Rational Emotive (Behavioral) Therapy
APS	Active Problem Solving
Cos	Change Objectives DT, Dynamic Tailoring
ST	Static Tailoring
RCT	Randomized Control Trial
YSR	Youth Self-Report.

PREFACE

Virtual violence carries potential, real consequences, and the average person becomes increasingly attached to this imaginary world. Therefore, a person becomes more and more exposed, and in many ways dependent on the Internet. Not long ago, clumsy attempts at fraud were the only threats online. In just a blink of an eye, social networks started to be the center of social events, and payments and purchases became inextricably linked to the global web. Naturally, in a moment when a big part of life moves to a new field, that brings along its negative sides as well. Crime accompanies the advancement of modern technologies because deviants are exposed to social trends and fast global changes as well.

The problem is not just generational or spatial, although it is possible to identify groups that are more likely to be endangered. Cyberbullying is an emerging issue in the context of higher education as information and communication technologies (ICT) increasingly become part of the daily life of the university. The paper in the first chapter presents findings from 1925 student surveys from four Canadian universities.

The explanations are certainly diverse and, of course, we should not keep ourselves grounded in an area that is continually evolving. In the second chapter, we will deal with the question of how to appropriately conceptualize peer-to-peer abuse in a cyber context. The very beginning of cyberbullying can have roots in harmless phenomena. Since violence is committed in a virtual world, perpetrators are not aware that someone could actually be hurt. Chapter 3 has a focus on how gaming interacts with cyberbullying and bullying. In addition, it creates a model grounded in enactivism to help us identify future areas of research and develop effective cyberbullying prevention programs.

If we single out younger children as a vulnerable group, the focus should be on the schools and whether they will have the same mechanisms to protect their students from the cyber reality. Next chapter deals with the consequences of cyber-teasing, although at the student level, these issues can equally apply to younger children as well.

The next chapter gives a modern theoretical explanation for the cyberbullying. Information about cyberbullying is presented in the study first, and then, the general views on the choice theory concerning human nature. Finally, there are evaluations of cyberbullying regarding the concepts of choice theory, such as basic needs, Quality World, successful and unsuccessful identity, choice and responsibility. In the later chapters, we will evaluate forms, awareness and moral reasoning against cyberbullying among youth and its consequences in working life. Since all forms of violence are present in all spheres of new networks, we will examine the example of the phenomenon of cyber violence on the Instagram.

We dedicate one separated chapter to the study that aimed to explore the effectiveness of the cyberbullying prevention WebQuest course implementation. Systematic abuse of power can be divided into six types: verbal-bullying, physical-bullying, sexual-bullying, social-bullying, defensive-bullying, and cyberbullying. Violent violence is just one of the forms, but it also has social, emotional, mental health and academic effects, and it can endanger the life of the victim. After that, we will deal with spiritual effects that children and youth may experience as a result of cyberbullying, and especially the most tragic consequence of this type of violent behavior.

We will finish with a description of an intervention that aims to reduce the number of cyberbully victims and their symptoms of depression and anxiety. The program goal is to teach victims how to cope in an adequate and effective manner with cyberbully incidents. Our last chapter deals with the criminological view on this topic. Comprehensive analysis of the criminological characteristics of computer crimes, which is the aim of this study, provides an opportunity to identify the motives of these crimes to determine the most effective ways to reduce them, as well as to work out the best ways and investigation means of criminal cases in this category. Since these are developing technologies with growing number of users, we need to develop skills for dealing with their negative aspects as well.

CHAPTER 1

CYBERBULLYING AMONG UNIVERSITY STUDENTS: GENDERED EXPERIENCES, IMPACTS, AND PERSPECTIVES

Chantal Faucher,[1] Margaret Jackson,[2] and Wanda Cassidy[3]

[1]Centre for Education, Law and Society, Simon Fraser University, 5288-13450-102 Avenue, Surrey, BC, Canada V3T 0A3

[2]School of Criminology, Simon Fraser University, 8888 University Drive, Burnaby, BC, Canada V5A 1S6

[3]Faculty of Education, Simon Fraser University, 8888 University Drive, Burnaby, BC, Canada V5A 1S6

ABSTRACT

Cyberbullying is an emerging issue in the context of higher education as information and communication technologies (ICT) increasingly become part of daily life in university. This paper presents findings from 1925 student

Citation: Chantal Faucher, Margaret Jackson, and Wanda Cassidy, "Cyberbullying among University Students: Gendered Experiences, Impacts, and Perspectives," Education Research International, vol. 2014, Article ID 698545, 10 pages, 2014. https://doi.org/10.1155/2014/698545.

surveys from four Canadian universities. The overall findings are broken down to determine gender similarities and differences that exist between male and female respondents' backgrounds, ICT usage, experiences with cyberbullying, opinions about the issue, and solutions to the problem. We also examine the continuities between these findings and those of earlier studies on cyberbullying among younger students. Our findings also suggest that gender differences, which do emerge, provide some support for each of the three theoretical frameworks considered for understanding this issue, that is, relational aggression, cognitive-affective deficits, and power and control. However, none of these three models offers a full explanation on its own. The study thus provides information about cyberbullying behaviour at the university level, which has the potential to inform the development of more appropriate policies and intervention programs/solutions to address the gendered nature of this behaviour.

INTRODUCTION

Over the last several years, both youth and adults have benefited from the advancement of information and communication technologies (ICT), including increased access to the Internet and mobile phones. Research on the relationship between "emerging adults" and ICT suggests that gender differences exist. It appears that young women are more involved than young men in emailing, social networking, and texting [1–3]. Young women's use of blogs, instant messaging, social networking, and so forth is marked by expressive language, with considerably more emotional content [4]; in some cases, it helps with their psychosocial development and social adjustment [5, 6]. According to research by Miltsov [7], even heavy Internet use (30 or more hours per week) does not detract from women's wellbeing, although the same is not true for men's wellbeing. On the other hand, research by Chen and Tzeng [8] suggests that it is the type of usage, rather than the amount, which is a better predictor of academic success and psychosocial adjustment. Further, the mobility of the devices can be more gratifying for young women who "may feel stronger ties to their cell phone than college aged [sic] males because it allows for independence to pursue their own interests while also being immediately accessible when they are needed by family members or friends" [9, page 2179].

Along with the advantages come certain disadvantages or risks, including the one that is the focus of this paper: cyberbullying. We start from our understanding of cyberbullying at the middle school and high school levels and move into a newer area of research, cyberbullying at the university level. Cyberbullying at the university level can be seen as a bridge in the continuum of this behaviour from childhood and youth into adulthood. Cyberbullying scholarship has begun to examine the continuities between the cyberbullying occurring in the K-12 sector, universities, workplaces, and beyond [10–17]. In this paper, we examine data from an ongoing study of cyberbullying at the university level and consider the gendered differences in university students' involvement with ICT and cyberbullying, their perspectives on cyberbullying, and solutions to the problem. Through this examination, we consider three theoretical frameworks that may be used to help explain these differences.

THEORETICAL PERSPECTIVES

Cyberbullying and Gender

Research suggests that females are more likely to be on the receiving end of cyberbullying than they are with traditional face-to-face bullying [18–21] and that new forms of sexual and gender harassment, such as "sexting," "morphing," "virtual rape," and "revenge porn," have emerged [22–26]. Some of the differences between face-to-face bullying and cyberbullying serve to exacerbate the impacts of the cyberbullying on victims. The longer "shelf life" of cyberbullying text or images, for example, can place the victim in harm's way for longer periods of time compared to face-to-face bullying. Previous studies of middle and high school students have found higher proportions of girls reporting that they have been victims of cyberbullying [19, 27–29]. Females are also more likely to be perpetrators of cyberbullying primarily targeting other females, sometimes within their "friendship groups" [19, 22, 26, 28, 30–32].

Three theoretical frameworks may assist us in understanding cyberbullying at the university level: relational aggression, deficits in affective and cognitive empathy, and the Power and Control model.

The relational aggression perspective is one that describes girls' bullying behaviour as being more covert and secretive than is true of boys' bullying behaviour. Relational aggression seeks to damage or disrupt friendships, group inclusion, or social status through such tactics as rumours, gossip, and slander [33]. The anonymity of the Internet therefore fits well with the girls' preferred "style" of bullying [19, 22, 34, 35]. The types of ICT usage described above for emerging adult women are also in line with a relational perspective.

The affective and cognitive deficits perspective has been used to explain boys' involvement [36]. In assessing its applicability to adults, we should consider that women generally have higher scores on measures of empathy [37] and greater ability with nonverbal skills, for example, identifying emotions and noticing paralinguistic cues such as changes in voice intonation and facial differences [3, 9]. As such, cyberbullying involvement may be impacted by

- the fact that online exchanges do not always immediately provide the feedback on the impact of one's words or actions, which is often useful in eliciting empathy;
- the fact that changes in voice tone and body language are not available in online exchanges, which may level the playing field for women whose superior language skills rest on the ability to decode those cues.

A third perspective to consider when examining the dynamic of cyberbullying is the Power and Control model [38]. This model is borrowed from the field of intimate partner violence but may assist in understanding cyberbullying that occurs in the university context where power imbalances exist between faculty and students, as well as between students in dating relationships, and/or between students of different ages and levels. There has also been research documenting the online components of intimate partner violence between college-aged individuals [39–43]. The model uses a Power and Control Wheel, which sets out the various elements that constitute abuse. Those elements that relate closely to cyberbullying abuse are those that use intimidation and threats, harmful language, social standing, exclusion, harassment, and technology to send unwanted messages, all within a relationship in which the abuser exerts control over the victim.

As a preliminary exercise, it is our intention in this paper to consider the relevance of these three theoretical models when examining our research findings on gender and cyberbullying at the university level.

Cyberbullying in Higher Education

Cyberbullying research has exploded in recent years but has for the most part been focused on cyberbullying behaviours at the middle school and high school levels (see Cassidy et al. [44] for a comprehensive review of this literature). Researchers, such as our team, are now looking into the continuation of this problem after high school, into postsecondary education, including the body of work about cyberbullying in the workplace.

The term "cyberbullying" may have a juvenile connotation, which is at odds with assumptions about adult behaviour. However, the types of threatening, degrading, harassing, and intimidating behaviours that adults undertake do fit within the scope of cyberbullying. Cyberbullying refers to online exchanges where there is an intent to harm the recipient. Currently "cyberbullying" is the term most often used when describing relevant behaviour at the university level [11–13, 16, 17, 45–60], as well as in the workplace [14, 15, 61–63], although other terms are also used. For example, online or cyberharassment has been used [10, 41, 64–66], as have cyberstalking [24, 39, 65] and technology-based sexual coercion [43].

Studies conducted to date on cyberbullying at the university level have documented highly variable prevalence rates for victimization and perpetration. The variations may be partially accounted for by differing definitions of cyberbullying, time frames, and methodologies. Table 1 summarizes the prevalence rates reported in these studies.

Table 1: Cyberbullying prevalence rates found in previous studies of undergraduate students

Study	n	Reported cyber-victimization (%)	Reported cyber-perpetration (%)
Beran et al. [10]	1368	8.6	4.1
Dilmaç [47]	666	55.3	22.5
Englander [13]	—	8	3
Finn [65]	339	10–15	—
Lindsay and Krysik [66]	420	43.3	—
Molluzzo and Lawler [48]	121	7	10
Schenk and Fremouw [49]	799	8.6	—
Turan et al. [51]	579	59.8	—
Walker et al. [52]	120	11	—
Wensley and Campbell [53]	528	11.6	3.8
Zalaquett and Chatters [17]	613	19	5
Zhang et al. [54]	134	62	40

Two Turkish studies specifically examined gender differences in cyberbullying among postsecondary students. Akbulut and Eristi [45] found that male students were more likely to be both cyberbully victims

For instance, both genders generally agreed that they would like to help create a more kind and respectful online world and that they would report cyberbullying if they could do it anonymously. The vast majority disagreed (somewhat or strongly) with the statement "Cyberbullying cannot hurt you; it's just words in virtual space."

However, there were responses to a few statements where gender differences emerged. Males were more likely than females to disagree (44% versus 38%) with the statement "It is the university's responsibility to stop or prevent on-line bullying." Female students were more likely than males to disagree with the statements "Cyberbullying is a normal part of the on-line world; it cannot be stopped" (47% versus 32%) and "I have the right to say anything I want on-line because of freedom of expression" (58% versus 43%).

While some gender differences in experiences with cyberbullying have been highlighted above, we found a relatively high degree of agreement between male and female students as far as solutions to the problem of cyberbullying at university. Respondents were provided with a list of 15 suggested solutions to cyberbullying at the university level and asked to rate their top five choices. Overall, the top five choices in descending order were to

- provide counselling/support services for cyberbullied victims;
- establish an anonymous phone-in line for reporting cyberbullying;
- develop a more respectful university culture where kind behaviour is modelled by all;
- suspend or expel students who participate in cyberbullying;
- engage the university community in developing a strong university anti-cyberbullying policy.

An analysis of the choices by gender revealed that male and female students both ranked these top five choices the highest; however, there were some variations in order. Counselling for victims was the number one choice for both male and female respondents. However, female students ranked the anonymous phone-in line second and policy third, while male students ranked a kinder culture second and the anonymous phone-in line third. Both groups ranked suspensions and expulsions fourth. Female students ranked a kinder culture fifth, whereas male students ranked policy fifth.

DISCUSSION AND CONCLUSION

The survey findings demonstrate the pervasiveness of ICT in the lives of university students. This starting point helps us to focus on the importance of the relationships and interactions that occur within this context. Well over 20% of student respondents to this survey have been victims of cyberbullying in the past 12 months. These numbers are consequential in making a case for cyberbullying as a key issue within the higher education context, just as it has been at the lower levels.

Continuity of Issue

We concur with the findings of Beran et al. [10] and Englander [13], as well as the suggestion made by others [11, 12, 15], that important continuities exist between cyberbullying at the lower levels of the education system and at university in terms of experiences, effects, and perceived solutions to the problem. Our findings suggest that same-gender targeting is more common than opposite-gender targeting, with females especially likely to target and be targeted by other females within their friendship groups. While this sort of cyberbullying is only one of the types of situations that arise, it is one that places cyberbullying at university on a continuum from what occurs among younger students, in middle and high school.

Female respondents in this study reported a wider range of ill effects stemming from their cyberbullying experiences than male respondents and they did so in greater numbers than the male respondents. Our earlier work also found that middle and high school girls were impacted by the cyberbullying they experienced to a greater degree than the boys [19, 27].

Female students were more likely to tell someone close to them about their cyberbullying experiences than were the males, but few respondents told university representatives about the cyberbullying. This finding too is consistent with what we noted among middle and high school students [19, 27, 28]. The majority would tell their friends, but far fewer would tell their parents and fewer still would tell school officials.

Also, in the survey responses about solutions to cyberbullying, we note that the anonymous phone line, which rates highly among university students, was also popular with the younger students [19, 27, 28].

Gender Differences

Female students responded to the survey in far greater numbers and also responded more readily to the calls for focus group volunteers than males. Male respondents tended to have a more hands-off attitude than the women, as demonstrated by their agreement with statements to the effect that cyberbullying is normal and that it is not the university's responsibility to stop or prevent it.

Male students were somewhat more likely to be targeted overall, but especially more likely to be targeted by someone they do not know and to be on the receiving end of extensive cyberbullying in a variety of online contexts. Also, based on our findings, male students are more likely to admit to cyberbullying others, whether other students or faculty members. Female students are more likely to be targeted by someone they thought was a friend and are also more likely to target their friends when they engage in cyberbullying, as was also found to be the case by Jackson et al. [19] with girls in grades 6 to 9.

Female respondents targeted by cyberbullying report a greater range of negative impacts on their academic and personal lives than do men and they are more likely than men to tell someone close to them if they have been targeted. The same finding also emerged from an earlier study of grade 6 to 9 students [19]. One possible explanation for the much higher survey participation level of women may be that, although they do not experience cyberbullying in greater numbers than men, they are more negatively impacted by it.

Gender-based targeting is reported by female respondents in addition to the other reasons for targeting reported by males as well. Shariff and Gouin [26] as well as Halder and Jaishankar [24] discuss the various forms of gender and sexual harassment to which girls and women are particularly vulnerable online. Cyberbullying is but one such category of the risks faced by women and girls online.

Theoretical Models

At the outset of this paper, we mentioned three theoretical models that may have some applicability to our understanding of cyberbullying at university. Each finds some initial support from our results, although no single model provides a full explanation of the variety of phenomena reported. Our findings suggest these models may be worthy of further in-depth study in subsequent research.

The relational aggression perspective addresses the relationships attacked by cyberbullying. Among the findings presented here, we note that the same-gender targeting, especially among female friendship groups, lends credence to this model for some of the university cyberbullying situations. Female students are more likely than males to experience cyberbullying over social networks and text messaging, suggesting a relationship between the victim and the person cyberbullying them. Female respondents' greater involvement with social media, notably with Facebook, does situate their ICT usage more firmly within the category of relationship-based usage. The research literature does suggest that this type of usage has many benefits for young women [4–7, 9]. On the other hand, when cyberbullying infiltrates these social media, young women are bound to be particularly affected.

Female respondents in our study also report that their relationships inside and outside the university have been impacted by the cyberbullying they have experienced. Such a finding is in accordance with the relational aggression perspective. It suggests that if the cyberbullying was intended to bring about friendship troubles, exclusion, or harm to reputations [33], it has been rather effective in reaching those goals.

The affective and cognitive empathy perspective suggests that males are involved in bullying to a greater extent due to lack of empathy for victims. We also see partial support for this model in some of the survey responses. Male students admit to engaging in cyberbullying in greater numbers than female students and they appear to be more aggressive than females when they are involved in cyberbullying as perpetrators. We noted more male respondents indicating intents such as humiliating, harassing, threatening, and wanting to hurt a faculty member or tarnish their reputation. Male students were also more likely than females to admit to engaging in cyberbullying as retaliation for prior bullying against them. Further, the opinions about cyberbullying expressed by the male respondents tended more towards cynicism than the females' opinions. For instance, "cyberbullying is normal, it cannot be stopped," and "freedom of expression means I can say anything I want online" were statements that garnered greater support among males than females. Furthermore, the empathy perspective may account for the higher female survey participation because even those who have not directly experienced the problem can see its potential harm.

The Power and Control model allows us to describe cyberbullying as a form of abuse where one party attempts to exert control over the other. Among the reasons cited by respondents for the cyberbullying they experienced, physical appearance, gender (for females), and ethnicity (for males) suggest that power dynamics may be at play in some of the exchanges. A small number of respondents also invoked "other" reasons and described cyberbullying as one of the ways in which power dynamics play out within the online gaming community. The intentions behind cyberbullying also suggest power and control: insulting, defaming, humiliating, harassing, threatening, and spreading rumours. Shariff and Gouin [26] also comment on the hierarchies of power, which exist in society and can manifest in a number of ways in online exchanges.

Additionally, however, there are significant parallels to be derived from the intimate partner violence literature, which are quite consistent with our own findings. From that research, it has been found that women are more concerned about their safety because of the abuse and experienced more serious harms resulting from the abuse than did male victims of abuse [70, 71]. Our own study results support those findings. Part of the issue, which emerges here, is the one of power and control. As noted above, one possible explanation for the much higher survey participation level of women may be that, although they do not experience cyberbullying in greater numbers than men, they are more negatively impacted by it. They do fear for their safety more than do the males. Such an explanation is also supported by our finding that female respondents were much more likely than male respondents to report having "unfriended" someone on Facebook for self-protection types of reasons. The emerging forms of online gender and sexual harassment may theoretically target male and female alike. However, the hierarchies of power in the online world seem to place women in a particularly vulnerable position, just as they do in the offline world [24, 26].

In the end, no one theoretical model may be adequate to explain those different gender dimensions of cyberbullying. But we have seen that it is important to consider the relationship issue, the cognitive-affective component, as well as the power and control dimension in order to understand more comprehensively the role gender differences play in the phenomenon itself. The consideration of the three perspectives represents an initial attempt to explain gender differences in cyberbullying at the university level.

This research represents a foundational step toward assisting university administrators and policymakers in their attempts to determine the nature, extent, and impacts of cyberbullying at the university level, as well as informing their development of more appropriate policies and intervention programs/solutions to address the gendered nature of this behaviour.

ACKNOWLEDGMENTS

The authors wish to express their gratitude to the students who completed the survey at the four institutions in this study. This work was supported by the Social Sciences and Humanities Research Council Standard Research Grant no. 401-2011-1800.

REFERENCES

1. B. M. Gucukoglu, M. Alsadi, M. Ocakdan, and F. Gürsul, "The effects of the social network sites on socialization: a survey study with the personal opinions and attitudes to socialization among university students," in Proceedings of the International Future-Learning Conference on Innovations in Learning for the Future: e-Learning, pp. 605–631, 2012.
2. F. T. McAndrew and H. S. Jeong, "Who does what on Facebook? Age, sex, and relationship status as predictors of Facebook use," Computers in Human Behavior, vol. 28, no. 6, pp. 2359–2365, 2012.
3. S. H. Thompson and E. Lougheed, "Frazzled by Facebook ? An exploratory study of gender differences in social network communication among undergraduate men and women," College Student Journal, vol. 46, no. 1, pp. 88–98, 2012.
4. A. B. Fox, D. Bukatko, M. Hallahan, and M. Crawford, "The medium makes a difference: gender similarities and differences in instant messaging," Journal of Language and Social Psychology, vol. 26, no. 4, pp. 389–397, 2007.
5. K. Davis, "Coming of age online: the developmental underpinnings of girls' blogs," Journal of Adolescent Research, vol. 25, no. 1, pp. 145–171, 2010.
6. C.-C. Yang and B. B. Brown, "Motives for using Facebook , patterns of Facebook activities, and late adolescents' social adjustment to college," Journal of Youth and Adolescence, vol. 42, no. 3, pp. 403–416, 2013.
7. A. Miltsov, "The internet in context: examining the interplay between internet use and personal well-being in New Brunswick," in Proceedings of the Annual Conference of the Canadian Sociological Association, Victoria, Canada, June 2013.
8. S.-Y. Chen and J.-Y. Tzeng, "College female and male heavy internet users' profiles of practices and their academic grades and psychosocial adjustment," Cyberpsychology, Behavior, and Social Networking, vol. 13, no. 3, pp. 257–262, 2010.
9. M. Grellhesl and N. M. Punyanunt-Carter, "Using the uses and gratifications theory to understand gratifications sought through text messaging practices of male and female undergraduate students," Computers in Human Behavior, vol. 28, no. 6, pp. 2175–2181, 2012.

10. T. N. Beran, C. Rinaldi, D. S. Bickham, and M. Rich, "Evidence for the need to support adolescents dealing with harassment and cyber-harassment: prevalence, progression, and impact," School Psychology International, vol. 33, no. 5, pp. 562–576, 2012.
11. S. Bauman, Cyberbullying: What Counselors Need to Know, American Counseling Association, Alexandria, Va, USA, 2011.
12. S. Bauman, "Research on cyberbullying: a lifespan perspective," in Keynote Presentation at International Conference on Cyberbullying: COST IS0801, Paris, France, June 2012.
13. E. K. Englander, "Cyberbullying and information exposure: user-generated content in post-secondary education," Paper 11, Massachusetts Aggression Research Center, Bridgewater, Mass, USA, 2008, http://vc.bridgew.edu/marc_pubs/11.
14. R. McKay, D. H. Arnold, J. Fratzl, and R. Thomas, "Workplace bullying in academia: a Canadian study," Employee Responsibilities and Rights Journal, vol. 20, no. 2, pp. 77–100, 2008.
15. S. C. McQuade, J. P. Colt, and N. B. B. Meyer, Cyber Bullying: Protecting Kids and Adults from Online Bullies, Praeger, Westport, Conn, USA, 2009.
16. H. Cowie, S. Bauman, I. Coyne, C. Myers, M. Pörhölä, and A. Almeida, "Cyberbullying among university students: an emergent cause for concern?" in Cyberbullying through the New Media: Findings from an International Network, P. K. Smith and G. Steffgen, Eds., pp. 165–177, Psychology Press, London, UK, 2013.
17. C. P. Zalaquett and S. J. Chatters, "Cyberbullying in college: frequency, characteristics, and practical implications," Sage Open, vol. 4, 2014.
18. J. J. Dooley, J. Pyzalski, and D. Cross, "Cyberbullying versus face-to-face bullying: a theoretical and conceptual review," Journal of Psychology, vol. 217, no. 4, pp. 182–188, 2009.
19. M. Jackson, W. Cassidy, and K. Brown, ""you were born ugly and youl die ugly too": cyber-bullying as relational aggression," In Education, vol. 15, no. 1, part 1, 2009.
20. R. M. Kowalski, C. A. Morgan, and S. P. Limber, "Traditional bullying as a potential warning sign of cyberbullying," School Psychology International, vol. 33, no. 5, pp. 505–519, 2012.
21. Q. Li, "New bottle but old wine: a research of cyberbullying in schools," Computers in Human Behavior, vol. 23, no. 4, pp. 1777–1791, 2007.

22. W. Cassidy, K. Brown, and M. Jackson, "'Under the radar': educators and cyberbullying in schools," School Psychology International, vol. 33, no. 5, pp. 520–532, 2012.
23. Coordinating Committee of Senior Officials (CCSO) Cybercrime Working Group, Cyberbullying and the Non-Consensual Distribution of Intimate Images, (Report to the Federal/Provincial/Territorial Ministers Responsible for Justice and Public Safety), Department of Justice, Canada, 2013, http://www.justice.gc.ca/eng/rp-pr/other-autre/cndii-cdncii/pdf/cndii-cdncii-eng.pdf.
24. D. Halder and K. Jaishankar, "Cyber socializing and victimization of women," Temida, vol. 12, no. 3, pp. 5–26, 2009.
25. S. Hinduja and J. W. Patchin, School Climate 2.0: Preventing Cyberbullying and Sexting One Classroom at a Time, Corwin, Thousand Oaks, Calif, USA, 2012.
26. S. Shariff and R. Gouin, "Cyber-Dilemmas: gendered hierarchies, free expression and cyber-safety in schools," in Proceedings of the Oxford Internet Institute International Conference Safety and Security in a Networked World, Oxford, UK, September 2005.
27. W. Cassidy, M. Jackson, and K. N. Brown, "Sticks and stones can break my bones, but how can pixels hurt me?: students' experiences with cyber-bullying," School Psychology International, vol. 30, no. 4, pp. 383–402, 2009.
28. W. Cassidy, K. Brown, and M. Jackson, "Moving from cyber-bullying to cyber-kindness: what do students, educators and parents say?" in Youth Culture and Net Culture: Online Social Practices, E. Dunkels, G.-M. Franberg, and C. Hallgren, Eds., pp. 256–277, Information Science Reference, Hershey, NY, USA, 2011.
29. A. Paglia-Boak, E. M. Adlaf, H. A. Hamilton, J. H. Beitchman, D. Wolfe, and R. E. Mann, The Mental Health and Well-Being of Ontario Students, 1991–2011: Detailed OSDUHS Findings, CAMH Research Document Series 34, Centre for Addiction and Mental Health, Toronto, Canada, 2012.
30. R. M. Kowalski and S. P. Limber, "Electronic bullying among middle school students," Journal of Adolescent Health, vol. 41, no. 6, pp. S22–S30, 2007.
31. P. K. Smith, J. Mahdavi, M. Carvalho, and N. Tippett, An investigation into cyber bullying, its forms, awareness and impact, and the

relationship between age and gender in cyber bullying (A report to th e Anti-Bullying Alliance), 2006, http://webarchive.nationalarchives.gov.uk/20130401151715/https://www.education.gov.uk/publications/eOrderingDownload/RBX03-06.pdf.

32. R. S. Tokunaga, "Following you home from school: a critical review and synthesis of research on cyberbullying victimization," Computers in Human Behavior, vol. 26, no. 3, pp. 277–287, 2010.
33. N. Crick, N. Werner, J. Casas et al., "Childhood aggression and gender: a new look at an old problem," in Proceedings of the Nebraska Symposium on Motivation, D. Bernstein, Ed., pp. 75–141, University of Nebraska Press, Lincoln, Neb, USA, 1999.
34. P. K. Smith, "Cyberbullying and cyber aggression," in Handbook of School Violence and School Safety: International Research and Practice, S. R. Jimerson, A. B. Nickerson, M. J. Mayer, and M. J. Furlong, Eds., pp. 93–103, Routledge, New York, NY, USA, 2nd edition, 2012.
35. C. Weeks, "The bullying gender gap: girls more likely to be targets," The Globe and Mail, 2012, http://www.theglobeandmail.com.
36. Ç. Topcu and Ö. Erdur-Baker, "Affective and cognitive empathy as mediators of gender differences in cyber and traditional bullying," School Psychology International, vol. 33, no. 5, pp. 550–561, 2012.
37. J. Andrew, M. Cooke, and S. J. Muncer, "The relationship between empathy and Machiavellianism: an alternative to empathizing-systemizing theory," Personality and Individual Differences, vol. 44, no. 5, pp. 1203–1211, 2008.
38. E. Pence and M. Paymar, Education Groups for Men Who Batter: The Duluth Model, Springer, New York, NY, USA, 1993.
39. E. M. Alexy, A. W. Burgess, T. Baker, and S. A. Smoyak, "Perceptions of cyberstalking among college students," Brief Treatment and Crisis Intervention, vol. 5, no. 3, pp. 279–289, 2005.
40. A. Lyndon, J. Bonds-Raacke, and A. D. Cratty, "College students' Facebook stalking of ex-partners," Cyberpsychology, Behavior, and Social Networking, vol. 14, no. 12, pp. 711–716, 2011.
41. L. A. Melander, "College students' perceptions of intimate partner cyber harassment," Cyberpsychology, Behavior, and Social Networking, vol. 13, no. 3, pp. 263–268, 2010.

42. K. S. Ménard and A. L. Pincus, "Predicting overt stalking perpetration by male and female college students," Journal of Interpersonal Violence, vol. 27, no. 11, pp. 2183–2207, 2011.
43. M. P. Thompson and D. J. Morrison, "Prospective predictors of technology-based sexual coercion by college males," Psychology of Violence, vol. 3, no. 3, pp. 233–246, 2013.
44. W. Cassidy, C. Faucher, and M. Jackson, "Cyberbullying among youth: a comprehensive review of current international research and its implications and application to policy and practice," School Psychology International, vol. 34, no. 6, pp. 575–612, 2013.
45. Y. Akbulut and B. Eristi, "Cyberbullying and victimisation among Turkish University students," Australasian Journal of Educational Technology, vol. 27, no. 7, pp. 1155–1170, 2011.
46. S. Çelik, H. Atak, and A. Erguzen, "The effect of personality on cyberbullying among university students in Turkey," Eurasian Journal of Educational Research, vol. 49, pp. 129–150, 2012. ·
47. B. Dilmaç, "Psychological needs as a predictor of cyber bullying: a preliminary report on college students," Educational Sciences: Theory and Practice, vol. 9, no. 3, pp. 1307–1325, 2009.
48. J. C. Molluzzo and J. P. Lawler, "A study of the perceptions of college students on cyberbullying," Information Systems Education Journal, vol. 10, no. 4, pp. 84–109, 2012.
49. A. M. Schenk and W. J. Fremouw, "Prevalence, psychological impact, and coping of cyberbully victims among college students," Journal of School Violence, vol. 11, no. 1, pp. 21–37, 2012.
50. P. A. Snell and E. K. Englander, "Cyberbullying victimization and behaviors among girls: applying research findings in the field," Journal of Social Sciences, vol. 6, no. 4, pp. 510–514, 2010.
51. N. Turan, O. Polat, M. Karapirli, C. Uysal, and S. G. Turan, "The new violence type of the era: cyber bullying among university students: violence among university students," Neurology Psychiatry and Brain Research, vol. 17, no. 1, pp. 21–26, 2011.
52. C. M. Walker, B. R. Sockman, and S. Koehn, "An exploratory study of cyberbullying with undergraduate university students," TechTrends, vol. 55, no. 2, pp. 31–38, 2011.
53. K. Wensley and M. Campbell, "Heterosexual and nonheterosexual young University Students' Involvement in traditional and cyber forms

of bullying," Cyberpsychology, Behavior, and Social Networking, vol. 15, no. 12, pp. 649–654, 2012.

54. A. T. Zhang, L. P. W. Land, and G. Dick, "Key influences of cyberbullying for university students," PACIS 2010 Proceedings Paper 83, 2010, http://aisel.aisnet.org/pacis2010/83.

55. L. M. Blizard, Faculty members' perceived experiences and impact of cyberbullying from students at a Canadian university: a mixed methods study [Ph.D. dissertation], Simon Fraser University, Burnaby, Canada, 2014, http://summit.sfu.ca/item/13897.

56. C. M. Clark, L. Werth, and S. Ahten, "Cyber-bullying and incivility in the online learning environment, part 1: addressing faculty and student perceptions," Nurse Educator, vol. 37, no. 4, pp. 150–156, 2012. ·

57. D. Daniloff, Cyberbullying Goes to College, Bostonia, 2009, http://www.bu.edu/bostonia/spring09/toc/.

58. J. C. Jones and S. Scott, "Cyberbullying in the university classroom: a multiplicity of issues," in Misbehavior Online in Higher Education (Cutting-Edge Technologies in Higher Education), L. A. Wankel and C. Wankel, Eds., pp. 157–182, Emerald, Bingley, UK, 2012.

59. Q. Martin and D. Olson, "College cyberbullying: The virtual bathroom wall," The Journal of Technology in Student Affairs, 2011.

60. M. A. Minor, G. S. Smith, and H. Brashen, "Cyberbullying in higher education," Journal of Educational Research and Practice, vol. 3, no. 1, pp. 15–29, 2013.

61. P. D'Cruz and E. Noronha, "Navigating the extended reach: target experiences of cyberbullying at work," Information and Organization, vol. 23, no. 4, pp. 324–343, 2013.

62. C. Piotrowski, "From workplace bullying to cyberbullying: the enigma of e-harassment in modern organizations," Organization Development Journal, vol. 30, no. 4, pp. 44–53, 2012. ·

63. C. Privitera and M. A. Campbell, "Cyberbullying: the new face of workplace bullying?" Cyberpsychology and Behavior, vol. 12, no. 4, pp. 395–400, 2009.

64. J. W. Vance, Cyber-harassment in higher education: online learning environment [Ph.D. dissertation], University of Southern California, Los Angeles, Calif, USA, 2010, http://digitallibrary.usc.edu/cdm/ref/collection/p15799coll127/id/309077.

65. J. Finn, "A survey of online harassment at a University Campus,"

Journal of Interpersonal Violence, vol. 19, no. 4, pp. 468–483, 2004.
66. M. Lindsay and J. Krysik, "Online harassment among college students: a replication incorporating new Internet trends," Information Communication and Society, vol. 15, no. 5, pp. 703–719, 2012.
67. R. M. Kowalski, S. P. Limber, and P. W. Agatston, Cyberbullying: Bullying in the Digital Age, Wiley-Blackwell, Malden, Mass, USA, 2nd edition, 2012.
68. C. Faucher, M. Jackson, and W. Cassidy, "When online exchanges byte: an examination of the policy environment governing cyberbullying at the university level," Canadian Journal of Higher Education.
69. W. Cassidy, C. Faucher, and M. Jackson, The Dark side of the Ivory Tower: Cyberbullying of University Faculty and Teaching Personnel.
70. H. Johnson and M. Dawson, Violence against Women in Canada: Research and Policy Perspectives, Oxford University Press, Ontario, Canada, 2011.
71. M. Sinha, "Measuring violence against women in Canada: statistical trends," Juristat Cat. no. 85-002-X, Statistics Canada, Minister of Industry, Ottawa, Canada, 2013, http://www.statcan.gc.ca/pub/85-002-x/2013001/article/11766-eng.pdf.

CHAPTER 2

CYBERBULLYING OR CYBER AGGRESSION?: A REVIEW OF EXISTING DEFINITIONS OF CYBER-BASED PEER-TO-PEER AGGRESSION

Lucie Corcoran [1], Conor Mc Guckin [2] and Garry Prentice [1]

[1]School of Arts, Dublin Business School, Dublin 2, Ireland

[2]School of Education, Trinity College Dublin, Dublin 2, Ireland

ABSTRACT

Due to the ongoing debate regarding the definitions and measurement of cyberbullying, the present article critically appraises the existing literature and offers direction regarding the question of how best to conceptualise peer-to-peer abuse in a cyber context. Variations across definitions are problematic as it has been argued that inconsistencies with regard to definitions result in

Citation: Lucie Corcoran, Conor Mc Guckin and Garry Prentice, "Cyberbullying or Cyber Aggression?: A Review of Existing Definitions of Cyber-Based Peer-to-Peer Aggression," doi:10.3390/soc5020245.

researchers examining different phenomena, whilst the absence of an agreed conceptualisation of the behaviour(s) involved hinders the development of reliable and valid measures. Existing definitions of cyberbullying often incorporate the criteria of traditional bullying such as intent to harm, repetition, and imbalance of power. However, due to the unique nature of cyber-based communication, it can be difficult to identify such criteria in relation to cyber-based abuse. Thus, for these reasons cyberbullying may not be the most appropriate term. Rather than attempting to "shoe-horn" this abusive behaviour into the preconceived conceptual framework that provides an understanding of traditional bullying, it is timely to take an alternative approach. We argue that it is now time to turn our attention to the broader issue of cyber aggression, rather than persist with the narrow focus that is cyberbullying.

Keywords: cyber aggression, cyberbullying, cyber victim, cyber victimization, definitions, bullying

INTRODUCTION

This paper asserts a position to progress the conceptualisation and definition of cyber-based aggressive behaviours, generally classed under the term cyberbullying. A review of definitional approaches to both traditional bullying and cyberbullying is provided so as to highlight the similarities but, also, crucially, the differences between the "real world" and cyber settings. In this way, it becomes evident that the traditional bullying definitional criteria do not provide an easy match to the cyber context. In addition, different theoretical perspectives on the conceptualisation of cyberbullying further emphasise the need to consider different perspectives on cyber-based aggression [1]. Whilst it is acknowledged that important contributions have been made to progressing the definition of cyberbullying [2], recent findings [3] have highlighted the need to adopt a different approach. Ultimately, we will present a synopsis of the problematic nature of the label "cyberbullying" and current definitions, and we will present a way forward for the research community. In order to gain insight regarding the rationale for cyberbullying definitions, it is important to first review the defining components of traditional bullying.

DEFINING BULLYING FOR A "REAL WORLD" SETTING

Presently there is an ongoing debate regarding the existence of cyberbullying, the extent of the problem, and the threat that cyber-based abuse carries (see Olweus and Smith for a scholarly engagement [4,5]). Central to this debate is how we delineate the behaviours and actions that are commonly labelled as "cyberbullying"; that is, how we identify the parameters of the phenomenon, what we recognise as the inclusion and exclusion criteria as part of the definitional stance, and importantly, how we conclude that cyberbullying is in fact the correct term for the behaviour that we are exploring.

Within the realm of "traditional bullying" research, sometimes referred to as face-to-face (f2f) bullying [6], there is wide consensus regarding the defining criteria, namely (a) intent to cause harm [7,8], (b) repetition of the behaviour over time [7,9,10], and (c) an imbalance of power between the victim(s) and bully(ies) [7,8,10]. However, with the emergence of cyberbullying, the central question for researchers and practitioners relates to the extent to which the same criteria could be "plugged into" a definition of cyberbullying.

Definitions of traditional bullying have reflected the static nature of the "real world" setting, which is characterised by boundaries of time and geography (e.g., school, home). However, abuse of peers is no longer confined to the school setting, nor is it restricted to the typical daily routines of human interaction; characteristics that bind instances of traditional bullying. Indeed, the capacity to use electronic devices and media to attack someone in almost any location, and at any time, is a distinctive feature of cyber-based abuse [11]. Moreover, there is the potential for abusive or humiliating content to be disseminated to an audience of unknown size and location [12]. This allows for the notion of "repetition" in operational definitions to take a different form in the cyber world, as abusive behaviour need not be repeated on the part of the aggressor [13] in order for the target to experience repeated victimization, as the bystanders take a central role in cyber-based abuse through their viewing, "sharing", and "liking" of humiliating content, such as comments (e.g., tweets, texts), pictures, and videos. Moreover, the element of "power", another central aspect of operational definitions of traditional bullying, is somewhat more difficult to determine in a cyber context. For example, power could be characterised by the ability to remain anonymous in cyberspace, or the ability to capitalise

would better serve our objectives. Indeed, the scale approach to assessing peer abuse in cyberspace revealed the incidence of behaviours which researchers and practitioners wish to better understand. Perhaps the term cyberbullying is in fact redundant and confusing. Fifth, the term cyberbullying may also carry a stigma which could account for the low incidence rate found by Corcoran and Mc Guckin [3]. This would further highlight the need for an alternative approach, and so a new focus on peer-directed cyber aggression is suggested.

CONCLUSION: A NEW WAY FORWARD

Whilst Menesini [27] poses the question "How and to what extent might cyberbullying be underestimated if we neglect its specificity?" (p. 544), the present article poses the question, to what extent might we be underestimating the incidence and effects of cyber-based peer-to-peer abuse by constraining its conceptualisation and operationalisation with inappropriate criteria and labels? Perhaps the definition of aggression [32] which states that aggression is "…any behavior intended to harm another person that the target person wants to avoid" (p. 222) could be adapted for the purposes of cyber aggression. Therefore, also considering Langos' suggestion regarding appraisal of intent [14] and Pyżalski's inclusion of intent (but not repetition or power imbalance) when measuring electronic aggression [24], the following definition is proposed—"Cyber aggression refers to any behaviour enacted through the use of information and communication technologies that is intended to harm another person(s) that the target person(s) wants to avoid. Intent to cause harm should be judged on the basis of how a reasonable person would assess intent." In this way, the shackles of the traditional bullying framework can be removed, allowing a different path forward. Combined with Pyżalski's approach of examining the identity of the targeted individual(s) [24], it is possible to distinguish between peer-directed cyber aggression and other-directed cyber aggression. There is already acknowledgement that cyber aggression is a behaviour which can be identified as, for example, online harassment or Internet harassment [2], and Grigg [1] has hinted at the "…vagueness, restrictiveness and ambiguity…" (p. 152) of the term cyberbullying and suggested that perhaps the focus needs to shift towards this broader approach—a suggestion worth considering as research, practice, and prevention work matures.

AUTHOR CONTRIBUTIONS

Lucie Corcoran was the primary author of this paper and was responsible for the write up and revisions to the manuscript. Conor Mc Guckin was involved in the planning of the paper and also contributed feedback, and editing throughout the writing process. Garry Prentice contributed feedback and editing throughout the writing process.

REFERENCES

1. Grigg, D.W. Cyber-Aggression: Definition and Concept of Cyberbullying. *Aust. J. Guid. Counsell.* **2010**, *20*, 143–156.
2. Menesini, E.; Nocentini, A.; Palladino, B.E.; Scheithauer, H.; Schultze-Krumbholz, A.; Frisén, A.; Berne, S.; Luik, P.; Naruskov, K.; Ortega, R.; *et al.* Definitions of cyberbullying. In *Cyberbullying through the New Media: Findings from An International Network*; Smith, P.K., Steffgen, G., Eds.; Psychology Press: Oxfordshire, UK, 2013; pp. 23–36.
3. Corcoran, L.; Mc Guckin, C. The incidence of bullying and aggression in Irish post-primary schools: An investigation of school and cyber settings. In Proceedings of Annual Conference of the Educational Studies Association of Ireland, Sheraton Hotel, Athlone, Ireland, 10–12 April 2014.
4. Olweus, D. Cyberbullying: An overrated phenomenon? *Eur. J. Dev. Psychol.***2012**, *9*, 520–538.
5. Smith, P.K. Cyberbullying: Challenges and opportunities for a research program—A response to Olweus (2012). *Eur. J. Dev. Psychol.* **2012**, *9*, 553–558.
6. Mc Guckin, C.; Cummins, P.K.; Lewis, C.A. f2f and cyberbullying among children in Northern Ireland: Data from the Kids Life and Times Surveys. *Psychol. Soc. Educ.* **2010**, *2*, 83–96.
7. Whitney, I.; Smith, P.K. A survey of the nature and extent of bullying in junior/middle and secondary schools. *Educ. Res.* **1993**, *35*, 3–25.
8. Campbell, M.A. Cyber Bullying: An Old Problem in a New Guise? *Aust. J. Guid. Counsell.* **2005**, *15*, 68–76.
9. Olweus, D. *Bullying At School: What We Know and What We Can Do*; Blackwell: Oxford, UK, 1993.
10. Farrington, D.P. Understanding and preventing bullying. *Crim. Justice* **1993**, *17*, 381–458.
11. O'Moore, M.; Minton, S.J. Cyber-bullying: The Irish experience. In *Handbook of Aggressive Behaviour Research*; Tawse, S., Quin, C., Eds.; Nova Science Publishers, Inc.: New York, NY, USA, 2009; pp. 269–292.
12. Kowalski, R.M.; Limber, S.P.; Agatston, P.W. *Cyber Bullying: Bullying in the Digital Age*; Blackwell: Malden, MA, USA, 2008.

13. Vandebosch, H.; Van Cleemput, K. Cyberbullying among youngsters: Profiles of bullies and victims. *New Media Soc.* **2009**, *11*, 1349–1371.
14. Langos, C. Cyberbullying: The challenge to define. *Cyberpsychol. Behav. Soc. Netw.* **2012**, *15*, 285–289.
15. Moore, G.E. Cramming more components onto integrated circuits. *Electronics***1965**, *38*, 114–117.
16. Drogin, E.Y.; Young, K. Forensic Mental Health Aspects of Adolescent Cyber Bullying: A Jurisprudent Science Perspective. *J. Psychiatr. Law* **2008**, *36*, 679–690.
17. Mc Guckin, C. School bullying amongst school pupils in Northern Ireland: How many are involved, what are the health effects, and what are the issues for school management? In *Bullying in Irish Education*; O'Moore, A.M., Stevens, P., Eds.; Cork University Press: Cork, Ireland, 2013; pp. 46–64.
18. O'Moore, M.; Cross, D.; Valimaki, M.; Almeida, A.; Berne, S.; Kurki, M.; Olenik-Shemesh, D.; Heiman, T.; Deboutte, G.; Fandrem, H.; *et al.* Guidelines to prevent cyber-bullying: A cross-national review. In *Cyberbullying through the New Media: Findings from An International Network*; Smith, P.K., Steffgen, G., Eds.; Psychology Press: Oxfordshire, UK, 2013; pp. 136–161.
19. Anti-Bullying Procedures for Primary and Post-Primary Schools. Available online: http://www.education.ie/en/Publications/Policy-Reports/Anti-Bullying-Procedures-for-Primary-and-Post-Primary-Schools.pdf (accessed on 10 September 2014).
20. Mc Guckin, C.; Perren, S.; Corcoran, L.; Cowie, H.; Dehue, F.; Ševčíková, A.; Tsatsou, P.; Völlink, T. Coping with cyberbullying: How can we prevent cyberbullying and how victims can cope with it. In *Cyberbullying through the New Media: Findings from An International Network*; Smith, P.K., Steffgen, G., Eds.; Psychology Press: Oxfordshire, UK, 2013; pp. 120–135.
21. Belsey, B. Cyberbullying.ca. Available online: http://www.cyberbullying.ca(accessed on 10 September 2014).
22. Smith, P.K.; Mahdavi, J.; Carvalho, M.; Fisher, S.; Russell, S.; Tippett, N. Cyberbullying: Its nature and impact in secondary school pupils. *J. Child Psychol. Psychiatr.* **2008**, *49*, 376–385.

23. Tokunaga, R.S. Following you home from school: A critical review and synthesis of research on cyberbullying victimization. *Comput. Hum. Behav.***2010**, *26*, 277–287.
24. Pyżalski, J. From cyberbullying to electronic aggression: Typology of the phenomenon. *Emot. Behav. Diffic.* **2012**, *17*, 305–317.
25. Carr-Fanning, K.; Mc Guckin, C.; Shevlin, M. Using student voice to escape the spider's web: A methodological approach to de-victimizing students with ADHD. *Trinity Educ. Papers* **2013**, *2*, 85–111.
26. Guerin, S.; Hennessy, E. Pupils' definitions of bullying. *Eur. J. Dev. Psychol.***2002**, *17*, 249–261.
27. Menesini, E. Cyberbullying: The right value of the phenomenon. Comments on the paper "Cyberbullying: An overrated phenomenon?". *Eur. J. Dev. Psychol.***2012**, *9*, 544–552.
28. Vandebosch, H.; Van Cleemput, K. Defining cyberbullying: A qualitative research into the perceptions of youngsters. *CyberPsycho. Behav.* **2008**, *11*, 499–503.
29. Sticca, F.; Ruggieri, S.; Alsaker, F.; Perren, S. Longitudinal risk factors for cyberbullying in adolescence. *J. Community Appl. Soc. Psychol.* **2013**, *23*, 52–67.
30. Nocentini, A.; Calmaestra, J.; Schultze-Krumbholz, A.; Scheithauer, H.; Ortega, R.; Menesini, E. Cyberbullying: Labels, Behaviours and Definition in Three European Countries. *Aust. J. Guid. Counsell.* **2010**, *20*, 129–142.
31. Björkqvist, K.; Ekman, K.; Lagerspetz, K. Bullies and victims: Their ego picture, ideal ego picture and normative ego picture. *Scand. J. Psychol.* **1982**, *23*, 307–313.
32. DeLamater, J.D.; Myers, D.J. *Social Psychology*; Wadsworth: Belmont, CA, USA, 2011.

CHAPTER 3

WHEN CYBERBULLYING AND BULLYING MEET GAMING: A SYSTEMIC REVIEW OF THE LITERATURE

Li Qing

Department of Educational Technology and Literacy, College of Education, Towson, USA

ABSTRACT

Bullying is an increasingly growing concern among children and adolescents; with the technology advances, youth has found more efficient ways to inflict harm to others via cyberbullying. The media is a relentless source for blaming violent video games as the 'cause' of bullying and cyberbullying. Despite this vast amount of research in all three individual areas, namely bullying, cyberbullying, and gaming, there is little research reviewing the connections between them. This study, therefore, systematically reviews

Citation: Qing L (2015) When Cyberbullying and Bullying Meet Gaming: A systemic Review of the Literature. J Psychol Psychother 5:195. doi:10.4172/2161-0487.1000195

the literature exploring the interconnectedness of these areas with a specific focus on how gaming interacts with cyberbullying and bullying. In addition, it creates a model grounded in enactivism to help us identify future areas of research and develop effective cyberbullying prevention programs.

Specifically, we conducted a literature search across 40 research databases to include, but not limited to PsycINFO, ERIC, Psycarticles, Teacher Reference Center, and Computer Science Index. Grounded in enactivism, we proposed the Enactivist Model of Cyberbullying, Bullying and Gaming, which suggests that the exploration of cyberbullying and bullying in relation to gaming should be conducted in a holistic fashion rather than limiting the focus on individuals' aggressive behavior. The model also provided a framework not only to make sense of but also to present the existing literature.

Keywords: Cyberbullying, Bullying, Gaming, Enactivism, Aggression

INTRODUCTION

It is widely recognized that bullying is a serious concern in schools and beyond. With the influx of technology and ever increasing prevalence of the Internet, people have found different ways to inflict harm on others via cyberbullying. Cyberbullying has gained increased attention as evidenced in various media reports, including a video address by President Obama and the First Lady Michelle Obama denouncing cyberbullying, posted on Facebook on March 9, 2011 [1]. Many review studies exist in multiple areas of bullying to include, but not limited to bullying in the workplace [2,3], schools [4,5], peer groups [6], special education populations [7], and parent prevention programs [8]. Some review studies have begun to address cyberbullying in relationship to bullying [9,10], with increasing amounts of systematic reviews of cyberbullying [11-13].

The media is a relentless source for blaming violent digital games (hereafter gaming) as the 'cause' of bullying and cyberbullying [14,15]. Past research has focused excessively on the effects of violent video games as exemplified by some systematic review studies [16-18] More recently, research has begun to emerge on the positive effects of gaming to include encouragement of motivation and learning enhancement, with several review studies summarizing such work [19-21]. Despite this vast amount of research in all three individual areas, namely gaming, cyberbullying, and bullying, there is little research reviewing the connections amongst all three at the same time. While we aim to bridge this gap, the focus on all three realms is too broad to do any thorough review, considering the limit of the available space. Since many studies exist reviewing bullying and cyberbullying, we narrowed our scope: 1) to systematically review the literature exploring the interconnectedness among the three domains, with a specific focus on gaming in relation to cyberbullying and bullying among children and young people, not considering the literature from adult populations; and 2) to propose a model grounded in enactivism to help us identify gaps and guide future research.

Specifically, we conducted a literature search across 40 research databases to include, but not limited to PsycINFO, ERIC, PsycARTICLES, Teacher Reference Center, and Computer Science Index, using initial key terms cyberbullying and gaming. These initial search results yielded approximately 23 articles including dissertations and books. Other key terms included games, cyberbullying, video games, and bullying. Using these additional key terms provided around 93 articles that related to individual key terms; however, only around 45 of those articles focused on a connection between games and bullying/cyberbullying. These papers comprised the basis of this literature review.

THEORETICAL FRAMEWORK AND A MODEL

Stemming from phenomenology and biological views, enactivism is an emerging philosophical perspective. It provides a means for conceptualizing gaming, cyberbullying, and bullying. Enactivism emphasizes embodiment and embodied cognition [22]. In addition, the biological perspective stresses that all living systems are evolved from the synthesis of the interplay of their parts [23]. From the enactivist point of view, our mind, body, and environment cannot be separated. We, including our actions and beliefs, always shape and are shaped by the environment in which we reside [24]. Examining cyberbullying, therefore, demands the exploration of the interactions among components at various levels including the meso-level (e.g. cyberbullying, gaming and bullying), the macro-level (e.g. society, schools, culture), and the micro-level (e.g. age, beliefs, self concept). The inseparability of our mind, body, and the surroundings further suggests that cyberbullying should be examined including different perspectives, from the bodily aspect (e.g. physical states), to the mind (e.g. mental health, personality, mood), to the surroundings (e.g. education).

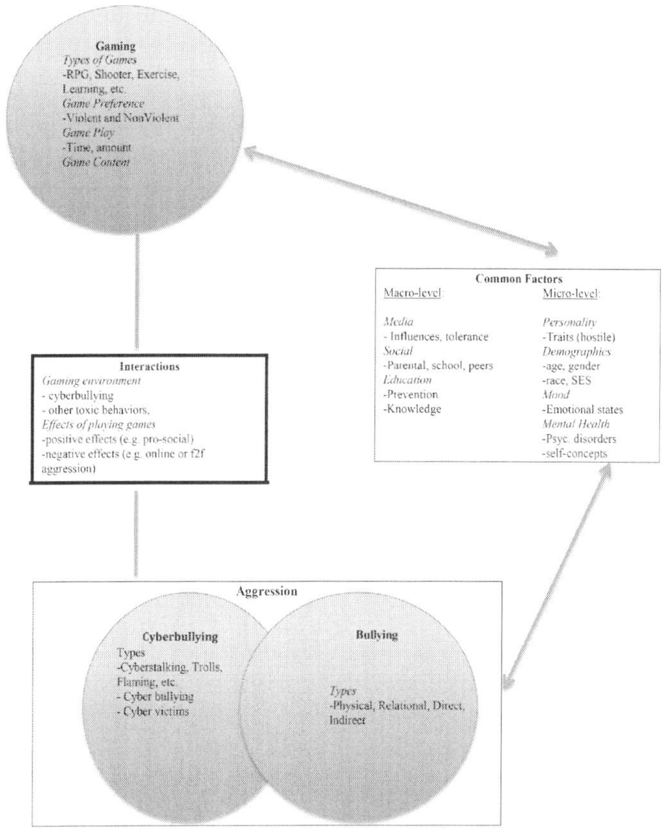

Figure 1: A model of cyberbullying, bullying and gaming.

Grounded in the enactivist perspective, we propose the Enactivist Model of Gaming, Cyberbullying, and Bullying (EMGCB) demonstrating the complex interplay of these three research domains (**Figure 1**). The evolvement of this model also reflects the enactivist view about cognition. The initial version of the model was inspired by the enactivist viewpoints and our previous knowledge about these research domains. After our preliminary review of the existing research papers, we contemplated on the functionality of such a model: should it be an analytical model to be presented at the beginning to provide theoretical guidance, or purely a rhetoric mechanism shared at the end of the paper to summarize the existing studies? Our iterative discussions with colleagues and reviewers as well as our further interaction with the existing literature made us decide to present the model early in this review as a device to assist readers in visualizing how several parts of the research literature relate to one another. As a sophisticated organizer for the topics and information presented in this review, this model also serves as a heuristic device that may be useful in making sense of the existing literature and identifying gaps. The nature of this recursive and dynamic, rather than a linear and static, development process of the model truly reflects the enactivist view about thinking. In fact, we expect that the model will continue to evolve that the current version of the model will guide future research, with new findings to further refine and reshape the model.

Some bullying research employs an ecological systems approach, which, at first blush, seems very similar to enactivism. We, however, argue the significance of our model based on enactivism for two important reasons: first, as convincingly argued by many scholars [25,26], enactivism is different from ecological systems perspectives, though these two viewpoints share some assumptions. Secondly, a unique aspect that differentiates this review from any other literature on cyberbullying/bullying lies in the intersection of gaming and cyberbullying/bullying. Our review therefore goes beyond the existing cyberbullying/bullying literature and the EMGCB model adds to our current understanding of the field.

Many variables are common factors that affect gaming, cyberbullying and bullying. Grouped under Common Factors, as represented by a rectangle, these variables include both macro-level (e.g. education) and micro-level (e.g. demographic) variables. The double-headed arrows between these variables suggest the reciprocal relationships. For example, individuals' personality and educational levels can shape their gaming experience. On the other hand, people's gaming experience can change to their mood or influence their way to interact with others in the social environment.

The last category – "interactions", also the main focus of this paper, is how gaming interacts with cyberbullying and bullying, which is presented by another rectangle but with dotted lines. The interactions between the variables are generally categorized into two areas: 1) gaming environment - cyberbullying and other aggressive behaviors can very much occur in gaming environments; and 2) effects – on one hand, cyberbullying and bullying, or other types of aggression may affect players' gaming experiences. On the other hand, games, especially violent games, may contribute to aggression, including bullying and cyberbullying.

In sum, the five categories in the model reflect the state of the field in research on cyberbullying and bullying in relation to gaming. Next, we first very briefly introduce each of the four categories in the model: gaming, cyberbullying, bullying, and common factors to set the stage. The focus then shifts to the "interaction" category, discussing the relationships amongst the three domains.

GAMING

Gaming industry has grown tremendously within the past decade. A 2001 study [27] suggested that 70% of children play computer games every week, with 68% of children playing on their phones. In 2006, a US national study found 85% of children play video games at home or school, with 50% of males reporting they play every day [28] The Pew study conducted in 2009 [29] stated that 97% of the US teens (12-17 years old) play digital games with rich gaming experience.

Many different types of games exist. [30] classified games into eight different types. The most popular games are action games (i.e., shooting) and adventure games (i.e., solving puzzles provided via narratives in order to progress through virtual worlds). Action games such as Call of Duty: Black Ops II has sold over ten million copies since its release in November 2012 [31]. Other game types include fighting games, puzzle games, sports games, strategy games, and role-playing games. Role-playing games include multiple settings where the human player assumes the role of the game character. These games are similar to simulation games; however, simulation games involve succeeding in a simplified version of an environment. Some games that do not neatly fit into one of these game type categories, and often time games may take on features from multiple categories [32].

Define games into seven categories: action/platform games, adventure games, fighting games, role-playing games, simulations, sports games, and strategy games. Again, these categories may not be mutually exclusive, meaning it is possible that one game belongs to more than one category [33]. Although many well-publicized violent games are shooting games, it is by no means the only type of game that can contain violent elements. On the flip side, even shooting games can be used to address cyberbullying and bullying issues. For example, schools can use educational shooting games to increase students' understanding of Internet safety and awareness of the negative consequences of cyberbullying.

CYBERBULLYING

What is cyberbullying?

Cyberbullying has increasingly gained attention both from media and research communities. More and more people have begun to realize the significant negative impact of cyberbullying and therefore are seeking prevention and intervention strategies. A clear, appropriate and accurate definition of cyberbullying is a precursor to effectively address the cyberbullying problem. To date, many definitions exist. For example, cyberbullying can be briefly defined as "sending or posting harmful or cruel text or images using the Internet or other digital communication devices" [34]. Another widely adapted definition is:

An aggressive, intentional act carried out by a group or individual, using electronic forms of contact, repeatedly and over time against a victim who cannot easily defend him or herself [35].

When the online gaming factor is introduced, similar definitions are adapted as exemplified by a study [36] on social experiences and online gaming referring cyberbullying as "an individual or group willfully using information and communication involving electronic technologies to facilitate deliberate and repeated harassment or threat to another individual or group by sending or posting cruel text and/ or graphics using technological means." (p. 160). Sometimes, the terms online harassment and cyberbullying were used interchangeably, essentially referring to threats or offensive behavior delivered via technology mediums (e.g., email, social networking sites) [37].

Many consider cyberbullying to be a special type of bullying. Logically some researchers derived their definition of cyberbullying from [38] classic definition of bullying. For example, [39] depicted cyberbullying as "willful and repeated harm inflicted through the use of e-mail, cell phone, instant messaging, and defamatory Web sites" (p. 388). While repetition is considered an important characteristic of bullying, researchers increasingly question this issue. Espelage [4] described several legal cases in which bullying victims committed suicide, yet school staff did not take actions because the alleged bullying behaviors were not repeated. She therefore challenges such definitions. Other scholars [35] raised similar questions concerning whether repetitiveness should be the essential characteristics of cyberbullying. One such strong argument is that cyberbullying behaviors can be repeatedly experienced even if it is one event because electronic materials can be easily preserved, quickly and widely distributed, and frequently shared.

As researchers agree the literature remains inconsistent with a universal definition for cyberbullying [40-42] argue that the increase in cyberbullying is in part due to the inconsistencies in the research.

Types of Cyberbullying

With technology introducing new forms of bullying within the virtual world, via offering the luxury of anonymity, many forms of cyberbullying have been explored. [43] called those who cyberbully as flamers and trolls. Flamers are individuals who make insulting, hurtful, and mean remarks to fellow online users, whereas, trolls are individuals who trick others into doing foolish things (e.g., breaking codes) and then making fun of them. A distinct characteristic of trolls is that they tend to blame the victim for their harm arguing that the victims are willing to be hurt. As a result of this vulnerability, it is the victims rather than the trolls that cause the online abuse [44]. Developed a cyberabuse model highlighting the multiple types of cyberbullying to include cyberstalking, masquerading, sexual harassment and coercion [45], threatening others, impersonation, exclusion of others, and trolling [46,47] categorized those who unintentionally hurt others via practical jokes as cyber mischief-makers, those who engage in deviant, dangerous behavior via posting threats or secret pictures as cyber rascals, and those who hack into other computers and spread explicit pictures and emails as cyber lords. While the technology continues to develop, people often find new ways to use and misuse those technological tools. Consequently, it is likely that cyberbullies will find new forms to abuse others. A critical question remains how do we operationally define cyberbullying in the research arena.

BULLYING

Bullying and cyberbullying are two closely connected fields with some studies [48,49] clearly describing the overlap of the two. Although some may disagree, a vast majority consider that cyberbullying is one type of bullying [35,50]. In fact, it is claimed that "one of the most well established findings in the literature on cyberbullying so far, is the substantial – but not complete – overlap between involvement in traditional and in cyber forms" [51].

There are multiple definitions for bullying, and a plethora of operational definitions used in theoretical arguments and empirical support [5].

Originally defined by [52], bullying is "unwanted, aggressive behavior among school aged children that involves a real or perceived power imbalance. The behavior is repeated, or has the potential to be repeated, over time," a definition stated on stopbullying. gov, a US federal government official website. Many subcategories have been identified including 'overt' and 'covert' acts of aggression [5]. A much-neglected area of bullying is sibling bullying, with a most recent review by Woke and colleagues [53]

Many factors influence aggression and bullying [14]. The Media Research Lab at Iowa State University reports that they can predict children at high risk of bullying behavior 80% of the time based on the following three factors: boys, involved in a fight in the past year, and consumed a lot of media violence. In addition, researchers report the best single predictor of future aggression is past aggression [54].

Multiple review studies exist [4,6,7] that systematically review the literature related to bullying. A detailed literature review about bullying, however, is beyond the scope of the current paper.

COMMON FACTORS

Our review of the related research shows that many factors (e.g., parental involvement, mental health, personality factors, etc.) influence all three main categories of this paper, namely cyberbullying, bullying and gaming. Needless to say the demographic variables play a significant role and many of the research studies described above have already confirmed this. The social environment, including parents, teachers, and peers, significantly shape people's behavior, therefore their involvement in cyberbullying, bullying or gaming is important. For example, some researchers [55] stated that parents often feel that children experience bullying as part of the childhood experience, and therefore, to some extent is expected. Yet, such parents' beliefs may unintentionally contribute to the cycle of cyberbullying and bullying. A study found that 90% of cyber victims do not tell their parents because they do not believe that their teachers and parents are equipped to handle these situations [56]. Another reason that the victims do not inform adults is the fear of consequences such as losing computer privileges [56,57]. Similar patterns were identified by a Canadian study [58] of 269 7th -12th grade students where over 40% of cyber-victims would do nothing and only about one in every 10 would inform adults. Students' distrust of adults and their fear that the cyberbullies could get back and escalate the problem were the top two reasons for the cybervictims' reluctance to report cyberbullying incidents to adults. Parents' beliefs have also been researched in relation to games. Studies in this area generally fall to two types: desirable and undesirable effects of video games [59]. Although understanding positive potentials of games, parents often concern about: 1) the balance between game playing and other activities, 2) game content, 3) possible negative impact of games, 4) mediation strategies [60].

With the increase of technology, studies show more Internet use, which leads to higher risks of cyberbullying, online harassment, and sexual solicitation; however, little is known about specific mediums of this exposure, including parental factors. One study [39] explored the effect of parent mediation, defined as "...the activities carried out by parents to protect their children from exposure to online dangers". Focusing on two types of mediation: restrictive mediation (i.e. the rules of Internet activity being determined by the parent), and evaluative mediation (i.e. open communication between the parent and child to joint create rules). They found that monitoring web sites and providing guidance were effective at decreasing the risk of cyberbullying, but only for boys. Surprisingly, the location of the computer does not have a significant effect. The results suggested that cyberbullying occurs in spaces already deemed 'safe' by parents, and/or children are better at hiding their activities. In turn, this can increase children's risk of cyber victimization.

The importance of bystanders has been widely researched in the field of bullying, but is under studied in cyberbullying. Bystanders refer to those who observe cyberbullying and/or bullying activities, yet fail to speak up especially in a peer setting. Much of the research reviewed in this paper suggests future research is needed in investigating the possible harmful effects of bystanders [5,36,61].

INTERACTIONS

Aggression is a concept closely linked to bullying or cyberbullying. While sometimes aggression and bullying are used interchangeably, we consider aggression a broader term to include bullying and cyberbullying. **Table 1** lists the studies reviewed in the paper that examine gaming in relation to aggression (including bullying and cyberbullying). The studies are listed in alphabetical order of the authors with the information related to the research focus of the study, country, research design, sample size, age range, and the specific games used in the studies. We also coded the level of each study based on the Model. The last column describes the results of the studies, indicating the effect of gaming on the players. The following discussion starts with the review of gaming in relation to aggression in general, delineating both the negative and positive effects. Then we focus on the interactions between gaming and the two specific types of aggression: cyberbullying and bullying.

GAMING AND AGGRESSION IN GENERAL

Negative Effects of Gaming

Many early research studies in video gaming focus on the negative effects and games increased association with violence. To date, the possible effects of violent video games remain a heated topic for debate among media and academics. On the one hand, media has often portrayed video games as evil, claiming that violent video game playing promotes violence. For example, after the Columbine shooting it was argued that playing Doom might have been a contributing factor; the Beltway Sniper shootings reported a connection to violent video games and training the sniper to kill. The courts argued he played Halo and other shooting games, in addition to watching violent media.

Many research studies have also approached this issue. A multitude of research suggests that violent video games are linked to aggression [16,17,36]. Anderson and colleagues conducted two systematic analyses of the existing literature in this area, first in 2001 and the second in 2010 [17]. Their first study was a meta-analysis of 33 empirical studies of video-game literature and violence. Their result suggested that violent video games increase aggressive behavior and thoughts in adolescents, in addition to decreasing prosocial behavior [16]. Their second metaanalysis review provided further support for linking violent video games to aggression and violence. It also added that violent video games may desensitize youth and create adolescents with less empathetic ability for others [17].

On the other hand, many scholars have argued against the idea that violent video game playing leads to violent behaviors in real life [62] despite America's tendency to blame mass tragedies and violent killings on violent video games. Recent studies have begun to demonstrate that there is no substantial evidence for long-term violent video game use and aggression [63-65].

In their book [66], discussed the correlation between video games and violence. They argued that numerous research studies have shown no connection between violent video game play and youth violent behavior. Since 1993 when video games have grown significantly, violent juvenile crime in the United States has been declining. In fact, arrests for murder, forcible rape, robbery, and aggravated assault dropped 49%. School violence has also decreased. Murder arrests plummeted 71% from 3,790 in 1993 to 1,110 by 2004 [66]. The Safe School Initiative Study by US government reviewed 37 incidences of school targeted violence between 1974-2000 in hopes to create a profile of potential problem youth [67]. In the end, no useful profile could be determined. The only commonalities suggested among potential attackers were being male with a history of suicide attempts and depression; video games were not even mentioned.

The inconsistent results suggest the lack of evidence linking real life violence to violent interactive games [68]. One criticism [63,68] of the current research in this area is that youth violence is not put into context with other factors and childhood predictors, along with experimental limitations in research methodologies. These limitations include the unrealistic amount of game play exposure (e.g., 10 minutes) compared to the actual amount of time spent playing video games. In addition, games are also usually played in a social setting (with friends), whereas, in research experiments they are often playing alone [69]. Limitations like these suggest that possible negative effects of violent games should not be so easily generalized.

Can Positive Gaming Negate Harmful Effects?

While the research literature to date has produced inconsistent results regarding aggression and violent video games, the positive effects of game playing (e.g., socialization, prosocial effects) should not be overlooked.

After reviewing the literature, a team [70] has advocated that more empirical research is needed investigating the positive effects of video games and whether or not these positive effects can begin to mitigate the negative effects of violent video game use. Games have powerful teaching capabilities that can capture emotions and embodied experiences [71]. Numerous violent games have engaging narrative and capturing entertainment, yet designers fail to produce the same engaging and capturing scenarios in game content in a positive medium [15]. Research in positive effects of gaming has begun to emerge recently exploring prosocial, neutral and violent games effects on both behaviors [72,73], and affect [74].

One study [73] investigated the short term effects of playing prosocial, neutral, or violent video games on helping behavior in a sample of 191 children between 9-14 years old using a tangram puzzle measure. Using an experimental design, participants were randomly assigned to a game type (i.e., violent, prosocial, neutral) condition and played for 30 minutes. Upon completion of game play, participants were asked to assign eleven tangram puzzles, either an easy, medium, or hard level, to their partner. In addition, they were told their partner would receive a $10 gift certificate if they completed ten of the puzzles in ten minutes. Results revealed that participants who played a prosocial video game were more helpful than those who played a violent video game, by assigning more easy puzzles. Those who played a violent video game were more likely to assign the more difficult puzzles, demonstrating hurtful behavior. The results also demonstrated that trait aggression is negatively related to helpful behavior, and positively correlated with hurtful behavior.

From a slightly different perspective, these researchers [74] explored state hostility and positive affect in relationship to different types of video games (e.g., prosocial, neutral, violent). A total of 332 participants completed measures assessing trait aggression and prosocialness, and then were randomly assigned to one of the three video game conditions (i.e., prosocial, violent, or neutral). There were a total of six games, two for each condition. Participants played for 20 minutes, then completed additional measures to include state affect and evaluation of the video game. They found that state hostility, aggravation, and mean feelings were reduced as positive affect increased while playing prosocial video games compared to the neutral and violent video game condition. In addition, the reverse was true when participants played violent video games. This research is one of the first to examine the result of affect on different types of video games in an experimental design.

GAMING AND CYBERBULLYING

Since cyberbullying is a relatively new phenomenon, limited studies exist that explore the relationships between cyberbullying and gaming. Among these studies, [39] analysized a telephone survey of 935 US students (12-17 year old). The results indicated that cyberbullying was not associated with playing online games. Tippet and conducted a pilot study with 193 Korean children to test the validity of a questionnaire. To their surprising, the results revealed that online games became a prominent area where children were experiencing bullying and harassment, which include three aspects: cyber victimization, cyberbullying, and observation of cyberbullying by bystanders. When cyber victimization was considered, about 43% of the participants had experienced this in the last two months. Of those, about half were bullied just once or twice over the previous months, but 30% had experienced on a regular basis, at least once a week. With respect to cyberbullies, about one third of the participants cyberbullied others in games in the last two months and close to half of them bullied others at least two to three times a month or more. For bystanders, every two out of five students having seen it occur within the previous two months. Of these, 17% said it had only taken place once or twice, while 12% witnessed online game bullying take place several times a week [61].

They then examined different forms of bullying (direct, indirect, mobile, internet, and online games), finding that anger was the most common feeling reported by the victim in all forms except online game bullying. 'Aggressive language', such as swearing or insults (reported by 64%), was the most frequent encounter of victims of online game bullying, followed by 'name calling' (44%), violence against one's avatar (16%), threats (12%), rumor spreading (4%), and social exclusion (2%). Interestingly, nearly half of those victims of online game bullying reported feelings of not being worried. Additionally, boys, compared to girls, were more likely to be online game bullies, victims and reported being more familiar with online game bullying [61].

[47] studied the relationship between online violent gaming and gender, preference for playing violent online games, hostility, and aggressive behavior in regards to bullying. The sample consisted of 1069 adolescents with moderate Internet experience and reported playing online games in the past. The results revealed that gender was significantly related to participant's preference for violent video games, and had a direct effect and predictive power for hostility. Compared to their female counterpart, males preferred and enjoyed violent online games and showed higher levels of aggressive behavior. Also, the more the male experiences cyberbullying, the easier to predict aggressive behavior in his daily life. [47] demonstrated that characteristics of the perpetrator and the victim overlap, and that some victims may become perpetrators after being attacked, creating a vicious cycle.

One study [75] surveyed 13-18 years old high school students in China. Of the 1278 (619 males) participants, over 40% reported spending less than one hour each day playing violent games, close to one third played one to two hours per day, and about one in every five played greater than 3 hours per day. Of those that played online games, only about 15% reported their games were moderate to severe in violent content. Final analysis suggests that those sharing roles of cyberbullies and victims were two times as likely as the ones not involved in cyberbullying, to have been moderately or severely exposed to violent online gaming. Compared to those who were not involved in cyberbullying either as a perpetrator or a victim, those cyberbullies (but not being victimized) were four times more likely to be exposed to moderate or severe violent online game content. Overall, this study demonstrated no associations between exposure to online violent games and being a victim of cyberbullying. Exposure to violent online games increased the odds of being a perpetrator or perpetrator-victim of cyberbullying, but not a victim alone.

A recent study [76] investigated cyberbullying in multi-player online gaming environments through a survey of 1025 adolescents and adults (age range 12-70, average age 22). The participants (about 62% female and 38% male) were recruited from an online gaming forum. The results showed that more than one third of the participants avoided a multiplayer game because of the concerns about cyberbullying behavior. Cyberbullying incidents in an online game also caused over half of the participants leaving that game. Close to 65% of the participants considered cyberbullying to be a serious problem in the online gaming world. With respect to the prevalence of cyberbullying in an online gaming world, nearly eighty percent of the participants were cyber victims, one in three were cyberbullies, and over 90% had involved in cyberbullying as a bystander. The examination of potential psychological impact indicated that both victims and predators were negatively impacted by cyberbullying behaviors, resulting a net decrease in social interaction and self-esteem. However, compared to the predator group, both social interaction and self-esteem dropped notably more for the victim group.

To date, the few research studies exploring cyberbullying and gaming show inconsistent, sometimes even conflicting results. This suggests that research can only begin to demonstrate the complexity in cyberbullying and gaming. Yet, it points out that online gaming seems to become a prominent area for people to cyberbully others. Many factors, like gender, contribute to the complex phenomenon related to cyberbullying and gaming.

GAMING AND BULLYING

Gaming and bullying is often portrait as negatively connected. A survey conducted in 2010 by the Josephson Institute on Ethics [77] indicated that children's exposure to violent video games can impede development of empathy and sympathy for others. In 2005, the American Psychological Association [15] stated that playing violent video games increases aggressive behavior and decreases helpful behavior, and hence not only called for a reduction of violence in video games and interactive media used by children and adolescents, but also endorsed teaching children to critically evaluate interactive media. The [78] in UK voiced concern about the influence of violent video games on primary school children. They reported that children as young as five are acting out violent scenes from video games on the school playground, reporting more observations of aggression, physical and relational, taking place in the classroom.

Researchers have also explored the effect of violent game playing through the lens of brain-based research. One study [78] examined violent video game effects via negative event-related potentials (nERPs) found within the brain. Their results suggested that those who are heavy players of violent video games display less empathetic sensitivity, and tend to display more aggressive tendencies in a laboratory task compared to controls.

While these results suggest a relationship between violence and violent games, the effect appears small and may be taken out of context [36]. Some [36,63,79] argue that we should not over simplifying findings by saying games are bad for children, but rather should pay attention to control the mediating effects. One study [80] investigated the relationship between frequent violent video game play and delinquent behavior among youth, controlling mediating factors such as trait anger, school performance, and aggressiveness. The participants were 1254 7th and 8th grade students who were asked to list the most recent games they played. Grand Theft Auto showed up consistently on the participant's top five lists. Results indicated that exposure to M-rated (mature - suitable for age 17+) games was a strong predictor of being bullies, which was compounded by the days played. M-rated game playing, however, was not connected with victimization. In addition, they found that trait anger, or aggressive personality was not a predictor of preference to M rated games. Gender effects were also identified showing that for boys, aggressive personality was the strongest predictor of bullying, while video game play was not a predictor. Interestingly, for girls,

M rated video game play became a strong predictor of bullying and fighting [80].

Building upon past research of mediating factors of aggression and violent video games, [63] assesses 302 students (mean age=12.34), a mostly Hispanic population, using clinically validated measures. The results revealed that current depressive symptoms were most predictive of violent outcomes in any of the models explored, while video game violence was not even a "trivial effect". In other words, violent game exposure had no long-term effects of aggression, rather depression may be the prevention key to serious aggression in youth.

Such mixed results from research highlight that we should not ignore the voice of the community of gamers, parents, and other adults who defended video games and reported that not everyone that plays violent games is violent.

CAN GAMING HELP FIGHT BULLYING AND CYBERBULLYING?

With the inconsistencies in whether violent video games increase aggression, it is important that we do not overlook the positive effects of game playing (i.e., socialization). For cxamplc, in Massive Multiplayer Online Games (MMOGs), players interact anonymously and simultaneously with each other, build identities, form relationships, and establish social networks. Based on past research that real friendships can act as a buffer to victimization, one study [36] investigated if online friendships can provide the same effects. Over 600 fifth and sixth grade students in Hong Kong participated in the study. Results revealed that 56% played MMOGs in the previous three months and boys played significantly more than girls. Over 93% reported having formed online friendships in MMOGs. Less than one eighth who played MMOG's reported being victims of cyberbullying. In addition, one eighth rated themselves as cyberbullies and reported engaging in the behavior frequently. Their analysis indicated that online friendships, similar to real life friendships, contributed significantly to all the psychosocial constructs measured. That is, friendships formed in online gaming environments could help boost children's overall psychological wellbeing. As well, online friendships benefit both gender group to the same degree [36].

The growing research regarding positive effects of game play leads to explorations of how video gaming can help in the prevention of bullying and cyberbullying. Though limited, game design has begun addressing these areas. For example, a game was developed and piloted with over 1000 children in Europe to explore how to reduce bullying [81]. The game is called "FearNot!" where kids can witness bullying situations without being directly involved. Each player takes the role of an invisible friend of the victimized character, discussing problems, possible solutions, and ways to cope. This influences the choices and narrative of where the game goes. Unfortunately no evaluation publications of this project could be found and hence the effect of such an approach cannot be determined.

In a similar vein, a team in Spain [82] created a 3D virtual world, Mii School (MS), to address substance abuse, bullying, and mental disorders in adolescents. Aming to help with early detection of these problem areas in youth, MS enabled players to experience emotions and feelings similar to real world scenarios in bullying, substance abuse, and mental disorders. In addition, this game can be used in a therapeutic setting where the therapist can change the stimuli in the game increasing the complexity of the levels. MS was piloted in a secondary school with 35 students (14 - 17 years old), with the MS program results being compared to a paper and pencil questionnaire. Interestingly, more students reported higher rates of being bullied on the paper questionnaire compared to the MS program. In the MS environment, when immersed in bullying situations, bullies often responded with feeling ashamed and simulated not listening to insults, but those who were not bullied answered insults from others sarcastically, with more insults, and some responses included violent threats.

Another group [83] explored the use of creating virtual scenarios in Second Life to educate students about cyberbullying. There were three phases investigating cyberbullying, implementation of the virtual world, and its effectiveness in educating young adults. Phase I consisted of a survey adapted from assessing cyberbullying. The survey results revealed that MySpace was the most prevalent source to experience cyberbullying. More than half of students on MySpace reported being a cyber-victim and around 70% reported being a cyberbully. Interestingly, one third of the students reported being a cyber-victim through virtual games, and one fourth reported being a cyberbully in games. Phase II consisted of a focus group stemming from data collected during phase I. The results revealed that high poverty schools displayed more aggression in their responses to bullying compared to the low poverty schools, which were more passive in their responses. Therefore, these researchers [83] suggest that socio economic status may play a mediating role in instances of cyberbullying. In the final phase, two participants viewed the virtual scenarios and evaluated them; the overall response suggested that the scenarios were realistic because kids often play interactive games.

CONCLUSIONS

Since cyberbullying is still a relatively new phenomenon, research studies, especially related to gaming, are scarce. Our review provides a first step towards a comprehensive understanding of the phenomena. This section first discusses the possible intervention strategies, linking them to the EMGCB model whenever appropriate. The focus then shifts to suggest future studies.

Intervention Strategies

Conforming to EMGCB, intervention strategies need to be considered in different levels, including mesa, micro, and macro levels. Previous meta-analysis demonstrated that training is strongly associated with reducing cyberbullying/bullying [84]. Training, therefore, need to not just focus on individual students, but also adults. For adults, while previous research emphasized on educating all school staff, parents, and families, our model suggests that members in gaming communities are also essential to be involved since cyberbullying occurs frequently in gaming environments. Educating adults need to consider not only cyberbulllying/ bullying related topics and technology use, but also knowledge about gaming. Adequate understanding of effective strategies to address cyberbullying and bullying should also include, but not limit to, knowledge about cyberbullying/bullying in relation to gaming, mental health, emotions, and demographic matters.

While improving young people's understanding and skills is equally important, the approaches to train young people should be different from adult training, because video and other multimedia methods prove to be more effective than regular curriculum integration for youth [85]. Given youths fascination with gaming and multimedia, the EMGCB suggest that one best approach may be to games as a platform for bullying/ cyberbullying prevention and intervention. There are two ways to implement such an approach. First, we can use existing gaming communities (e.g. World of Warcraft community) to impart knowledge about ways to respond effectively to cyberbullying/bullying. Secondly, we can build anti-bullying games to teach people needed information and skills. It is optimal that both youth and adults are involved in such gaming environments.

Proactive policies, plans and practices are key factors as identified in earlier review studies [84,85] to reduce cyberbullying/bullying. Based on our model, we recommend that a whole-school formal anti-bullying policy should also consider people's gaming behaviors to send clear and consistent messages to guide actions of people for the prevention and intervention of cyberbullying/bullying behaviors.

Building and sustaining a safe and supportive environment, in both real and virtual worlds, is another factor that can reduce cyberbullying/bullying [51]. Students need a positive climate that goes beyond school boundaries. Earlier studies [57] found that extracurricular activities, such as sport and recreation, can lead youth to report cyberbullying incidents as well as decreasing their chance to retaliate others when they are cyberbullied. Gaming is such a wonderful media for recreation and entertainment, hence provides a great way to increase school connectedness and social networks for youth and adults. One possible strategy, as our model implied, is to create games that involve students and their teachers, parents, family members, or even administrators to help build a supportive social environment in schools and gaming worlds.

Collaboration amongst schools, families, and communities is a must to effectively address cyberbullying/bullying issues [51]. Building partnerships amongst schools and communities can help develop a comprehensive and coordinate approach to cyberbullying/ bullying prevention. According to our model, forming partnerships should involve not just students, teachers, and parents, but also professionals in the area of mental health, physicians and drug and alcohol counselors, gaming experts, and technology experts.

Future Research

In this review, we have proposed the Enactivist Model of Cyberbullying, Bullying and Gaming, which suggests that the exploration of cyberbullying and bullying in relation to gaming should be conducted in a holistic fashion rather than limiting the focus on individuals' aggressive behavior. Enactivism stresses the importance of the interplay of systems' parts. Therefore, macro, meso and micro level variables should all be examined with a focus on the interactions of them. The investigation should not only concentrate on individuals' acts and mind (including their behavior, attitude, emotions, mental health), but also the social environment in which they situate (e.g., their victims, their peers, their schools, their technology access, their game buddies). For example, longitudinal studies can investigate the interactions of students (including cyberbullies, their victims), their peers (including their game buddies), and parents, through multiple-point surveys, and continued observation of the student behaviors (including cyberbullying/bullying and gaming) in different environments (e.g. home, school). Another possibility is designing research-supported games addressing cyberbullying/bullying problems and then conducting experimental studies involving students, parents, school personnel to examine the effects of such games. Employing design based research considering variables at the micro, meso, and macro levels (e.g. student demographics, school environments, gaming behaviors) can provide another lens to explore potentials of digital games in addressing cyberbullying/bullying issues. Combating cyberbullying and bullying should be a collective effort on the part of schools, families, peers, and society.

Table 1: List of studies examining gaming and aggression

Year	Author(s)	Focus of Research (Level**)	Country	Design/ Sample Size	Age Range	Games	Effect of gaming
2001*	Anderson & Bushman [16]	Games & Aggression (Meso & Micro)	USA	Meta-Analysis	Mixed	General Violent Video Games	Negative
2010*	Anderson et. al [17]	Games & Aggression (Meso & Micro)	Primary USA (Mixed)	Meta-Analysis	Mixed	General Violent Video Games	Negative
2006	Bartholow, Bushman, & Sestir [78]	Games & Aggression (Macro & Micro)	USA	Experimental, n=39	Mean age = 19.5	General Violent Video Games	Negative
2011	Carmona, Espinola, Cangas, & Iribarne [81]	Cyberbullying (Macro)	Spain	Survey, n = 35	Mean age = 15.29	Virtual Worlds	Positive
2012*	Connolly, Boyle, MacArthur, Hainey, & Boyle [20]	Games (Meso)	USA	Review, 129 papers	Mixed	General Games	Positive
2007*	Ferguson [79]	Games (Meso)	USA	Meta-Analysis	Mixed	General Violent Video Games	Mixed
2011	Ferguson [63]	Bullying & Games (Micro)	USA, Hispanic population	Survey n=302	Mean age = 12.34	General Violent Video Games	No long term effects
2014	Frying, et al. [76]	Cyberbullying & games (micro)	Unknown (Gaming community)	Survey n=1025	Mean age=22	General game	negative
2012	Gentile & Bushman [54]	Games & Aggression (Macro)	USA	Survey n=430	Mean age = 9.7	General Violent Video Games	Negative
2009	Gentile et. al [72]	Games (Macro & Meso)	Singapore	Survey, n= 727	7th-8th graders	General Games	Mixed
			Japan	Survey n=1830	5th-8th-11th graders	General Games	Mixed
			USA	Experimental n=161	Undergraduates	Super Mario Sunshine, Chibi Robo, Ty2, Crash Twinsanity, Pure Pinball, Super Monkey Ball Deluxe	Mixed
2013	Lam, Cheng, & Liu [75]	Cyberbullying (Macro)	Northeast China	Survey n=1278	Mean age = 14.7	General Games	Negative
2013	Leung & McBride-Chang [36]	Cyberbullying (Macro & Micro)	Hong Kong	Survey n=626	Mean age = 10.8	MMOG	Mixed
2011	Mark & Ratliffe [56]	Cyberbullying (Macro & Meso)	USA	Survey n=265	Middle school	Role-playing games	Negative
2009	Mesch [39]	Cyberbullying (Macro)	USA	Survey n= 935	12-17 y/o	General games	no effect
2009	Olson, Kutner, Baer, Beresin, Warner, & Nicholi [80]	Bullying (Meso & Micro)	USA	Survey, n= 1254	7th-8th graders	General Violent Video Games: Grand Theft Auto	Negative
2012a	Saleem, Anderson, & Gentile [73]	Games & Behavior (Meso & Micro)	USA	Experimental n=191	Mean age = 11.4	Super Mario Sunshine, Chibi Robo, Ty2, Crash Twinsanity, Pure Pinball, Super Monkey Ball Deluxe	Mixed
2012b	Saleem, Anderson, & Gentile [74]	Games & Affect (Meso & Micro)	USA	Experimental n=330	Mean age = 19.57	Super Mario Sunshine, Chibi Robo, Ty2, Crash Twinsanity, Pure Pinball, Super Monkey Ball Deluxe	Mixed
2012	Tippett & Kwak [61]	Cyberbullying (Macro)	South Korea	Survey n=416	Mean age = 14.0	General Games	Negative
2009	Wright, Burnham, Inman & Ogorchock [82]	Cyberbullying (Macro)	USA	Mixed Methods, n=114	Middle school	General games, Virtual world	Positive
2012	Yang [47]	Bullying (Meso & Micro)	Taiwan	Survey, n= 1069	Adolescents	General Violent Video Games	Negative

Note. * Review studies. ** Levels as described in the theoretical framework

There is still much to be explored, examined, and investigated in regards to cyberbullying and its relationship to gaming. As an overview of the research represented in **Table 1** indicates, the existing empirical studies on cyberbullying in connections with gaming are predominantly using survey design, with just a few studies employing experimental design approach. Other research designs such as qualitative approach to explore cyberbullying, bullying in connection with gaming is virtually nonexistent. This calls for future research adapting a more diverse design, especially experimental design and or qualitative or mixed research to broaden our understanding about this phenomenon. In addition, longitudinal studies may help elucidate the different patterns of change or stability of people and consequently will shed light on the controversy about the long-term effect of gaming on aggression.

As well, this review reveals that virtually no study examining the connections between gaming and cyberbullying/bullying has looked at variables from all three levels (i.e. macro, meso, micro), let alone the interactions amongst the variables. Future studies are recommended not only to holistically analyze the phenomenon from all 3 levels but also to pay particular attention to the interplay of these factors.

As indicated in **Table 1**, a majority of the current studies in the field are US studies, with only a handful of Asian studies, and one European study. While it is well documented that cyberbullying is an international phenomenon [40], apparently there is a lack of international studies focusing on cyberbullying and gaming. Researchers need to expand the landscape with international perspectives on studies examining the association between bullying/cyberbullying and gaming. Comparative studies juxtaposing data from different countries and even continents will also deepen our understanding of the phenomena.

Another area of research yet to be developed is investigating the effects of the actual game content itself [17,72,73]. Some [80] suggest that parents should play video games with their children in order to better understand the appeal of the game and motivation of playing, which may help stop bullying and other acts of aggression.

Consistent throughout the literature is the need for education of students, teachers, parents, and higher education institutions in order to prevent cyberbullying. Yet, almost all of the studies in the field have centered the attention on the negative effects of gaming and its connection with aggression. This review highlights the lack of empirical studies and the limited knowledge on whether and how gaming can have positive effects on players. Very few studies explored the potential of gaming and how we can harness the power of gaming to educate or help address cyberbullying and bullying issues. For example, can we develop educational games to address cyberbullying by teaching students how to fight cyberbullies or by educating bystanders? Future studies on positive effects of gaming in relation to cyberbullying and bullying are highly recommended. As well, design based research integrating game design into cyberbullying/bullying studies will provide useful information for the development of intervention and prevention programs.

A comprehensive understanding of the phenomenon from all perspectives is the precursor to the development of successful prevention strategies and intervention programs to address cyberbullying and bullying. Until then, we may be able to develop education that supports children's healthy lifestyles inside and outside of schools, in real life or out in cyberspace.

REFERENCES

1. FoxNews.com (2011) White House Ready to Rumble with Cyberbullies, Online article.
2. Bartlett JE, Bartlett ME (2011) Workplace bullying: An integrative literature review. Advances InDeveloping Human Resources 13: 69-84.
3. Catanzaro MF (2011)Indirect aggression, bullying and female teen victimization: A literature review. Pastoral Care In Education 29: 83-101.
4. Espelage D, De La Rue L (2012) School bullying: its nature and ecology. International Journal Of Adolescent Medicine & Health 24: 3-10.
5. Hong J, Espelage DL (2012) A review of research on bullying and peer victimization in school: An ecological system analysis. Aggression & Violent Behavior 17: 311-322.
6. Salmivalli C (2010) Bullying and the peer group: A review. Aggression & Violent Behavior 15: 112-120.
7. Rose CA, Monda-Amaya LE, Espelage DL (2011) Bullying perpetration and victimization in special education: A review of the literature. Remedial And Special Education 32: 114-130.
8. Jordan K, Austin J (2012) A review of the literature on bullying in U.S. schools and how a parent–educator partnership can be an effective way to handle bullying. Journal Of Aggression, Maltreatment & Trauma 21: 440-458.
9. Dooley JJ, Pyzalski J, Cross D (2009) Cyberbullying versus face-to-face bullying: A theoretical and conceptual review. ZeitschriftFürPsychologie/Journal Of Psychology 217: 182-188.
10. Sticca F, Perren S (2013)Is cyberbullying worse than traditional bullying? Examining the differential roles of medium, publicity, and anonymity for the perceived severity of bullying. Journal Of Youth And Adolescence 42: 739-750.
11. Cassidy W, Faucher C, Jackson M (2013) Cyberbullying among youth: A comprehensive review of current international research and its implications and applications to policy and practice. School Psychology International 34: 575-612.
12. Kowalski R, Giumetti G, Schroeder A, Lattanner M (2014) Bullying in the digital age: a critical review and meta-analysis of cyberbullying

research among youth. Psychology Bulletin 140.

13. Notar C, Padgett S, Roden J (2013) Cyberbullying: A review of the literature. Universal Journal of educational Research 1: 1-9
14. Kaplan A (2012) Violence in the media: What effects on behavior?. Psychiatric Times 29: 1-11.
15. Power MR (2009) Video games and a culture of conflict. Journal Of Children & Media 3: 90-94.
16. Anderson CA, Bushman BJ (2001) Effects of violent video games on aggressive behavior, aggressive cognition, aggressive affect, physiological arousal, and prosocial behavior: A meta-analytic review of the scientific literature. Psychological Science 12: 353.
17. Anderson CA, Shibuya A, Ihori N, Swing EL, Bushman BJ, et al. (2010) Violent video game effects on aggression, empathy, and prosocial behavior in Eastern and Western countries: A meta-analytic review. Psychological Bulletin 136: 151-173.
18. Sim T, Gentile DA, Bricolo F, Serpelloni G, Gulamoydeen F(2012) A conceptual review of research on the pathological use of computers, video Games, and the internet. International JournalOf Mental Health And Addiction 10: 748-769.
19. Barlett CP, Anderson CA, Swing EL (2009) Video game effects--Confirmed, suspected, and speculative: A review of the evidence. Simulation & Gaming 40: 377-403.
20. Connolly TM, Boyle EA, MacArthur E, Hainey T, Boyle JM (2012) A systematic literature review of empirical evidence on computer games and serious games. Computers & Education 59: 661-686.
21. Felicia P (2012) Motivation in games: A literature review. International Journal Of Computer Science In Sport 11: 4-14.
22. Varela, Thompson E, Rosch E (1991a)The embodied mind: Cognitive science and human experience. Massachusetts Institute of Technology Press, Cambridge, MA.
23. Maturana HR, Varela FJ (1980)Autopoiesis and cognition: The realization of the living. D. Reidel Publishing Company, Dordrecht, Holland.
24. Li Q, Clark B, Winchester I (2010) Instructional design and technology grounded in enactivism: A paradigm shift? British Journal of Educational Technology 41: 403-419

25. McGann M (2014) Enacting a social ecology: radically embodied intersubjectivity. Frontiers in Psychology 5:0 13-21.
26. Varela F, Thompson E, Rosch E (1991d)The embodied mind: Cognitive science and human experience. Massachusetts Institute of Technology Press, Cambridge, MA.
27. Facer K (2001)Children's out of school use of computers A Report for the InterActive Education Project. FutureLab, Berkshire.
28. Sandford R, Ulicsak M, Facer K, Rudd T (2006) Teaching with games: Using commercial off-the-shelf computer games in formal education (pp. 66). Bristol, UK: FutureLab.
29. Lenhart A, Kahne J, Middaugh E, Macgill A, Evans C, Vitak J (2009) Teens, video games, and civics. (Vol. 2008). Washington, DC: PEW Internet & American Life Project.
30. Herz JC (1997) Joystick nation: Little, Brown & Company
31. Activision (Producer). (2013, July 25, 2013). Call of Duty: Black Ops II.
32. Kirriemuir J, McFarlane A (2004) Literature review in games and learning. Bristol: NestaFuturelab.
33. Gros B (2007) Digital games in education: The design of game-based learning environment. Journal of Research on TEchnology in Education, 40(1), 23-38
34. Willard N (2004) Educator's Guide to Cyberbullying: Addressing the Harm Caused by Online Social Cruelty Retrieved July 11, 2005,
35. Smith PK, Mahdavi J, Carvalho M, Fisher S, Russell S, Tippett N (2008) Cyberbullying: its nature and impact in secondary school pupils. Journal of Child Psychology & Psychiatry 49: 376-385.
36. Leung A, McBride-Chang C (2013) Game on? Online friendship, cyberbullying, and psychosocial adjustment in Hong Kong Chinese children. Journal Of Social & Clinical Psychology 32: 159-185.
37. Jones LM, Mitchell KJ, Finkelhor D (2013) Online harassment in context: Trends from three youth internet safety surveys (2000, 2005, 2010). Psychology Of Violence 3: 53-69.
38. Olweus D (2003) A profile of bullying at school. Educational Leadership 60: 12-19.
39. Mesch GS (2009) Parental mediation, online activities, and cyberbullying. Cyberpsychology& Behavior 12: 387-393.

40. Li Q, Cross D, Smith P (2012) Cyberbullying in the Global Playground: Research from Interntational Perspective. Boston: Blackwell Publishing.
41. Wingate V, Minney JA, Guadagno RE (2013) Sticks and stones may break your bones, but words will always hurt you: A review of cyberbullying. Social Influence 8: 87-106.
42. Sugarman DB, Willoughby T (2013) Technology and violence: Conceptual issues raised by the rapidly changing social environment. Psychology Of Violence 3: 1-8.
43. McDermott IE (2012) Trolls, Cyberbullies, and Other Offenders. Searcher 20: 7.
44. Hanewald R (2009) Cyberbullying research: The current state. Australian Educational Computing, 24: 10-15.
45. Barack L (2010)The thin line on digital abuse. School Library Journal 56: 11.
46. Kowalski R, Limber S, Agatston P (2008) Cyberbullying: Bullying in the digital age. Blackwell Publishing Ltd, Malden, MA.
47. Yang S (2012) Paths to bullying in online gaming: The effects of gender, preference for playing violent games, hostility, and aggressive behavior on bullying. Journal Of Educational Computing Research 47: 235-249.
48. Mehari K, Farrell A, Le A (2014) Cyberbullying among adolescents: Measures in search of a construct. Psychology of Violence 4: 399-415.
49. Waasdorp T, Bradshaw C (2015)Theoverlop between cyberbullying and traditional bullying. Journal of Adolescent Health 56: 483-488.
50. Li Q, Lambert D (2012)Cyberbulling behaviors. In: Y. Zhen (Eds.), Encyclopedia of Cyber Behavior. IGI Global Publisher, Hershey, PA.
51. Cross D, Li Q, Smith P, Monks H (2012) Understanding and preventing cyberbullying: Where have we been and where should we be going? In: Q. Li, D. Cross & P. Smith (Eds.), Bullying in the Global Playground: Research from International Perspectives. Wiley-Blackwell, London.
52. Olweus D (1993) Bullying at school: What we know and what we can do. Blackwell Publishers, Inc, Cambridge, MA.
53. Wolke D, Tippett N, Dantchev S (2015) Bullying in the family : sibling bullying. The Lancet Psychiatry

54. Gentile DA, Bushman BJ (2012) Reassessing media violence effects using a risk and resilience approach to understanding aggression. Psychology Of Popular Media Culture 1: 138-151.
55. Pellegrini A, Bartini M (2002) A longitudinal study of bullying, victimization, and peer affiliation during the transition from primary school to middle school. American Educational Research Journal, 37: 699-725.
56. Mark L, Ratliffe KT (2011) Cyber worlds: New playgrounds for bullying. Computers In The Schools, 28: 92-116.
57. Li Q, Fung T (2012) Predicting student behaviors: Cyberbullies, cybervictims, and bystanders. In: Q. Li, D. Cross & P. Smith (Eds.), Bullying in the Global Village. Wiley-Blackwell Publishing, Boston.
58. Li Q (2010) Cyberbullying in High Schools: A Study of Students' Behaviors and Beliefs about This New Phenomenon. Journal of Aggression, Maltreatment, and Trauma 19: 372-392.
59. Bourgonjon J, Valcke M, Soetaert R, Wever B, Schellens T (2011) Parental acceptance of digital game based learning. Computers,& Education 57: 1434-1444.
60. Kutner L, Olson C, Warner D, Hertzog S (2008) Parents' and sons' perspectives on video game play – a qualitative study. Journal of Adolescent Research 23: 76-96.
61. Tippett N, Kwak K (2012) Cyberbullying in South Korea. In: Q. Li, D. Cross & P. K. Smith (Eds.), Cyberbullying in the global playground: Research from international perspectives. Wiley-Blackwell, London.
62. Gee J (2008)What video games have to teach us about learning and literacy (2nd ed.): Palgrave Macmillan.
63. Ferguson C (2011) Video games and youth violence: a prospective analysis in adolescents. Journal Of Youth And Adolescence 40: 377-391.
64. Ferguson C, Kilburn J (2009)The public health risks of media violence: a meta-analytic review. The Journal Of Pediatrics 154: 759-763.
65. Sherry J (2007)Violent video games and aggression: Why can't we find effects? In: R. W. Preiss, B. Gayle, N. Burrell, M. Allen & J. Bryant (Eds.), Mass media effects research: Advances through meta-analysis (pp. 245-262). Lawrence Erlbaum Associates Publishers, Mahwah, NJ.
66. Kutner L, Olson C (2008) Grand Theft Childhood: The Surprising Truth About Violent Video Games and What Parents Can Do: Simon

& Schuster.

67. Vossekuil B, Fein RA, Reddy M, Borum R, Modzeleski W (2002) The final report and findings of the "Safe School Initiative": Implications for the prevention of school attacks in the US. Department of Education & US Secret Service, Washington, DC.
68. Olson CK (2004) Media violence research and youth violence data: Why do they conflict? Academic Psychiatry 28: 144-150.
69. Griffiths M (1997) Video games and aggression. The Psychologist 10: 397-401.
70. Dill KE, Redding RE, Smith PK, Surette R, Cornell DG (2011) Recurrent issues in efforts to prevent homicidal youth violence in schools: Expert opinions. New Directions for Youth Development 129: 113-128.
71. Squire (2006)From content to context: Videogames as designed experience. Educational Researcher, 35: 19-29.
72. Gentile DA, Anderson CA, Yukawa S, Ihori N, Saleem M, et al. (2009) The effects of prosocial video games on prosocial behaviors: International evidence from correlational, longitudinal, and experimental studies. Personality And Social Psychology Bulletin 35: 752-763.
73. Saleem M, Anderson CA, Gentile DA (2012) Effects of prosocial, neutral, and violent video games on children's helpful and hurtful behaviors. Aggressive Behavior 38: 281-287.
74. Saleem M, Anderson CA, Gentile DA (2012) Effects of prosocial, neutral, and violent video games on college students' affect. Aggressive Behavior 38: 263-271.
75. Lam LT, Cheng Z, Liu X (2013)Violent online games exposure and cyberbullying/victimization among adolescents. Cyberpsychology, Behavior & Social Networking 16: 159-165.
76. Fryling M, Cotler J, Rivituso J, Mathews L, Pratico S (2014) Cyberbullying or normal game play? Impact of age, gender, and experience on cyberbullying in multiplayer online gaming environments: Perceptions from one gaming forum. Paper presented at the Conference for Information Systems Applied Research, Baltimore, MD.
77. Hicks MT (2011) Video games and bullying. The Washington Times 6.
78. Bartholow BD, Bushman BJ, Sestir MA (2006)Chronic violent video

game exposure and desensitization to violence: Behavioral and event-related brain potential data. Journal of Experimental Social Psychology 42: 532-539.

79. Ferguson C (2007)The good, the bad and the ugly: A meta-analytic review of positive and negative effects of violent video games. Psychiatric Quarterly 78: 309-316.
80. Olson CK, Kutner LA, Baer L, Beresin EV, Warner DE, et al. (2009) M-Rated video games and aggressive or problem behavior among young adolescents. Applied Developmental Science 13: 188-198.
81. ICWE International Conferences (2007) Preventing Bullying At Schools With Computer Role Play Game, ScienceDaily.
82. Carmona J, Espinola M, Cangas A, Iribarne L (2011) MII-School: A 3d videogame for the early detection of abuse of substances, bullying, and mental disorders in adolescents. European Journal of Education and Psychology 4: 75-85.
83. Wright VH, Burnham JJ, Inman CT, Ogorchock HN (2009) Cyberbullying: Using virtual scenarios to educate and raise awareness. Journal Of Computing In Teacher Education 26:35-42.
84. Farrington DP, Ttofi MM (2009) Reducing school bullying: Evidence-based implications for policy. Crime and Justice 38: 281-345.
85. Farrington DP, Ttofi MM (2009) School-based programs to reduce bullying and victimization Campbell Systematic Reviews. The Campbell Collaboration, Oslo.

CHAPTER 4

PREVALENCE AND PATTERNS OF TRADITIONAL BULLYING VICTIMIZATION AND CYBER-TEASING AMONG COLLEGE POPULATION IN SPAIN

Francisco Caravaca Sánchez, María Falcón Romero, Javier Navarro-Zaragoza, Aurelio Luna Ruiz-Cabello, Oriali Rodriges Frantzisko and Aurelio Luna Maldonado

Department of Social and Health Sciences, University of Murcia, 30100 Campus of Espinardo, Murcia, Spain

Citation: Francisco Caravaca Sánchez, María Falcón Romero, Javier Navarro-Zaragoza, Aurelio Luna Ruiz-Cabello, Oriali Rodriges Frantzisko and Aurelio Luna Maldonado, "Prevalence and patterns of traditional bullying victimization and cyber-teasing among college population in Spain," DOI 10.1186/s12889-016-2857-8.

ABSTRACT

Background

Traditional bullying victimization and the growing number of cyber-teasing victims during the last decade is a major public health concern. The objective of this study was to examine the relationship between students' experiences of traditional bullying victimization and cyber-teasing and the sociodemographic characteristics of a sample composed of college students in Spain.

Methods

In the fall of 2014, 543 sixth-grade students from southeast Spain completed an anonymous survey on their experience of both kinds of to ascertain any relationship with sociodemographic characteristics, including gender, nationality, economic problems, family conflicts and alcohol and cannabis use.

Results

A total of 62.2 % of the students reported to having suffered traditional bullying victimization and 52.7 % reported that they had been subject to cyber-teasing. 40.7 % of participants had been victims of traditional bullying victimization and cyber-teasing in the past 12 months. Most (65.7 %) of the victims were at the same time cyber-teasing victims; 77.6 % of cyber-teasing victims were also victimized in a different manner. Traditional bullying victimization was higher among boys than among girls, while female students were more likely to have been subjected to cyber-teasing than male students. The characteristics that most heavily influenced suffering traditional bullying victimization were economic problems, family conflicts and cannabis use.

Conclusions

Our findings confirm overlapping results in the risk factors that influence suffering both traditional bullying victimization and cyber-teasing: there was a strong influence of certain sociodemographic and individual characteristics of the college population, suggesting that specific policies are necessary to improve college students' environment in Spain.

Keywords: College Student, Sociodemographic Characteristic, Family Conflict, Foreign Student, College Population

BACKGROUND

In the recent years, awareness of new young victims of cyber-bullying has increased [1, 2] due to the *boom* in information and communications technology and the use of social network. The internet and other electronic media offer many benefits to adolescents, even though previous cross-sectional studies have shown that cyber-bullying and cyber-teasing among the school population is associated with mental health problems such as depression, suicidal thoughts and non-fatal suicidal behavior among school students [3, 4, 5].

Cyber-bullying, also known as electronic bullying or online bullying is defined as intentional and repeated harm inflicted on individuals through the use of electronic devices such as mobile phones or computers [6]. Similar to definitions of traditional bullying, cyber-bullying also implies that the offender's behavior is usually aggressive with intention to harm the victims [7]. Cyber-teasing is a related phenomenon defined as hurtful teasing sent via technology that includes messages resulting in psychological abuse, verbal aggression or social rejection that has received less attention that cyber-bullying [8].

Previous studies have found rates of cyber-bullying among young regular Internet users (between 10 and 17 years old) that range from 4 to 72 % [9, 10], and lower rates among college population compared to adolescent samples ranging from 9 to 20 % [11, 12, 13, 14]. Cyber-bullying and cyber-teasing are known to cause higher level of depression disorders in victims that traditional ways of bullying among adolescents [15]. Finally, victims frequently suffer additional problems involving aggressiveness, substance use or delinquency [15].

Cyber-bullying can occur in several ways [16], and its effects are intensified by the audience reached or the ability to attack at any time or in any place [7, 15]. Nevertheless, schools still lack of information on the effects and consequences of this problem, which they tend not to distinguish from traditional bullying [7].

According to Olweus [17], bullying is defined as a repeated negative behavior that occurs along time in a relationship characterized by an imbalance of strength and power. However, approximately three decades of

gender, nationality, grade, economic problems, family conflicts, alcohol use and cannabis use in the last twelve months.

RESULTS

Prevalence and Overlap Of Traditional Bullying Victimization And Cyber-teasing

Table 1 describes the sociodemographic characteristics of the survey college population for full sample and by gender. The prevalence of cyber-teasing and traditional bullying victimization for the whole sample and according to gender is shown in Table 2. Overall, 52.7 % (95 % confidence interval [CI]: 48.3–57.1 %) of students reported cyber-teasing, 62.2 % (95 % CI: 58.0–66.1 %) reported traditional bullying victimization during the previous twelve months, and 40.7 % (95 % CI: 36.8–44.6 %) were victims of both types of victimization (traditional bullying victimization and cyber-teasing) in the last twelve months. Analyzing the overlap between both types of victimization, there was a statistically significant difference: 65.7 % of traditional bullying victims were also victims of cyber-teasing, and 77.6 % of cyber-teasing victims suffered also traditional bullying victimization (χ^2=60.789, p <0.001). Categorizing these reports into two, we obtained the following results: 21.3 % suffered traditional bullying victimization only and 12 % victims of cyber-teased only.

Table 1: Sociodemographics characteristics of study sample for full sample and by gender

Variables	Total	Male	Female
	N=543	*N*=138	*N*=405
	No. (%)	No. (%)	No. (%)
Nationality			
Spanish	499 (91.9)	132 (95.7)	367 (90.6)
Non-Spanish	44 (8.1)	6 (4.3)	38 (9.4)
Grade			
2nd	195 (35.9)	36 (26.1)	159 (39.3)
3rd	144 (26.5)	26 (18.8)	118 (29.1)
4th	82 (15.1)	36 (26.1)	46 (11.4)
5th	58 (10.7)	12 (8.7)	46 (11.4)
6th	64 (11.8)	28 (20.3)	36 (8.9)
Economic problems***			

Yes	183 (33.7)	28 (20.3)	155 (38.3)
No	360 (66.3)	110 (79.7)	250 (61.7)
Family conflicts*			
Yes	99 (18.3)	19 (13.8)	85 (21.0)
No	444 (81.7)	119 (86.2)	320 (79.0)
Alcohol use			
Yes	438 (80.7)	111 (80.4)	327 (80.7)
No	105 (19.3)	27 (19.6)	78 (19.3)
Cannabis use**			
Yes	88 (16.2)	34 (24.6)	54 (13.3)
No	455 (83.8)	104 (75.4)	351 (86.7)

Statistically significant difference between male and female students; *$p \leq .05$, **$P \leq .01$, ***$P \leq .001$

Table 2: Prevalence of cyber-teasing and traditional bullying victimization during the past twelve months in full sample and by gender

	Total	**Male**	**Female**
	***N*=543**	***N*=138**	***N*=405**
	No. (%) and 95 % CI[a]	**No. (%) and 95 % CI[a]**	**No. (%) and 95 % CI[a]**
Cyber-teasing			
None victims	257 (47.3) 42.9–51.7	73 (52.9) 44.4–60.8	184 (45.4) 40.4–50.4
Victims	286 (52.7) 48.3–57.1	65 (47.1) 39.2–55.6	221 (54.6) 49.6–59.6
1 time	137 (25.2) 21.6–29.1	33 (23.9) 16.5–31.9	104 (25.7) 21.7–29.9
2 time	45 (8.3) 5.9–10.7	14 (10.1) 5.6–15.0	31 (7.7) 5.2–10.2
More than 2 times	104 (19.2) 15.8–22.3	18 (13.0) 7.5–18.6	86 (21.2) 17.5–25.1
Traditional bullying victimization			
None victims	205 (37.8) 33.9–42.0	40 (29.0) 21.9–36.4	165 (40.7) 36.0–45.7
Victims*	338 (62.2) 58.0–66.1	98 (71.0) 63.6–78.1	240 (59.3) 54.3–64.0
1 time*	177 (32.6) 28.9–36.6	58 (42.0) 34.1–50.4	119 (29.4) 25.1–33.8
2 time	36 (6.6) 4.6–8.8	6 (4.3) 1.3–8.1	30 (7.4) 5.0–10.1
More than 2 times	125 (23.0) 19.5–26.5	34 (24.6) 17.7–32.1	91 (22.5) 18.4–26.5
Cyber and traditional bullying victimization			
None victims	322 (59.3) 55.4–63.2	77 (55.8) 47.3–63.7	245 (60.5) 55.9–65.4
Victims	221 (40.7) 36.8–44.6	61 (44.2) 36.3–52.7	160 (39.5) 34.6–44.1
1 time*	68 (12.5) 9.5–15.5	26 (18.8) 12.8–25.8	42 (10.4) 7.6–13.4

2 time	82 (15.1) 12.3–18.4	22 (15.9) 10.3–22.0	60 (14.8) 10.9–18.3
More than 2 times	71 (13.1) 10.1–16.0	13 (9.4) 4.6–14.6	58 (14.3) 10.7–17.8

[a]Confidence interval

Statistically significant difference between male and female students; *$p \leq .05$

Correlates of Traditional Bullying Victimization and Cyber-teasing

Table 3 displays the demographic characteristics of victimization when they are categorized into the following four groups: cyber-teasing victim only, traditional bullying victimization only, cyber-teasing and traditional bullying victimization, and neither. Reports of traditional bullying victimization were higher among boys than among girls (26.8 % vs. 19.5 %, χ^2=6.052, p=0.014) while cyber-teasing was more prevalent among girls than among boys (15.0 % vs. 2.8 %, χ^2=10.352, $p \leq 0.001$).

Table 3: Sociodemographic correlations of traditional bullying victimization and cyber-teasing of study sample

Variables	Cyber-teasing victim only	Traditional bullying victimization only	Cyber-teasing and traditional bullying victimization	Neither
	No. (%)	No. (%)	No. (%)	No. (%)
Gender				
Girl	61 (15.0)***	79 (19.5)*	160 (39.5)	105 (25.9)
Boy	4 (2.8)	37 (26.8)	61 (44.2)	36 (26.0)
Nationality				
Spanish	61 (12.2)	111 (22.2)**	200 (40.0)	127 (25.4)
Non-Spanish	4 (9.0)	5 (11.3)	21 (47.7)	14 (31.8)
Grade				
2°	29 (14.8)	40 (20.5)	85 (43.5)	195 (21.1)
3°	25 (17.3)	26 (18.0)	59 (40.9)	34 (23.6)
4°	2 (2.4)	20 (13.8)	33 (40.2)	27 (32.9)
5°	5 (8.6)	16 (27.5)	24 (41.3)	13 (7.5)
6°	4 (6.2)	14 (21.8)	20 (31.2)	26 (40.6)
Economic problems				
Yes	35 (19.1)**	28 (15.3)**	80 (43.7)	40 (21.8)

No	30 (8.3)	88 (24.4)	141 (39.1)	101 (28)
Family conflicts				
Yes	61 (21.3)***	70 (20.7)	51 (49.0)*	26 (25.0)
No	43 (16.7)	34 (32.6)	170 (38.7)	116 (26.4)
Alcohol use				
Yes	52 (11.8)	101 (23.0)*	179 (40.8)	106 (24.2)
No	13 (12.3)	15 (14.2)	42 (40.0)	35 (33.3)
Cannabis use				
Yes	10 (11.3)	24 (27.2)	30 (34.0)	24 (27.2)
No	55 (12.0)	92 (20.1)	191 (41.9)	117 (25.7)

Statistically significant difference between victims and non-victims; $*p \leq .05$, $**P \leq .01$, $***P \leq .001$

According to the nationality of the college students, traditional bullying victimization was almost twice more frequent in the case of Spanish students compared with foreign students (22.2 % vs. 11.3 %, $\chi^2=8.052$, $p=0.003$). As regards the economic situation, cyber-teasing (19.1 % vs. 8.3 %, $\chi^2=11.45$, $p \leq 0.001$) and traditional bullying victimization (24.4 % vs. 15.3 %, $\chi^2=6.678$, $p=0.009$) was higher among participants with low financial resources. Family conflicts were also higher among college students who suffered traditional bullying victimization and cyber-teasing (49.0 % vs. 38.7 %, $\chi^2=6.124$, $p=0.016$). Analyzing the substance use data, 80 % of the college students had drunk alcohol during the last year, and, among these students, traditional bullying victimization was more common than among non-drinkers (23.0 % vs. 14.2 %, $\chi^2=5.831$, $p=0.023$).

Table 4 present the logistic regressions which regulate the relationship of the different ways of victimization (cyber-teasing victim only, traditional bullying victimization only, cyber-teasing and traditional bullying victimization, or neither of them) for the sociodemographic characteristics. There was a strong relationship between the grade of the students and suffering cyber-teasing only. For example, the college students of 2nd (adjusted odds ratio [AOR] =3.86; 95 % CI: 1.19, 12.48, p-value=0.004) and 3rd grade (AOR=3.94; 95 % CI: 1.20–12.94, p-value=0.006) were almost 4 times more likely to report cyber-teasing than students of 6th grade. Economic problems among the college students were also a risk factor for suffering cyber-teasing only (AOR=2.46; 95 % CI: 1.29–4.71, p-value=0.008). Finally, family conflicts were a risk factor for both cyber-teasing and traditional bullying victimization (AOR=1.62; 95 % CI: 1.10–2.34, p-value≤0.001).

Table 4: Associations between traditional bullying victimization and cyber-teasing and sociodemographic characteristics of study sample

Characteristics	Cyber-teasing victim only	Traditional bullying victimization only	Cyber-teasing and traditional bullying victimization	Neither
	AOR[a] (95 % CI[b])	AOR[a] (95 % CI)	AOR (95 % CI)	Ref.
Gender				
Girl	0.26 (0.08–0.79)	1.49 (0.84–2.64)	1.34 (0.81–2.23)	1.00
Boy (ref)	1.00	1.00	1.00	1.00
Nationality				
Spanish	1.92 (0.59–6.24)	2.50 (0.86–7.23)	1.08 (0.52–2.23)	1.00
Foreigner (ref)	1.00	1.00	1.00	1.00
Grade				
2°	3.86 (1.19–12.48)*	2.10 (0.96–4.68)	2.92 (1.44–5.94)*	1.00
3°	3.94 (1.20–12.94)*	1.60 (0.69–3.73)	2.44 (1.17–5.05)*	1.00
4°	0.50 (0.84, 3.01)	1.46 (0.61–3.52)	1.61 (0.64–3.50)	1.00
5°	2.14 (0.48–9.51)	2.67 (0.98–7.22)	2.60 (1.05–6.43)*	1.00
6° (ref)	1.00	1.00	1.00	1.00
Economic problems				
Yes	2.46 (1.29–4.71)**	1.54 (0.70–2.51)	1.17 (0.72–1.91)	1.00
No (ref)	1.00	1.00	1.00	1.00
Family conflicts				
Yes	1.34 (0.87–2.08)	1.31 (0.83–2.06)	1.62 (1.10–2.34)*	1.00
No (ref)	1.00	1.00	1.00	1.00
Alcohol use				
Yes	0.84 (0.38–1.87)	1.63 (0.80–3.31)	1.16 (0.66–2.03)	1.00
No (ref)	1.00	1.00	1.00	1.00
Cannabis use				
Yes	1.61 (0.48–2.80)	1.31 (0.66–2.60)	0.74 (0.39–1.40)	1.00
No (ref)	1.00	1.00	1.00	1.00

[a]Adjusted Odds Ratio;[b]Confidence interval

Statistically significant difference between victims and non-victims; *$p \leq .05$, **$P \leq .01$

DISCUSSION AND CONCLUSIONS

The aim of the present study was to analyze for the first time in Spain the prevalence and the different characteristics of traditional bullying victimization and cyber-teasing in a university population, and to assess how sociodemographic characteristics might be a protective or risk factor for suffering both types of violence. Data from this research support and extend findings from previous studies about the nature and prevalence of traditional bullying victimization and cyber-teasing. More specifically, we found that over a half of the subjects suffered traditional bullying victimization (62.2 %), cyber-teased (52.7 %), or had suffered both cyber-teasing and traditional bullying victimization (40.7 %) during the past 12 months.

Previous studies among adolescent and college students in United States and European countries such as Finland and Sweden observed substantially lower prevalence of traditional bullying victimization or cyber-teasing than we did (e.g. cyber-bullying: approximately 7 % and 5 %) [16, 41, 43]. However, other cross-national studies in Spain among adolescents between 13 and 17 years old [45] and in other countries have found a similar prevalence of traditional bullying victimization or cyber-teasing to that which we observed, ranging from 24 to 40 % over a 6- to 12-month time period [16, 42]. Methodological differences, more specifically the definition and measure of traditional bullying victimization and cyber-teasing and the time frame of this research contributed to the variation in estimated rates [50].

Our results show that prevalence of cyber-teasing was higher than traditional bullying victimization; however, most of the previous studies reported that cyber-teasing was much less prevalent than traditional bullying victimization among school and adolescents students [3, 15, 25, 51]. It should be noted that in the current research teasing was included in the measure for cyber-bullying, but not for victimization, which might explain this finding. In fact, a previous study showed that teasing is one of the most common types of victimization among adolescents' samples [15, 52].

We found that most cyber-teasing victims also reported that they experienced traditional bullying victimization (and *vice versa*) during the previous twelve months, suggesting that there is a clear overlap between traditional bullying victimization and suffering cyber-teasing in at any moment. In fact, 65.7 % of traditional bullying victims were also cyber-teasing victims, and 77.6 % of cyber-teasing victims also suffered traditional bullying victimization. This finding is consistent with previous literature about studies in school and high school students [27, 28].

Our results also found differences according to gender, in agreement with previous studies in adolescents [15, 53] and college [19] students, female being more likely than male students to report cyber-teasing. Perhaps this finding can be explained by the fact that female university students are more likely to use their mobile phone [54]. Indeed the increased use of mobile phones in recent years has been linked to suffering cyber victimization among adolescents [55]. Rates of traditional bullying victimization were higher among boys than girls (71 % vs. 59.3 %), while previous studies showed the opposite [56]. However high school girls are more likely to run for conflict resolution strategies [57].

An interest finding was that Spanish students were more often victimized (traditional bullying victimization only or cyber-teasing only) than foreigner students, what is contradictory to previous research from Finnish adolescents [43] or school students in the United States [58]. Perhaps this finding might be explained by the socioeconomic status: exchange college students may be more wealthy than Spanish students, but school and young foreigner students and their families might have a lower socioeconomic background. This difference between foreigner college students and foreigner school students is explained because of the phenomenon of immigration which implicates poverty. In fact, in the current research, economic position was associated with both ways of victimization, as seen in earlier research conducted in children [52] and adolescents [59]. Family conflicts were also associated with traditional bullying victimization and cyber-teasing during the last twelve months, coinciding with previous research developed in schools [36].

Finally, our data support previous research that found high rates of legal and illegal drug use among college students [29, 60]: 80.7 % of our sample population had drunk alcohol and 16.2 % smoked cannabis during the previous twelve months at university. Contrarily to previous research, alcohol or cannabis use were not a predictor of suffering traditional bullying victimization and/or cyber-teasing in this study [26, 61, 62].

Limitations and Strengths of the Study

This study has a certain number of limitations. Firstly, because we were unable to use a longitudinal design, a cross-sectional study was conducted, so that it was only possible to measure the study variables at a given time and not follow their evolution. Secondly, our time period referred to the last 12 months, whereas most research refers to the past 6 months [48] and the last 2 months [15], which would explain a higher frequency of traditional bullying victimization or cyber-teasing. We decided to use a longer time frame than previous studies among adolescents because we expected a lower prevalence of traditional bullying victimization and cyber-teasing in college students based on previous studies [15, 16, 19]; nevertheless, we found a high prevalence of both types of victimization. Thus our hypothesis was not sustained. Thirdly, we did not have the possibility to analyze psychological and physical consequences of traditional bullying victimization and cyber-teasing in our sample [63]. Moreover, the demographics of our sample were limited by gender distribution (because of the low representation of males, approximately 25 %), potentially limiting the generalizability of our results. However, the prevalence of women students in the current research is similar to previous studies among college population [13]. Despite these limitations, this study addresses gaps in the literature and is one of the first to examine the association among traditional bullying victimization and cyber-teasing, and the risk factors associated to these problems among Spanish college students.

The main strength of the present study is the fact that it is the first carried out in Spain to examine traditional bullying victimization and cyber-teasing among college students, so that the results and conclusion might serve as a guide for future research in our country to examine and prevent victimization among this collective. Another important strength of the study is that was developed among a college population, whereas most studies worldwide on victimization and cyber-bullying have targeted elementary, middle, and high school students [16, 25, 64, 65, 66]. Although there is a large number of programs aimed at reducing traditional bullying victimization and cyber-bullying among youth in the United States [9, 67], Asia [2], Europe [68], and specifically Spain [69], it is still not clear what techniques and programs would be effective in order to reduce traditional bullying victimization and cyber-bullying because of the few representative studies focused on this population [16, 70]. Nowadays, different prevention programs are taking place worldwide in order to increase traditional bullying victimization and cyber-bullying knowledge such as the Olweus Bullying Prevention Program [71], the KiVa anti-bullying programme [72] or "zero tolerance" policies [73] demonstrating reductions in both types of victimization for different age groups. However, studies about the patterns and programs on college samples are underdeveloped compared to younger generations. Besides, very often these programs are not relevant because they were developed in schools [74] in spite of that previous studies have shown that cyberbullying in high school may also lead to cyberbullying during college [12, 75]. Moreover, the few specific prevention programs and awareness campaigns created in universities by different developers (counselling office, student organisations [76] or video program [70] were effective and reduced traditional bullying and cyber-bullying rates. Furthermore, prevention and intervention programs should not be limited to school and adolescents samples, and should be extended to college students.

Practice and Policy

In summary, the current research increases our knowledge of the association between traditional bullying victimization, cyber-teasing and demographic and behavioral characteristics. These findings have several implications for interventions. Regarding the prevention, there is an association of both types of victimization with other risk behaviors such as substance use and family conflicts (including economic problems). Given that, it could be important to include strategies to prevent bullying based on these patterns. Those strategies could be implemented in college age students, providing counseling services for legal and illegal substance use.

Future research with longitudinal designs is needed in order to investigate associations between traditional bullying victimization and cyber-teasing and subsequent exposure to demographics and substance risk factor exposure, as well as to examine the relationship between cyber-teasing and traditional bullying victimization (and *vice versa*) among college population, who show similar patterns and risk factors to adolescent samples [23, 35, 38]. Previous studies in this field have shown that traditional bullying victimization and cyber-teasing are an increasing phenomenon and a growing health problem among young people. This study found a strong association between traditional bullying victimization and cyber-teasing (and *vice versa*), as well as the importance of demographics and individual characteristics as risk factors associated.

ACKNOWLEDGEMENTS

Thanks to the Department of Social and Health Sciences, University of Murcia, and especially to the students who participated in the study.

AUTHORS' CONTRIBUTIONS

FCS and ALM designed, planned, and oversaw all scientific aspects of the study. MFR oversaw program coordination and data acquisition. JNZ was involved in devising the analytic plan and in study design. ALRC and FCS were responsible for database management. ORF participated in the revision of the manuscript. All authors read and approved the final manuscript.

71. Olweus D, Limber SP. Olweus bullying prevention program. 2007.
72. Salmivalli C, Kärnä A, Poskiparta E. Counteracting bullying in Finland: the KiVa program and its effects on different forms of being bullied. Int J Behav Dev. 2011;35(5):405–11.
73. American Psychological Association Zero Tolerance Task Force. Are zero tolerance policies effective in the schools?: an evidentiary review and recommendations. Am Psychol. 2008;63(9):852–62.
74. Foody M, Samara M, Carlbring P. A review of cyberbullying and suggestions for online psychological therapy. Internet Interv. 2015;2(3):235–42.
75. Zalaquett CP, Chatters SJ. Cyberbullying in college: frequency, characteristics, and practical implications. SAGE Open. 2014;4(1):1–8.
76. Crosslin K, Golman M. "Maybe you don't want to face it" college students' perspectives on cyberbullying. Comput Hum Behav. 2014;41:14–20.

CHAPTER 5

DUTCH CYBERBULLYING VICTIMS' EXPERIENCES, PERCEPTIONS, ATTITUDES AND MOTIVATIONS RELATED TO (COPING WITH) CYBERBULLYING: FOCUS GROUP INTERVIEWS

Niels C.L. Jacobs, Linda Goossens, Francine Dehue, Trijntje Völlink, and Lilian Lechner

Faculty of Psychology and Educational Sciences, Open University The Netherlands, Valkenburgerweg 177, 6419 AT Heerlen, The Netherlands

ABSTRACT

Because of the negative effects of cyberbullying; and because of its unique characteristics; interventions to stop cyberbullying are needed. For this purpose, more insightful information is needed about cyberbullying victims'

Citation: Jacobs, N.C.; Goossens, L.; Dehue, F.; Völlink, T.; Lechner, L. Dutch Cyberbullying Victims' Experiences, Perceptions, Attitudes and Motivations Related to (Coping with) Cyberbullying: Focus Group Interviews. *Societies* **2015**, *5*, 43-64.

(*i.e.,* the target group) experiences, perceptions, attitudes and motivations related to (coping with) cyberbullying. Five schools with 66 low-educated Dutch adolescents between 12 and 15 (53% female) participated in 10 focus group interviews. Results show that victims do not perceive all behaviors as cyberbullying and traditional bullying is generally perceived as worse than cyberbullying. Cyberbullies are perceived as sad, cowards and embarrassing themselves. Victims are perceived as easy targets; they wear strange clothes, act in a provocative manner and have a bad appearance. These perceptions often depend on context, the level of anonymity, being in a fight or not, the person sending the message and his/her behavior. Further, victims reacted to cyberbullying by acting nonchalant, by not actually saying anything and seeking help from others (*i.e.*, parents are not often asked for help because they do not want to bother them; fear of restricted Internet privileges). It can be concluded that asking cyberbullying victims about their experiences in an open manner, and allowing them to discuss these experiences, likely results in new and insightful information compared to using self-reports. In this questioning the perception of adolescents is key to see what is perceived as cyberbullying.

Keywords: cyberbullying, adolescents, experiences, attitudes, perceptions, coping strategies, qualitative results

INTRODUCTION

Worldwide, between 20% and 40% of adolescents are the victim of cyberbullying [1]. In the Netherlands, this percentage lies around 20% [2], which is similar to the worldwide prevalence. In addition, the Netherlands appears to have the highest percentage of Internet use among children between 9 and 16 years old [3]. Since heavy Internet use is related to cyberbullying and victimization [4,5], Dutch children have an increased risk of being involved in cyberbullying. Cyberbullying is a repeated aggressive and intentional act, carried out by a group or an individual, using electronic forms of contact. This act is directed towards a victim who cannot easily defend him or herself [6]. Cyberbullying victimization appears to be related to a variety of negative consequences (e.g., anxiety [7], depression, emotional distress [8], suicidality [9,10], school violence and delinquency [11]). Because of the negative consequences, and because of the unique characteristics of cyberbullying (e.g., the bully can stay anonymous and reach a large audience in a relatively short amount of time [12]), some suggest that specific intervention programs are needed [13,14].

Nowadays, there are many anti-bullying websites and programs that are intended for adolescents, their parents and teachers. However, adolescents often do not (want to) talk to adults about their cyberbullying experiences [15,16,17,18,19]. Further, the interventions that currently exist do not specifically target cyberbullying [20], are often based on practical beliefs or commonsense approaches (*i.e.*, without a basis in theory or results of effectiveness [21]), are school-based anti-bullying interventions and/or aim at changing online risk and safety behaviors [22]. Research shows that participation in these interventions is not significantly related to change in Internet risk attitudes or behavior and, in case of the school-based anti-bullying interventions that were researched by Mishna *et al.* [22], do not affect the number of cyberbullying experiences had by students.

Until now (*i.e.*, to the authors knowledge), there are no specific anti-cyberbullying programs in the Netherlands (see the database of the Netherlands Youth Institute, www.nji.nl). A well-known program, the Finnish school-based anti-bullying program KiVa that is also implemented in the Netherlands, appears to be efficacious in addressing both traditional [23] and cyberbullying [24]. However, the unique effects of KiVa on traditional and cyberbullying are conditional on age (*i.e.*, once students were older than approximately 12.87 years, the effect of the treatment condition was no longer significant), and the effects on cyberbullying and cyber victimization were modest in size [23,24]. Williford *et al.* [24] therefore suggest that school-based anti-bullying interventions (e.g., KiVa) may need to incorporate additional components that aim specifically at reducing cyberbullying.

Hence, it is important to develop effective and evidence-based anti-cyberbullying interventions, preferably in a planned, systematic and theory-based manner [25]. These interventions should be based on thorough research and recommendations from the literature as well as directly from the target-group, and should: (1) not only increase victims' awareness of possible dangers but also give advice based on what victims need [21]; (2) increase victims' knowledge of effective coping strategies [26]; (3) reduce both traditional and cyberbullying because they often occur together [27]; and (4) use personalized information based on unique characteristics of a person [28,29]. Because most of the cyberbullying victims attend lower educational levels (*i.e.*, secondary vocational education as opposed to higher general secondary education and higher academic education) and are transferring to (junior) high school [30,31], an intervention should focus on this specific aged target-group. As mentioned before, KiVa appears to have no effects in this specific aged target-group. We therefore aim to develop a cyberbullying-specific intervention for Dutch adolescents (12–15 years) who start attending secondary vocational education [32].

To develop an intervention based on the above mentioned recommendations, insight is needed into cyberbullying victims' experiences, perceptions, attitudes and motivations related to (coping with) cyberbullying. It is important to consider these topics in adolescents' own language and words [33]. Focus group interviews could help in gaining more insightful information into what is already known, and to add this information to the current discussion about cyberbullying. A focus group interview is a guided discussion between people who share a number of characteristics. It is an adequate method for obtaining information about the ideas, feelings, attitudes and preferences of a target group. The interaction between participants often results in "in depth" information [34,35]. Focus group interviews are likely to enhance insight into the uniqueness of online experiences and needs of Dutch cyberbullying victims that will help them to combat cyberbullying.

The literature already provides general information about cyberbullying victims' experiences: they are called names, insulted, ignored, misled, hacked, and gossiped about via e-mail and messenger services [2,15,36,37,38,39]. They receive pornographic content (*i.e.*, pictures, videos), (their) pictures are forwarded [40] and manipulated, and humiliating websites are created [41]. The most common forms of cyberbullying victimization are name calling and insulting [19] or being contacted by strangers [41]. However, it is not always clear what these experiences constitute and how they take place. Researchers often use self-report questionnaires in which adolescents are not able to give detailed information about their experiences and perceptions concerning cyberbullying. In addition, these questionnaires are developed by researchers, leading to the possibility that some bullying behaviors are overseen, wrongly described, or that some online experiences are wrongly perceived as cyberbullying. It is also unknown whether cyberbullying experiences found in other countries or populations are without exceptions applicable to Dutch cyberbullying victims. Therefore, this study sets out to find more detailed information related to research question (RQ) 1:

(1) What kind of experiences do Dutch low-educated cyberbullying victims have with cyberbullying victimization and perpetration, and what do they look like?

The (qualitative) literature provides some information about adolescents' perceptions of cyberbullying. Adolescents, for example, perceive repeated, public and anonymous cyberbullying as worse than repeated, public and anonymous traditional bullying [42]. Some adolescents perceive picture and video clip bullying as worse than traditional bullying; email, instant messaging, website and chat room bullying as comparable to traditional bullying; and phone call and text message bullying as less severe than traditional bullying [6,39]. Some negative online behaviors are not considered as cyberbullying but as "another way to bully just over the computer" [37] (p. 1224) or as teasing [2], cyber-teasing or cyber-arguing [41]. Vandebosch and van Cleemput [41] found that adolescents' perception of cyberbullying heavily depends on the context in which it takes place, and—in line with the definition of cyberbullying—on the power imbalance and intention to hurt. Although these studies provide important information about adolescents' perceptions, this information is not always conclusive. More information is needed (e.g., for intervention development) that is applicable to the target group, obtained without the use of self-developed and self-report questionnaires. RQ2 therefore is:

(2) How do Dutch low-educated cyberbullying victims perceive/consider experiences with cyberbullying and what is perceived as worse (traditional bullying, cyberbullying, different forms)?

Some studies suggest that a primary motivation for adolescents to cyberbully is anonymity [14,43,44,45,46], while for others it is not [19,47]. Apparently, the feeling of anonymity that many online activities entail may contribute to cyberbullying [48]. Other motivations to cyberbully that were found in individual interviews among high-school students (15–19 years) are for example jealousy, rejection, revenge, boredom, to make cyberbullies feel better about themselves, to try out new persona, and to seek approval [47]. Additionally, adolescents mentioned the lack of consequences and confrontation as reasons to cyberbully. Other studies suggest avoiding retaliation or punishment [49] and boy/girlfriend break ups [50] as motivations. Further, according to adolescents, people will become the victim of (traditional) bullying when they have a different appearance, and a bully when they have low self-esteem [51]. However, these sometimes inconclusive results—often found with self-developed self-report questionnaires—are yet to be found among Dutch victims of cyberbullying. RQ3 therefore is:

(3) Why do Dutch low-educated cyberbullying victims think people (cyber) bully (i.e., traditional and cyberbully) each other, who becomes/is a victim and who is a bully?

Research shows that having a positive attitude towards cyberbullying (e.g., cyberbullying is cool, fun, good) is associated with verbal, physical and cyberbullying and negative bystander behavior [14]. One study even found that the attitude towards cyberbullying was the strongest predictor (*i.e.*, compared to subjective norm and perceived behavioral control) of adolescents' intention to cyberbully [52]. Similarly, adolescents who have the tendency to think that aggression is appropriate are more likely to be a cyberbully [53]. Self-reported cyberbullies think that their actions are funny while cyberbully victims perceive their actions as hurtful [54], and those who are less concerned about the possible impact of cyberbullying are more likely to perpetrate in cyberbullying [31]. Although this information can (partly) be used in, for example, intervention development, more information—applicable to Dutch cyberbullying victims—is needed that is obtained without the use of self-developed and self-report questionnaires. RQ4 therefore is:

(4) Which attitudes do Dutch low-educated cyberbullying victims have towards cyberbullying?

Questionnaire-research provides information about adolescents' reactions to cyberbullying. In general, there are two types of ineffective reactions: victims either react passively (*i.e.*, one relinquishes the control of- and reactions to the stressful situation to others, or one lets other areas of life to be adversely affected by the stressful situation [55]) or aggressively (*i.e.*, one reacts to a stressful situation by physically/instrumentally, verbally or emotionally inflicting harm to oneself, another person or object). Examples of passive reactions are crying [15], doing nothing or feeling depressed/bad [56]. Examples of aggressive reactions are getting mad/angry or retaliating [2,57,58]. When victims do not react effectively, an incident can quickly and repeatedly reach a large audience [54,59]. There are, however, effective reactions that are considered to be helpful (e.g., confronting the bully [15], seeking social support [6,15,16,60,61] and blocking and deleting the bully [15,17,19]). Although many adolescents recommend asking parents for help [15,61], there are also adolescents who do not [4,16]. Asking teachers for help is generally not recommended [15,38]. Asking peers for help, [15,61] however, and acting in an assertive manner [62] are often recommended and commonly used. Again, it is unknown whether these findings—which are often collected with self-developed self-report questionnaires—are applicable to Dutch cyberbullying victims. RQ5 therefore is:

(5) How do Dutch low-educated cyberbullying victims cope with cyberbullying, and how do they perceive these coping strategies?

MATERIALS AND METHODS

Recruitment and Participants

Twenty schools were contacted via e-mail, and were asked to contribute to the discontinuation of cyberbullying by participating in the focus group interviews. The schools were asked to seek for cyberbullying victims (*i.e.*, adolescents who (have) experience(d) cyberbullying), to provide a classroom and time to conduct the interviews. The students were subsequently told that we wanted to talk about their experiences with cyberbullying, and that their information could help us and other adolescents in combating cyberbullying. In total, five schools (response rate: 25%) located in the south of the Netherlands (provinces Limburg and Noord-Brabant) with 66 adolescents between 12 and 15 years old, participated in 10 focus group interviews; 53% was female. All participating students were attending the first class of secondary vocational education.

Procedure

Before the interviews took place, schools received informed consent forms (ICs). Students were instructed to sign the ICs, and to let their parents sign the ICs.

Each focus group consisted of six to eight (former) cyberbullying victims, with one group of four adolescents. In all interviews, two researchers were present: one as interviewer and discussion leader, the other taking notes and checking whether all questions/topics were discussed. The victims were asked permission to record the interview. We explained that no one else but the researchers had access to the recordings, and that they would be used only for research purposes. It was also stressed that all opinions and comments were welcome, and that there were no right or wrong answers. Furthermore, the rules of the focus group interviews were pointed out (e.g., respect each other's opinion, do not talk when someone else is talking). Four interviews were conducted as a pilot test for the intervention, two of them focusing solely on questions from the pilot test. These two interviews were not used in the analysis for this article.

The interviews lasted between 30 min and 1.5 h (M = 59.1 min, SD = 23.35 min), were semi-structured, but all included questions about experiences with-, perceptions of-, coping with- and attitudes about cyberbullying. Research indicates that a direct approach of asking about cyberbullying experiences (e.g., "Did you experience cyberbullying?") often results in low prevalence figures, because adolescents do not perceive all behaviors as cyberbullying [2,41], and because perception of cyberbullying appears to depend on context [54]. Because perceptions and contexts often differ between persons, we used an indirect approach (e.g., "Which of the following behaviors did you experience?"), in which we did not provide the adolescents with a definition of cyberbullying. This approach allowed us to ask follow-up questions about perceptions and contexts, and enables the adolescents to adjust their answers based on others' opinions.

The questions were printed out on paper prior to the interviews, to facilitate the interviewer and assistant in checking whether all topics were asked, and to allow for similarity in the main questions in each group. To ensure and stimulate discussion about cyberbullying, mostly open-ended questions were used. The main topics and example questions of the interviews are summarized in Table 1. When all questions were exhaustively answered the victims were thanked for their cooperation, and received some drinks and sweets.

Table 1. Interview schedule with predefined themes

Theme	Example Questions
Experiencing cyberbullying	Which of the following cyberbullying events did you experience? What kind of cyberbullying event did you experience? What are the consequences of cyberbullying?
Performing cyberbullying	Which of the following cyberbullying events did you perform? Who cyberbullied someone else? What did you do? Why did you cyberbully someone else?
Perception of cyberbullying	How do you perceive cyberbullying? Did you perceive this behavior as cyberbullying? Why? What do you perceive as worse? Traditional or cyberbullying? Why?
Attitude about cyberbullying	What do you think about cyberbullying? What is worse? Traditional or cyberbullying? What is the worst thing about cyberbullying?
Motives for cyberbullying	Why do (you think) people cyberbully each other? Which characteristics does a victim of cyberbullying have? Which characteristics does a cyberbully have?
Coping with cyberbullying	How do you react to cyberbullying? How did your cyberbully react to your reaction? What are other possible reactions towards cyberbullying? Which reactions do you think are effective in stopping cyberbullying? Why? Do you talk about experiences with cyberbullying? With whom? Why (not)?

Data Analysis

All interviews were recorded and transcribed by the first and second author. In order to become familiar with the data, these two researchers read the transcripts repeatedly. Based on this process, and based on the questions asked in the interviews, a coding scheme was developed with main themes and subthemes (see first and second columns of Table 3, Table 4, Table 5, Table 6, Table 7 and Table 8), using a data-driven thematic approach [63] in which we sought to find insightful information related to the research questions.

Victims talked about traditional bullying as well. Therefore, additional codes for traditional bullying were developed. Moreover, it was not always evident whether victims were talking about traditional or cyberbullying, in which case we refer to (cyber)bullying (*i.e.*, traditional and cyberbullying). The transcripts were subsequently analyzed independently by the first and second author using Qualicoder (www.qualicoder.com). Disagreement in coding was discussed. When no consensus could be reached, the third author was asked for her opinion until consensus was reached. During this process, the coding scheme was adjusted if necessary (*i.e.*, adding more elaborate definitions of categories and codes, adding additional codes). In Table 2, an overview of the (dis)agreements between coders can be found.

Table 2. Agreement and disagreement between coders

Focus group	Coder 1		Coder 2		Agreement	Fragments without Consensus
	Number of fragments coded	Disagreement with coder 2	Number of fragments coded	Disagreement with coder 1		
Interview 1	197	74 (37,56%)	224	101 (45,09%)	123	19
Interview 2	88	20 (22,72%)	89	21 (23,60%)	68	0
Interview 3	220	31 (14,09%)	226	37 (16,37%)	189	0
Interview 4	128	19 (14,84%)	134	25 (18,66%)	109	0
Interview 5	24	6 (25%)	27	11 (40,74%)	18	0
Interview 6	41	5 (12,20%)	45	9 (20%)	36	0
Interview 7	4	0 (0%)	4	0 (0%)	4	0
Interview 8	18	1 (5,56%)	19	3 (15,79%)	17	0

Ethics Approval

The Ethical Commission of the psychology department of the Open University in the Netherlands judged the focus group interviews as nonmedical research and concluded that the victims were not "subjected to procedures or required to follow certain rules of behavior" [64]. Therefore, ethical approval of the Regional Medical Ethics committee in the Netherlands was not necessary.

RESULTS

First, experiences (*i.e.*, victimization and perpetration) with cyberbullying and traditional bullying will be discussed (3.1). Next, victims' perceptions of (cyber)bullying (*i.e.*, what is (not) seen as (cyber)bullying and characteristics of victims and bullies) is discussed (3.2), followed by motivations to cyberbully (3.3), attitudes (3.4), and coping strategies used in response to cyberbullying (3.5)). Although we did not set out to find information about consequences, victims talked about consequences (3.6). Each topic (1–5) has a table with (additional) examples (*i.e.*, Table 3, Table 4, Table 5, Table 6, Table 7, Table 8 and Table 9).

Experiences with Victimization and Perpetration in (Cyber) bullying

What Kind of Experiences do Dutch Low-Educated Cyberbullying Victims Have with Cyberbullying Victimization in Cyberbullying, and What do They Look Like?

Victims indicated having experienced 16 different forms (see Table 3 "subthemes") of cyberbullying victimization. The most common forms of cyberbullying victimization in several groups were being called names and being ridiculed. Being ignored by someone else and being threatened also occurred quite often, however, more among boys than girls. In four groups, victims experienced that someone—known (e.g., brother) or unknown to them—pretended to be someone else (*i.e.*, impersonation), which made it possible to bully anonymously. In three groups, victims experienced that others lied to them. In five groups, some victims received anonymous e-mails or phone-calls. Less common forms of cyberbullying victimization were, for example, one's picture being placed upon a voting website (two groups), receiving mail bombs (one group), being misled by someone else (one group), breaking into the computer (one group), receiving pornographic content (two groups), and being deleted by someone (one group).

Table 3. Main themes, subthemes and examples for experiences with traditional and cyberbullying

Final Themes	Subthemes	Examples
Experiences with cyberbullying	Being called names	Boy: "On the Internet I was playing around on Facebook, and this girl from my old school started calling me names…"
	Being ignored	Girl: "… I was in a fight with someone, I think, and then they ignored me."
	Being deleted	Girl: "… she deleted me, now she isn't talking to me anymore, thank god!"
	Being gossiped about	No examples, only raised hands
	Being threatened	Boy: "Once, I received a text message which stated that someone would enter my room around midnight. However, it didn't happen."
	Being mislead	No examples, only raised hands
	Being lied to	Girl: "Yeah, they just lied to me."
	Impersonation	Boy: "And from someone else, I don't know exactly who it was, but he sent me messages with four-letter words."
	Being placed upon a voting website	No examples, only raised hands
	Being threatened	Girl: "…I got in a fight with a girl via Hyves* and she was calling me names and said: 'When I see you, I'll hit you in the face'."
	Uploading unwanted pictures	Girl: "They posted a picture of me on Hyves* while I was sleeping."
	Breaking in	Boy: "Nothing happened to my computer, but now and again someone took over the control over my mouse."
	Changing passwords	Girl: "On my MSN messenger, I don't know who it was. I wanted to log in but it didn't work anymore."
Experiences with traditional bullying	Receiving mail bombs	Boy: "Yesterday I checked my Inbox and then there were 493 unread messages about stuff you can buy."
	Receiving pornographic materials	Boy: "Once I went to Hyves* and someone added me and started sending me nasty pictures."
	Receiving anonymous e-mails/ phone-calls	Boy: "The past few weeks someone was calling me and then my phone displays 'Blocked number'. The caller has a thing, a strange voice. And then I think I know who it is, but then he isn't."
	Being called names	Girl: "They call everybody hooker and bitch and so on."
	Being beaten up/ physical bullying	Boy: "Continuously calling me names, pushing me, stuff like that. They tried to throw me on the floor, stuff like that. Eight kids standing around me."
	Being threatened	Girl: "In this class, some girls came to my house."
	Being excluded	Girl: "They started making noises I didn't like and started gossiping about me and counting me out. I really didn't like that."

* Hyves was (until December 2013) a Dutch social networking site.

Inevitably, victims also talked about traditional bullying victimization. Victims from six groups indicated being bullied in a non-specified way. In the same six groups, victims were physically bullied (e.g., kicking, hitting, pushing), and in five groups they were called names. Other, less occurring traditional forms of bullying victimization were being threatened, being excluded and being gossiped about.

What Kind of Experiences do Dutch Low-Educated Cyberbullying Victims Have with Cyberbullying Perpetration, and What do They Look Like?

Victims mentioned performing nine specific forms of (cyber)bullying (*i.e.*, it was not always apparent whether they were talking about traditional or cyberbullying, some behaviors occur in both forms of bullying). For instance, in one group, all girls have ridiculed or called someone names. In another group, a girl said: "sometimes as a joke.". In a third group, a common form of perpetrating in traditional bullying was insulting someone. In the same group, some girls also gossiped about someone. Victims from three groups ignored someone once or twice. Almost all victims from one group also lied to someone. Other, less occurring perpetrations of cyberbullying were threatening someone, changing passwords and uploading unwanted pictures. Additionally, two boys impersonated themselves.

How do Dutch Low-Educated Cyberbullying Victims Perceive/ Consider Experiences with Cyberbullying and What is Perceived as Worse?

In five groups, victims mostly talked about what was (not) seen as (cyber) bullying. There was no agreement on, for example, receiving a mail bomb and calling names, since a girl said: "Some people think the word 'loser' is calling names. However, when I call ----1 a loser, she won't get angry. Right this morning I called her loser. I don't think that's bullying.". However, another girl said: "It depends, when you're in a fight you call each other names and offend each other as well, that doesn't mean that it's bullying. However, when they always do that, and with more people, then I think it is.". Similarly, there was no agreement on threatening. One girl said: "With threatening, people try to scare you and with bullying this isn't the case.

Therefore I think it isn't bullying." and another girl said "... when you say 'Watch out, tonight at eight o clock I will be standing in front of your house', then I think this is pretty bad.". Some even consider threatening as being worse than (cyber) bullying. In addition, on being offended no agreement was found. There was agreement on talking negative about family, which victims from different groups always considered as cyberbullying, and lying, which victims do not considered as cyberbullying, even when it is done repeatedly or by an unknown person.

Table 4. Main themes, subthemes and examples for cyberbullying perpetration

Final Themes	Subthemes	Examples
Performing cyberbullying	Calling names/ridiculing	Girl: "Calling names and ignoring, and ridiculing and stuff..."
	Changing passwords	Girl: "On my brother's phone, just as a joke."
	Gossiping	Girl: "For example gossiping, or directly to the person, just like ----."
	Ignoring	No examples, only raised hands
	Insulting someone	Boy: "And, I don't know how I said it, but I think I said 'It doesn't smell so nice over here' while I was standing next to him. Well, like 'It smells over here'. It wasn't really nice."
	Lying to someone	No examples, only raised hands
	Misleading/imperson-ation	Boy: "A friend of mine received a text message, and then I send a message to the sender pretending to be my brother. I told him I was 17 and that I would get to him. He then stopped texting."
	Threatening	Boy: "... with a friend, we anonymously send a mail mentioning 'if you don't stop you'll die'."
	Uploading unwanted pictures	Girl: "Once I was in a bad fight with a girl, and then I Photo shopped her head on Lolo Ferrari and posted the picture on Hyves*, and stuff like that."

* Hyves was (until December 2013) a Dutch social networking site. ---- Anonymized name.

Table 5. Main themes, subthemes and examples for perceptions of (cyber)bullying

Final Themes	Subthemes	Examples
Perception of (cyber)bullying	Characteristics of a victim	Boy: "…they're insecure, but they also often walk alone. And that's an appearance like, I am just saying, I don't have any friends and thus I'm kind of bait."
	Characteristics of a bully	Girl: "Yes everybody can be a bully. Whether it's someone who's very small with glasses and whatever, or someone who's very tall and who looks like a bully…")
	Seen as (cyber) bullying	Boy: "When you just had a fight, and when someone isn't talking back to you on Hyves*. I think this is cyberbullying because you try to make it up and that person perhaps doesn't even see your attempts, he just clicks your message away."
	Not seen as (cyber)bullying	Girl: "Sometimes I think calling names isn't bullying, sometimes you do that as friends..."

* Hyves was (until December 2013) a Dutch social networking site.

Whether something was seen as (cyber)bullying depended on: (1) the context: for example, repetitiveness, anonymity and the person sending the message were mentioned; (2) the content of the message or photo; and (3) whether the person was willing to delete it (e.g., boys and girls: "It depends on what kind of picture it is and who posted the picture. It also depends on whether that person deletes the picture immediately when you ask for it.").

Why do Dutch Low-Educated Cyberbullying Victims Think People (Cyber)Bully Each Other, Who Becomes/Is a Victim and Who is a Bully?

Victims mentioned several possible reasons why others are (cyber)bullied; for example, clothing, having a bad appearance, and being an (easy) target (e.g., girl: "People sent out a certain message or ask for it."). In two groups, victims mentioned that others bully because they are in a bad mood, they want to be popular, they want to feel better about themselves, they are jealous or they act out on someone. Some said that bullies are insecure, while others said they are not. In one group, all victims agreed that everybody can be a bully.

Table 6. Main themes, subthemes and examples for motivations for (cyber) bullying

Final Themes	Subthemes	Examples
Motivations to bully/being bullied	Cyberbullying victims	Girl: "So provoking others and being lonely, then you're being an easy target."
	Cyberbullying bullies	Girl: "A bully is insecure at the moment, I think."

Which Attitudes do Dutch Low-Educated Cyberbullying Victims have towards Cyberbullying?

When talking about being (cyber)bullied, a lot of negative attitudes were given (e.g., boy: "No, once I got bullied really bad, and now I know how it feels. It really isn't funny.") In several groups, victims considered both traditional and cyberbullying as cowardly. Other opinions about cyberbullies were given in response to someone talking about being cyberbullied (e.g., boy: "Then you're a really sad person."; and boy: "… I think they embarrass themselves."). In response to the question whether cyberbullying is worse than traditional bullying, a girl answered: "Yes, I think it is.". Others thought that traditional bullying was worse. Additionally, when talking about performing bullying, a girl mentioned: "I don't do that. When I don't like it myself, I'll not do it to others.".

Table 7. Main themes, subthemes and examples of attitudes about (cyber)bullying

Final Themes	Subthemes	Examples
Attitudes	Cyberbullying	Girl: "I think it's cowardly when you don't have the balls to say something to me in real life, like 'you're a hooker'. When someone says that to me via the Internet, than he's a coward."
	Specific forms of (cyber)bullying	Girl: "When the four-letter words aren't that bad I don't mind that much."
	Cyberbullying compared to traditional bullying	Boy: "When they kick you or hit you offline, then I think it's worse than online."

How do Dutch Low-Educated Cyberbullying Victims Cope with Cyberbullying, and How do They Perceive These Coping Strategies?

Aggressive Coping

A wide variety of aggressive coping responses were given. In some groups, some of the victims got angry after being cyberbullied. However, the most often used and discussed aggressive coping strategy was retaliation, which was mentioned in four groups (e.g., girl: "...when someone does that (*i.e.*, offending or calling names) to me, yeah then I have the tendency to do the same."). The most used strategies in response to traditional bullying were fighting back (*i.e.*, getting physical), and retaliating (*i.e.*, calling names), which were mentioned in four groups. Many victims also got angry in response to traditional bullying. Only one girl mentioned that she once agreed to meet for a fight.

Passive Coping

In seven groups, the most often discussed passive coping strategy was doing nothing or ignoring the cyberbullying. Another way of doing nothing that was mentioned was sending the word "OK", as was described by a girl: "One reaction that works really well is sending an 'O' and a 'K'. 'OK' means okay, nobody likes that. Like you aren't responding.". Later on she told us: "Yes it's just on Twitter, when someone calls me a hooker, then I just say 'OK'.". Another passive coping strategy that was often mentioned in four groups was acting nonchalant or thinking "I don't care". A third, less often used passive coping strategy was thinking positive or putting things in perspective, which was mentioned in three groups.

Active Coping

Victims mentioned several strategies that can be considered as active coping. For example, in four groups, blocking and deleting was mentioned. Other frequently used strategies (*i.e.*, mentioned in five groups) were standing up for oneself, and sometimes the adolescents stood up for someone else. Additionally, victims also mentioned talking about the event. One girl mentioned that seeming self-assured is a good strategy to use, and a boy mentioned: "You could save it in your history, then it will be mentioned in history and then your parents and police will be able to read it.".

Seeking Support Coping

A lot of victims considered seeking social support as a good strategy to use. They mentioned support in general, but also specified their source of support (e.g., parents, teachers, siblings/family, friends). When talking about parents as a source of support, there was a lot of ambiguity. On the one hand, victims told us that they went to their parents and received effective help (e.g., boy:

"Then my mother found out and went to my school. Since then they never bullied me again and I don't suffer from it anymore.") or did not receive help. On the other hand, some victims mentioned that they did not want to bother their parents (e.g., boy: "No, but I'll not tell my parents. It would only be bad for them, because they'll stress out and stuff. While that's not necessary at all, I think.") or that their help would be irritating (e.g., girl: "When you tell your parents they'll react like a parent. That's really annoying!"). When asked who turns to their friends for help, a boy mentioned: "Yes, I think that everybody does that.". Otherwise, mostly girls mentioned that they turned to their friends for help. Teachers were mentioned in six groups, however, talking to teachers was not always perceived as useful (e.g., boy: "Occasionally, I went to a teacher, however they hardly did something about it. They only said 'We'll keep an eye out' and even that they didn't do."). Other sources of support are siblings (*i.e.*, brothers and sisters) or family (*i.e.*, aunts, nephews). Some victims did not seek help. When asked whether they turn to someone for help a girl said: "No, I think it's my own problem, I can solve it myself.".

Table 8. Main themes, subthemes and examples of coping with cyberbullying

Final Themes	Subthemes	Examples
Aggressive coping	Getting angry online	Girl: "It doesn't make me sad, I just get really angry when people do stuff like that..."
	Retaliating/calling names online	Boy: "When someone does that to me, I do it back, to be honest."
	Agreeing to meet for a fight offline	Girl: "Very stupid, but then we waylaid for her. We did not really waylaid for her but agreed to waylay, this sounds really stupid, however different things happened."
	Fighting back/getting physical offline	Boy: "Only then he kept doing it. Okay, I wasn't supposed to do that, but I grabbed him in his neck, well not lifting him up, and I pushed him with his head against the door. And then I just reacted really angry. Anger attack. Because I warned him, but he kept doing it and kept provoking me."
	Getting angry offline	Girl: "Getting angry. Then I start yelling, hitting and I grab the nearest painful object and throw it at their heads."
	Retaliating/calling names offline	Boy: "When they call me names, then I do it back three times worse."

Active coping	Blocking and deleting	Boy: "Once I was on Hyves* and someone added me and started sending me nasty pictures. Then I told my mom. After that, I immediately deleted and blocked him."
	Seem self-assured	Girl: "Loosen up a little bit in class and try to not look insecure. People will respect you more and they'll stop bullying you eventually. That's how it went with me."
	Standing up for oneself	Boy: "Yeah I once said 'What you're saying to me, you wouldn't like it when I said that to you…"
	Standing up for someone else	Girl: "Then I completely freaked out on him and told him 'Go and cry to your mommy'. Because I don't stand it when they do something like that to my friends. I was really angry!"
	Talking about it	Girl: "After a time you just try to talk, because then you both will be more calm and will be able to talk about it. However, it depends on what the person said."
Passive coping	Doing nothing/ignoring (the message)	Boy: "Someone, I don't know who, called me names on Twitter and then I just let it happen, I didn't know him so I didn't reacted to it."
	Nonchalance/I do not care	Girl: "When they call me for example a hooker via the Internet, then I just let that happen. I don't care. I just know that I am not."
	Quitting school	Girl: "…when it happened at my old school, I just thought 'I'll go to another school'…"
	Putting things in perspective/positive thinking	Boy: "When they call me names, I always think ' Yeah, you can call me names, but the only thing you do is making yourself look smaller and you make a fool out of yourself."
Seeking support coping	Friends	Girl: "Most of my friends help me pretty good."
	Parents	Boy: "I just go to my mom, then I tell my mom and dad what's going on and they tell me what I should do."
	Teachers	Girl: "I went to talk to my mentor."
	Siblings/family	Girl: "Once my sister came to this school, they did not dare to bully me anymore. I wouldn't tell her, but when she hears I'm in trouble, she immediately comes and helps me."
	Not seeking support/ loneliness	Girl: "Most of the time I don't talk about it to no one, really no one. And I keep it to myself."

* Hyves was (until December 2013) a Dutch social networking site.

Consequences

Although we did not set out to find information concerning consequences, there were two types of consequences mentioned by the victims. The first type are the consequences of (cyber)bullying victimization. Several victims from different groups mentioned feeling depressed, bad and angry. Some said that the consequences of experiencing (cyber)bullying could last a lifetime (e.g., boy: "Most of the bullies forget the event, but victims experience the consequences for the rest of their lives.").

The second type were consequences of certain coping strategies in response to cyberbullying. Consequences of getting angry were, for example, fights or the bully going offline. For some, getting angry helped, for others it did not. Additionally, a boy mentioned that ignoring and positive thinking helped. Active coping and seeking support often resulted in the discontinuation of cyberbullying (e.g., girl: "I just say to them: 'If you want to call me names, come and find me and say it to my face.' Then they stop saying things to me." or boy: "On the Internet I was just playing around on Facebook and then there was a girl who attended my previous school, and she started calling me names and then I then blocked her and didn't accept her on my profile."). After that, the bullying stopped. However, in some cases acting active/effectively did not help (e.g., boy: "Yeah I once said 'What you're saying to me, you wouldn't like it when I said that to you', however it didn't help.").

Table 9. Main themes, subthemes and examples of consequences of (coping with) (cyber)bullying victimization

Final Themes	Subthemes	Examples
Consequences	Victimiza-tion	Girl: "A really bad feeling..."
	Coping	Boy: "I became more angry and angry, so eventually there was a big fight, however since then they don't do anything anymore."

DISCUSSION & CONCLUSIONS

In this study, we aimed to find relevant insightful information into Dutch cyberbullying victims' experiences, perceptions, attitudes and motivations related to (coping with) cyberbullying. We expected that focus group interviews would enable us to get this information. Indeed, this study found new and insightful information that, for example, can be used in intervention development. Before discussing the results, however, a notable finding was made: a lot of victims spontaneously talked about experiences with traditional bullying as well (*i.e.*, physical bullying, being called names, being threatened, and being excluded). This finding can be explained by the large overlap between involvement in traditional and cyberbullying [4,65]: about 40% of the adolescents who had experienced online harassment did also experienced traditional bullying [66]. Subsequently, cyberbullying is seen as another form of bullying [39,43]. This suggests that interventions should focus on both forms of bullying [27].

In answering RQ1 (*i.e.*, What kind of experiences do Dutch low-educated cyberbullying victims have with cyberbullying victimization and perpetration, and what do they look like?), all participants were victimized but many also perpetrated in cyberbullying (often in response to someone else bullying them). Indeed, the literature shows correlations between victimization and perpetration of cyberbullying [67]. Similar to Juvonen and Gross [19], this study found that being called names and being ridiculed (*i.e.*, insulted) were the most often mentioned victimization behaviors. Besides confirming earlier findings, this study also found new cyberbullying victimization (e.g., being posted upon a voting website, breaking into the computer) and perpetration behaviors (e.g., lying to someone else, changing passwords). It seems that when asking victims about their experiences in an open manner, and allowing them to discuss these experiences, more information is found compared to using self-report questionnaires. Additionally, victims automatically talked about possible consequences (e.g., feeling depressed, bad, angry) of being victimized online. Furthermore, although some research mentions that boys are more often the perpetrators of cyberbullying [2,68], a prominent finding of the present study is that mostly girls perpetrated in the above mentioned behaviors. A possible explanation could be that cyberbullying is in some respects like indirect bullying, in which girls are more often involved [6].

Several studies (e.g., [69,70]) recommend that one should explicitly ask participants about their involvement in specific negative behaviors. In relation to RQ2 (*i.e.*, How do Dutch low-educated cyberbullying victims perceive/consider experiences with cyberbullying and what is perceived as worse?), this study found that victims do not perceive all specific negative behaviors as cyberbullying (*i.e.*, being lied to online, calling names) and thus this approach could give a distorted picture. Apparently, calling names is considered as "normal" communication (*i.e.*, even friends call each other names). Victims do not agree with each other on perceiving certain behaviors as cyberbullying (e.g., calling names/being offended, receiving mail bombs, threatening). Victims did perceive—and agreed on—talking negatively about family as cyberbullying. Additionally, being deleted by someone was not completely perceived as negative (*i.e.*, adolescent experienced relief) as was found in [42]. Although some victims perceived cyberbullying as worse than traditional bullying (as was found in [42]), most agreed on traditional bullying being worse than cyberbullying: offline, a message cannot be deleted or ignored, and people can physically hurt you. Furthermore, considering something as cyberbullying in this study indeed depends on the context [4,41] and the level of anonymity [48]. A new finding is that it depends whether the persons involved are in a fight (or not) and on the behavior of the person sending the message (e.g., willing to delete it).

Regarding RQ3 (*i.e.*, Why do Dutch low-educated cyberbullying victims think people (cyber)bully each other, who becomes/is a victim and who is a bully?) this study found motivations to cyberbully reported in previous studies (e.g., jealousy, boredom, to redirect feelings, to feel better, to seek approval, confrontation). Although victims indicated being an occasional victim or bully of cyberbullying, they mostly mentioned motivations why others are being cyberbullied or why others cyberbully, not motivations why they got bullied or why they bully. When talking about motivations, the perspective changes from talking about personal experiences (RQ1) to talking about what others experienced (RQ3). Apparently, victims do not see themselves as cyberbullying victims, but rather as adolescents who once or twice experienced cyberbullying. Similarly, they do not see themselves as cyberbullies but rather as adolescents who occasionally tease someone else, and therefore cannot be called bullies. These findings suggest that the repeated nature, as mentioned in Smith's *et al.* [6] definition of cyberbullying, really is important in the perception of cyberbullying: single or occasional events are not often perceived as cyberbullying. Future studies should look into which frequency of cyberbullying determines when and if an adolescent perceives something as cyberbullying. In addition, as discussed before, some behaviors are not seen as cyberbullying (e.g., gossiping, calling each other names while being friends), and perception depends on the context and/or being in a fight. In case of these behaviors—contexts and being in a fight—apparently adolescents do not always see themselves as cyberbully or cyberbullying victim. Nevertheless, according to the majority of the participants of this study, everybody can be a cyberbully, and cyberbullies are often insecure. Further, victims mentioned that one's appearance (e.g., easy targets, wear strange clothes, provoke and have a bad appearance) determines becoming a (cyber)bullying victim, which was previously found in traditional bullying [51]. Unfortunately, it was not always clear whether the victims were talking about cyberbullying or only about traditional bullying.

In relation to RQ4 (*i.e.*, Which attitudes do Dutch low-educated cyberbullying victims have towards cyberbullying?), victims provided several negative attitudes (e.g., someone who perpetrates in cyberbullying is sad, a coward and embarrasses him/herself). However, some of these victims also perpetrated (once or twice) in (cyber)bullying, suggesting that having a negative attitude towards (cyber)bullying does not mean that one will not (cyber)bully themselves. A possible explanation—found in response to asking victims about motivations—could be that victims do not perceive themselves as (cyber)bully when they, for example, retaliate or bully occasionally (*i.e.*, once or twice). Further, and new to the literature, some victims disapproved of perpetrating cyberbullying behavior because of reciprocal reasons (e.g., "When I don't like it myself, I'll not do it to others.").

In exploring RQ5 (*i.e.*, How do Dutch low-educated cyberbullying victims cope with cyberbullying, and how do they perceive these strategies?), this study found aggressive, passive as well as active/effective strategies. The most often mentioned aggressive strategies that were also found in the literature were getting angry [58] —which often resulted in the bully going offline, the message being changed or deleted by the bully, or in a fight—and retaliating [2,71]. The most often mentioned passive strategy that was also found in the literature was doing nothing or ignoring the bully [2], which appeared to be a successful strategy. New to the literature were acting nonchalant and reacting by not actually saying anything (e.g., sending "OK" as a response), which was perceived as helpful.

The most often used active/effective strategies that were also previously found in the literature were blocking and deleting [15,17,19], confronting the bully or standing up for oneself [15], and seeking parents', teachers', siblings/family's and friends' support [6,15,16,60,61]. In general, these strategies are effective in discontinuing bullying, although some adolescents also experienced that the cyberbullying continued. Additionally, victims also stood up for someone else. Further, victims either mentioned talking to adults and receiving effective help (e.g., comfort, parents intervening) or mentioned not wanting to talk to adults because they (as found in the literature): (1) do not want to bother their parents [16]; (2) have the feeling that adults would not be able to help them [72]; (3) have the perception that their friends are more tech-savvy [15]; (4) have experienced that teachers would not react [16]; (5) have the feeling that parents were able to restrict or deny their access to the internet, which could isolate them from their friends and peers [4]; and (6) wanted to solve the problem themselves. Moreover, adolescents mentioned a preference of turning to their friends and other family members (e.g., siblings, nieces/nephews) for support [72].

This study has several strengths and limitations. This study seemed to result into more insightful information than when using a quantitative design. Subsequently, this led to some findings that are not previously reported in the literature. However, this study did not compare qualitative with quantitative designs but merely compared qualitative with quantitative results, suggesting that we cannot conclude that qualitative designs result in more information than quantitative designs. Furthermore, this study is one of the first qualitative studies that included adolescents that had just started to attend lower secondary vocational education. A limitation of this study, on the other hand, is the voluntary cooperation of participants. This may bias the results in that the opinions of victims who do not want/dare to talk about their experiences are overseen. Another limitation is the fact that there were no "pure cyberbullies" included in this study, which may have led to one-sided views. Future research should focus on the views of "pure cyberbullies", because this information might be helpful in reducing cyberbullying as well. Additionally, in this study we did not ask specifically who perceived themselves as a bully or as a victim, and when one perceived themselves as a bully or victim, which may have led to less interpretable results. Future research should also consider these self-perceptions.

In conclusion, the focus group method seems to be promising in finding unstudied concepts related to cyberbullying. It appears that victims perceive traditional and cyberbullying to be related, suggesting that interventions should focus on both forms of bullying. Furthermore, an indirect approach of asking about experiences (e.g., Which of the following behaviors did you experience?) could result in an overestimation of prevalence figures, because victims do not perceive all behaviors as cyberbullying. A direct approach (e.g., How many times were you cyberbullied?) could result in an underestimation of prevalence figure. Therefore, victims should be asked whether they perceive certain behaviors as (cyber)bullying, and they should be given a clear definition of cyberbullying, in addition to asking them indirectly about cyberbullying. Further, both boys and girls are victims and perpetrators of cyberbullying, suggesting that interventions should offer a wide variety of information to both boys and girls. Furthermore, an intervention should not communicate that it focuses on victims of cyberbullying, because a lot of adolescents do not perceive themselves as victims. It appears that the focus group method results in at least the same findings as questionnaire research; however, this study also found some new and unstudied concepts. These results can be used in the development of effective interventions with a primary focus on cyberbullying. However, since a lot of overlap exists between traditional and cyberbullying, as suggested by this study, these interventions can have a secondary focus and effect on traditional bullying as well. These results can also directly provide content for a program in a language that members of the target group speak and understand.

AUTHOR CONTRIBUTIONS

N.J. and L.G. conceived of the study, recruited participants and drafted the manuscript. N.J. conducted the interviews, T.V. (twice) and L.G. (six times) assisted N.J. in conducting the interviews. N.J. and L.G. independently coded the transcripts, compared the coding and adjusted the coding scheme. F.D. and T.V. served as back-up coders in case of disagreement between N.J. and L.G., F.D. and T.V. helped recruiting participants, helped to draft the manuscript and helped in drafting the final manuscript. L.L. supervised the whole research and helped with drafting and writing the final manuscript. N.J. processed all feedback from the other authors and reviewers. All authors read and approved of the final manuscript.

REFERENCES

1. Tokunaga, R.S. Following you home from school: A critical review and synthesis of research on cyberbullying victimization. *Comput. Human Behav.*2010, *26*, 277–287.
2. Dehue, F.; Bolman, C.; Völlink, T. Cyberbullying: Youngsters' experiences and parental perception. *Cyberpsychol. Behav.* 2008, *11*, 217–223.
3. Livingstone, S.; Haddon, L.; Görzig, A.; Olafsson, K. *Risks and Safety on the Internet: The Perspective of European Children: Full Findings and Policy Implications from the EU Kids Online Survey of 9–16 Year Olds and Their Parents in 25 Countries 2011*; LSE: London, UK.
4. Kowalski, R.M.; Limber, S.P.; Agatston, P.W. *Cyber Bullying: Bullying in the Digital Age*; Blackwell Publishing: Malden, MA, USA, 2008.
5. Ybarra, M.L.; Mitchell, K.J. Youth engaging in online harassment: Associations with caregiver-child relationships, Internet use, and personal characteristics. *J. Adolesc.* 2004, *27*, 319–336.
6. Smith, P.K.; Mahdavi, J.; Carvalho, M.; Fisher, S.; Russell, S.; Tippett, N. Cyberbullying: Its nature and impact in secondary school pupils. *J. Child Psychol. Psychiatry* 2008, *49*, 376–385.
7. Campbell, M.A.; Spears, B.; Slee, P.; Butler, D.; Kift, S. Victims' perceptions of traditional and cyberbullying, and the psychosocial correlates of their victimisation. *Emot. Behav. Difficulties* 2012, *17*, 389–401.
8. Perren, S.; Dooley, J.; Shaw, T.; Cross, D. Bullying in school and cyberspace: Associations with depressive symptoms in Swiss and Australian adolescents. *Child Adolesc. Psychiatry Ment. Health* 2010, *4*, 1–10.
9. Hinduja, S.; Patchin, J.W. Bullying, Cyberbullying, and Suicide. *Arch. Suicide Res.* 2010, *14*, 206–221.
10. Schneider, S.K.; O'Donnell, L.; Stueve, A.; Coulter, R.W.S. Cyberbullying, school bullying, and psychological distress: A regional census of high school students. *Am. J. Public Health* 2012, *102*, 171–177.
11. Hinduja, S.; Patchin, J.W. Offline Consequences ofOnline Victimization. *J. Sch. Violence* 2007, *6*, 89–112.
12. Smith, P.K.; del Barrio, C.; Tokunaga, R.S. Definitions of bullying and cyberbullying: How useful are the terms. In *Principles of Cyberbullying*

sense, one of the reasons for cyberbullying is the individual's inadequacy to take responsibilities. In this sense, it can be stated that characteristics of unsuccessful identity can be observed in people who cyberbully.

Forcing the person to withdraw from social contexts and weakening his initiative power for change are other characteristics of unsuccessful identity (Palancı, 2014). People who are alone and who have low levels of self-esteem, peer optimism, social acceptance and the ability to make friends have been observed to have high levels of cyberbullying behaviors (Schoffstall and Cohen, 2011). Besides, a relationship between being open to change and cyberbullying was found, too (Çelik et al., 2012). Findings of this study, which are related to unsuccessful identity, indicate that people who cyberbully have characteristics of unsuccessful identity.

According to Glasser, psychological problems can be explained by characteristics of unsuccessful identity (Kaner, 1993). Findings of this study also present us similar information showing that cyberbullying behaviors can be explained by having unsuccessful identity.

CONCLUSION

The relationship between cyberbullying behaviors and basic needs shows that cyberbullying behaviors aim to satisfy the needs of entertainment and power, two of the five basic needs in choice theory. Cyberbullying, in this sense, can be regarded as an abnormal behavior stemming from a person's inability to realistically satisfy the needs of power and entertainment. Therefore, it can be stated that pictures in the picture album of people displaying cyberbullying behaviors consist of images of cyberbullying. From the point of successful and unsuccessful identity, people displaying cyberbullying behaviors have characteristics of unsuccessful identity, such as feeling worthless and having low self-confidence. From the point of choice theory, cyberbullying behaviors can also be explained by a person's inability to develop healthy and satisfying commitments. Another reason is a person's deficiency in taking responsibilities.

In this study, along with cyber-bullying behaviors analyzed from the perspective of choice theory, some limitations of the theory should be taken into consideration as well. In choice theory, William Glasser does not accept psychiatric classifications of misbehaviors and rejects psychopathological explanations as well (Cameron, 2009). Moreover, cyber-bullying behaviors were stated to be predicted by some psychiatric symptoms (Arıcak, 2009).

Another limitation of choice theory and reality therapy on cyber-bullying behaviors is about not giving importance to the effects of past and focusing on present in relation to the source of behaviors (Corey, 2009). Studies show that those with cyber-bullying behaviors were exposed to cyber or traditional bullying in their past (König et al., 2010). In addition, another finding of studies is that cyber-bullying and parental attitudes during childhood are related (Dilmaç and Aydogan, 2010). Another limitation of the theory used in this analysis is related to its rejection of unconscious processes (Corey, 2009). In this case, the possible unconscious causes of the behavior cannot be explained with those who have healthy relationships, whose basic needs are met adequately and who do not have any observable reason leading to cyberbullying behaviors.

REFERENCES

1. Agatston PW, Kowalski R, Limber S (2007). Students' perspectives on cyberbullying. J. Adolesc. Health 41:59-60.
2. Anderson WL (2010). Cyber stalking (cyberbullying) proof and punishment. Insights to a Changing World J. (4):18-23.
3. Ang RP, Goh DH (2010). Cyberbullying among adolescents: the role of affective and cognitive empathy, and gender. Child Psychiatry Hum. Dev. 41(4):387-397. doi: 10.1007/s10578-010-0176-3
4. Aoyama I, Saxon, TF, Fearon, DD (2011). Internalizing problems among cyberbullying victims and moderator effects of friendship quality. Multicult. Educ. Technol. J. 5(2):92-105. doi:10.1108/17504971111142637
5. Arıcak OT (2009). Psychiatric symptomatology as a predictor of cyberbullying among university students, Eurasian J. Educ. Res. 34:167-184.
6. Arıcak OT (2011). Cyberbullying: The new danger waiting for adolescents. [Siber zorbalık: gençlerimizi bekleyen yeni tehlike.] [Career Win¬dow]. Kariyer Penceresi. 2(6):10-12.
7. Ayas T, Horzum MB (2010). Cyber bully/victim scale development study. Akademik Bakış Dergisi [Academic Sight]. 19:1-1.
8. Cameron A (Spring 2009). Regret, choice theory and reality therapy. Int. J. Reality Ther. 28(2):40-42
9. Corey G (2009). Theory and practice of counseling and psychotherapy. Belmont: Cengage Learning.
10. Çelik S, Atak H, Erguzen A (2012). The effect of personality on cyberbullying among university students in turkey. Eurasian J. Educ. Res. 49:129-150.
11. Çetin B, Eroğlu Y, Peker A, Akbaba S, Persoy S (2012). The investigation of relationship among relational-interdependent self-construal, cyberbullying, and psychological disharmony in adolescents: an investigation of structural equation modeling. Educational Sciences: Theory Practice (ESTP) 12(2):637-653.
12. Çetin B, Peker A, Eroğlu Y, Çetimel N (2011). Interpersonal cognitive distortions as a predictor of cyber victimization and bullying: A preliminary report in adolescents. Int. Online J. Educ. Sci. 3(3):1064-1080.

13. Deci EL, Ryan RM (2000). The 'what' and 'why' of goal pursuits: human needs and the self-determination of behavior. Psychol. Inquiry 11:227-268.
14. Didden R, Scholte RHJ, Korzilius H, de Moor JMH, Vermeulen A, O'Reilly M, Lang R, et al (2009). Cyberbullying among students with intellectual and developmental disability in special education settings. Dev. Neurorehabil. 12(3):146-151. doi:10.1080/17518420902971356
15. Dilmaç B, Aydogan D (2010). Parental attitudes as a predictor of cyber bullying among primary school children. World Acad. Sci. Engi. Technol. 67:167-171.
16. Dooley JJ, Gradinger P, Strohmeier D, Cross D, Spiel C (2010). Cyber-victimization: the association between help-seeking behaviors and self-reported emotional symptoms in Australia and Austria. Austr. J. Guidance Couns. 20(2):194-209. doi:10.1375/ajgc.20.2.194
17. Dooley JJ, Pyżalski J, Cross D (2009). Cyberbullying versus face-to-face bullying. Zeitschrift für Psychologie/J. Psychol. 217(4):182-188. doi:10.1027/0044-3409.217.4.182
18. Eroğlu Y (2011). The investigation relationships among contingencies of self-worth, risky internet behaviors, and cyberbullying/cyber victimization. (Master Thesis). Sakarya University, Sakarya.
19. Gradinger P, Strohmeier D, Spiel CH (2010). Definition and Measurement of Cyberbullying. Cyberpsychology: J. Psychosocial Res. Cyberspace 4(2):1-13
20. Grigg DW (2010). Cyber-aggression: definition and concept of cyberbullying. Austr. J. Guidance Counsel. 20(2):143-156. doi:10.1375/ajgc.20.2.143
21. Glasser W (1985). Discipline has never been the problem and isn't the problem now. Theory into Practice. 24(4):241–246. doi:10.1080/00405848509543181
22. Glasser W (1997). Choice theory and student success. Educ. Digest. 63(3):16-22
23. Glasser W (1998a). The quality school: managing students without coercion. New York: Harper Collins Publishers
24. Glasser W (1998b). Choice theory: a new psychology of personal freedom. New York: Harper Collins Publishers.
25. Glasser W (2000). School violence from the perspective of William Glasser. Professional Sch. Couns. 4(2):77-80.

26. Haight M, Shaughnessy MF (2003). An interview with William Glasser. North Am. J. Psychol. 3(5):407-416.
27. Jose PE, Kljakovic M, Scheib E, Notter O (2011). The joint development of traditional bullying and victimization with cyber bullying and victimization in adolescence. J. Res. Adolesc. 22(2):301-309. doi:10.1111/j.1532-7795.2011.00764.x
28. Kaner S (1993). Kontrol kuramı ve gerçeklik terapisi [Control theory and reality therapy]. J. Faculty Educ. Sci. 26(2):569-585.
29. Kiriakidis SP, Kavoura A (2010). Cyberbullying A Review of the Literature on Harassment Through the Internet and Other Electronic Means. Family Commun. Health 33(2):82-93.
30. Kowalski RM, Limber SP (2013). Psychological, Physical, and Academic Correlates of Cyberbullying and Traditional Bullying. J. Adolesc. Health 53(1):13-20. doi:10.1016/j.jadohealth.2012.09.018
31. König A, Gollwitzer M, Steffgen G (2010). Cyberbullying as an act of revenge? Austr. J. Guidance Couns. 20(2):210-224. doi:10.1375/ajgc.20.2.210
32. Li Q (2007). Bullying in the new playground: research into cyberbullying and cyber victimization. Austr. J. Educ. Technol. 23:435-454.
33. Mason KL (2008). Cyberbullying: a preliminary assessment for school personnel. Psychol. Schools 45(4):323-348. doi:10.1002/pits.20301
34. Menesini E, Nocentini A. (2009). Cyberbullying Definition and Measurement. Zeitschrift für Psychologie/J. Psychol. 217(4):230-232. doi:10.1027/0044-3409.217.4.230
35. Navarro R, Yubero S, Larra-aga E, Martínez V (2011). Children's cyberbullying victimization: associations with social anxiety and social competence in a Spanish sample. Child Indicators Res. 5(2):281-295. doi:10.1007/s12187-011-9132-4
36. NCES (National Center for Education Statistic) (2011). Student Reports Of Bullying And Cyber-Bullying: Results From The 2007 School Crime Supplement To The National Crime Victimization Survey. (NCES 2011 -316), Washington, DC: U.S. Department of Education.
37. Özmen A (2004) The impact of "coping with anger training program" based on choice theory and realty therapy and "encounter group experience" on students skills in coping with anger. Doctoral Thesis. Ankara University, Ankara.

38. Palancı M (2004). A reality therapy oriented helping model for explaining and reducing collage students' social anxiety. Doctoral Thesis. Karadeniz Technical University, Trabzon.

39. Patchin JW, Hinduja S (2006). Bullies move beyond the schoolyard: a preliminary look at cyberbullying. Youth Violence Juvenile Justice 4(2):148-169.

40. Patchin JW, Hinduja S (2010a). Cyberbullying and self-esteem. J. Sch. Health 80(12):614-621. doi:10.1111/j.1746-1561.2010.00548.x

41. Patchin JW, Hinduja S (2010b). Traditional and nontraditional bullying among youth: a test of general strain theory. Youth & Society. 43(2):727-751. doi:10.1177/0044118X10366951

42. Raskauskas J, Stoltz AD (2007). Involvement in traditional and electronic bullying among adolescents. Dev. Psychol. 43:564-575.

43. Schoffstall CL, Cohen R (2011). Cyber aggression: the relation between online offenders and offline social competence. Social Dev. 20(3):587-604. doi:10.1111/j.1467-9507.2011.00609.x

44. Schultze-Krumbholz A, Scheithauer H (2009). Social-behavioral correlates of cyberbullying in a German student sample. Zeitschrift für Psychologie/J. Psychol. 217(4):224-226. doi:10.1027/0044-3409.217.4.224

45. Sourander A, Brunstein Klomek A, Ikonen M, Lindroos J, Luntamo T, Koskelainen M, Ristkari T, et al. (2010). Psychosocial risk factors associated with cyberbullying among adolescents: a population-based study. Arch. General Psychiatry 67(7):720-728. doi:10.1001/archgenpsychiatry.2010.79

46. Totan T (2007). Implications for educators and parents on prevention of school bullying. Abant İzzet Baysan Üniversitesi Eğitim Fakültesi Dergisi [Abant İzzet Baysan University J. Faculty Educ. 7(2):190-202.

47. Vandebosch H, Van Cleemput K (2008). Defining cyberbullying: a qualitative research into the perceptions of youngsters. Cyber Psychol. Behav. 11(4):499-503. doi:10.1089/cpb.2007.0042

48. Vandebosch H, Van Cleemput K (2009). Cyberbullying among youngsters: profiles of bullies and victims. New Media Soc. 11(8):1349-1371. doi:10.1177/1461444809341263

49. Walter SM, Lambie GW, Ngazimbi EE (2008). A choice theory counseling group succeeds with middle school students who displayed disciplinary problems. Middle Sch. J. 40(2):4-12.

50. Wright VH, Joy JB, Christopher TI, Heather NO (2009). Cyberbullying: using virtual scenarios to educate and raise awareness. J. Comput. Teacher Educ. 26(1):35-42.
51. Wong-Lo M, Bullock LM, Gable RA (2011). Cyber bullying: practices to face digital aggression. Emotional Behav. Diff. 16(3):317-325. doi: 10.1080/13632752.2011.595098
52. Yaman E, Peker A (2012). The Perceptions of adolescents about cyberbullying and cyber victimization. Gaziantep University J. Soc. Sci. 11(3):819–833.
53. Zeeman RD (Fall 2006). Glasser's choice theory and purkey's invitational education allied approaches to counseling and schooling Int. J. Reality Ther. 26(1):14-17.

CHAPTER 7

VIRTUOUS REALITY: MORAL THEORY AND RESEARCH INTO CYBER-BULLYING

Tom Harrison

Jubilee Centre for Character and Virtues, School of Education, University of Birmingham, Birmingham B15 2TT, UK

ABSTRACT

This article draws on a study investigating how 11–14 year olds growing up in England understand cyber-bullying as a moral concern. Three prominent moral theories: deontology, utilitarianism and virtue ethics, informed the development of a semi-structured interview schedule which enabled young people, in their own words, to describe their experiences of online and offline bullying. Sixty 11–14 year olds from six schools across England were involved with the research. Themes emerging from the interviews included anonymity; the absence of rules, monitoring and guidance and, the

Citation: Tom Harrison, Virtuous reality: moral theory and research into cyber-bullying, DOI: 10.1080/02643944.2016.1202307.

challenges associated with determining the consequences of online actions. The findings demonstrate the advantages of adopting a character-based moral theory to compliment rules and/or consequence based moral theories as the basis for future research into cyber-bullying. The findings evoke some wider implications for future research into cyber-bullying that might equally be applied to investigations into other Internet related moral concerns.

Keywords: Virtue ethics, Cyber-bullying, Character, Moral concern

INTRODUCTION

Research into the impact of the Internet on children and young peoples' morality has struggled to keep up with technology's rapid development and innovation. The existing body of research on how the Internet influences young people does not paint a clear picture and is often polemical (Harrison 2014; Livingston 2009). Interpretations oscillate between extremes; young people online are depicted as either predominantly truthful or dishonest, compassionate or callous, selfless or selfish, altruistic or egotistical, courageous or cowardly, or as modest or vain. What is clear is that the Internet appears to influence young people in a number of complex ways, and that it is not obvious if such influence is predominantly positive or negative. The only common ground in the literature is a broad agreement that the Internet is, in some way, having an effect on the morality of children and young people (Harrison 2014).

What is missing from many empirical studies attempting to determine what this effect might be is a philosophical foundation on which to ground the research. Recent articles have explored the Internet from deontological, utilitarian and virtue ethical lines of normative enquiry (see, for example Plaisance 2013; Vallor 2010; Lievens 2011), although the arguments expressed in them have not been put to an empirical test. The research reported in this article describes an attempt to do exactly that. It draws on an empirical study that prioritised young peoples' perspectives of cyber-bullying, with the aim of suggesting what the best moral philosophical framework for researching the pervasive issue might be. The findings of this study raise some wider implications for future research into cyber-bullying, which might equally be applied to investigations into other moral concerns found on the Internet.

Cyber-bullying as a Moral Concern

Despite varying definitions of bullying and more specifically cyber-bullying (Tokunaga 2010), it is understood by many to be deliberate and hostile behaviour that is intended to harm others and as such, a moral concern (Belsey 2005; Menesini et al. 2011). The concern is great due to the high rates of cyber-bullying (Hasebrink et al. 2009) and also because of the emotional, psychological and at times, physical damage it causes its victims (Layard and Dunn 2009). Despite this, moral development and cyber-bullying research have largely been undertaken independently. Although studies have shown that the processes and reasons behind cyber-bullying do not differ much from face-to-face bullying (Froese-Germain 2008; Lenhart 2007), there is also a specific body of research that draws on moral disengagement theory (Bandura 2002) to explain why young people might bully others on the Internet. Empirical research supports a claim that the Internet acts as a 'moral disengagement mechanism' so that young people feel they are doing less moral wrong if they bully online than if they bully face-to-face (Gini 2006; Perren and Gutzwiller-Helfenfinger 2012; Menesini et al. 2013). Studies have also shown that cyber-bullies have less shame and guilt than offline bullies (Menesini and Camodeca 2008) and a corresponding lack of moral compassion (Pozzoli and Gini 2010).

Despite such promising research, none of these studies have sought to ground their findings in any established moral theory. This state of affairs persists despite accounts drawn from wider research into the Internet, demonstrating why such an approach might be beneficial. Several recent articles consider the rights and duties of Internet users, adopting largely deontological lines of enquiry (see, for example, Lievens 2011; Granitz and Loewy 2007; Zhang 2010; Lyu 2012). The preponderance of deontological approaches is not surprising, given that Kantianism (in some form of another) has been the moral theory of choice, until recently at least, in many areas of applied ethics (Arthur et al. 2015). Articles that explore pleasure, happiness or subjective wellbeing as a consequence of web-based interactions, adopting consequentialist lines of enquiry, are also common in the literature (see, for example, Valkenburg et al. 2006; Ali 2013; Cross et al. 2012). There has been growing awareness of virtue ethics as a serious moral rival to deontological and utilitarian theories ever since the publication of Elizabeth Anscombe's influential article Modern Moral Philosophy (1958) and Alasdair MacIntyre's book *After Virtue* (1981). Examples of recent articles that apply a virtue ethics theory to the Internet include: Elder (2014) who presents an Aristotelian defence of friendships online and argues that the concept of a shared life can equally be applied to online and offline friendships; and McFall (2012) who also adopts an Aristotelian conception of friendship to argue that online friendships are 'character friendships'.

In short, virtue ethics is a character based moral theory that offers an alternative framework for research into the Internet to the more directly action-guiding theories of deontology and utilitarianism. Vallor (2010) believes that several distinctive features of virtue ethics make it uniquely applicable to the domain of Internet ethics—and, furthermore, that a virtue-based perspective is needed to balance a strong utilitarian bias in the literature. Couldry (2010) agrees and argues that virtue ethics offers a more compelling and useful basis from which to study the Internet, than deontology. In particular, since rules are hard to establish and uphold online, and consequences are hard to predict, an approach to morality that is based on individual own character virtues has immediate appeal. As Plaisance (2013: 92) argues, 'rather than getting mired in the philosophical thicket regarding the motives and duties of actors in an online world we should focus on what behaviour and guidelines contribute to the flourishing of digital lives'. In this view, a virtue ethical approach offers a promising way to explore the specific moral issues found online. It is also useful to those interested in developing practical solutions for dealing with such moral issues, as it provides general guidance regarding appropriate virtue- or character-based behaviour, without reducing it to a set of codifiable rules that tend to be insensitive to particularities and contexts.

All the same, recognising Williams (1985) call for a non-reductionist approach to moral philosophy, there are merits in considering how each of the classical moral theories might be applied to a specific problem such as cyber-bullying. In doing so, the basis for pluralistic models that integrate notions of duty, consequence and virtue into future moral enquiries might well be sought. The research reported on here attempts to consider the potential interplay between different moral theories by attending to young peoples' own perspectives on cyber bullying. It holds that by taking into account the actual views of young people on the realities of their daily experience we might come to a more informed position that may be useful for further studies into the issue. Still, this study has a particular interest in exploring the potential of virtue ethics to better understand the influence of the Internet on young people, regarding it as providing an attractive and fruitful lens though which to question why people do good and/or bad things online.

Research Methodology

The research reported on here is part of a larger project that investigated the influence of the Internet on the character and virtues of 11–14 year olds. This study is reported on in more general terms elsewhere (Harrison 2014) whereas this paper focuses on one section of the qualitative findings of that piece in greater detail and depth.

The study described here sought to learn from 11 to 14 year olds, growing up in England and how they conceived the motivations of cyber-bullies. It was deemed important to hear the actual voice of the young people at both the data collection and data analysis stages. Semi-structured group interviews are widely used with young people for this purpose. Unlike individual interviews, group interviews reduce adult influence in data collection methods (Heary and Hennessy 2002) by providing children of like age with the opportunity to share perceptions and experiences with peers. Horner (2000: 510) suggests that children 'are more relaxed and willing to share perceptions when discussions are held with a group of peers'. When conducting group interviews with young people, it is important to try to avoid 'answer dialogue' (Heath et al. 2009) in which young people try to answer questions in the 'expected' way, for fear of negative consequences if they get things wrong. The aim was therefore to encourage participants to speak freely and honestly about their cyber-bullying experiences.

Twelve group interviews were undertaken in six schools between September and November 2013. In total, sixty 11 to 14 year olds were interviewed, of whom thirty-five were female and twenty-five male. The group interviews lasted between 30 and 45 min. On average, there were six students in each group (smallest number was 4, largest 7), since a group of this size is considered small enough to be manageable, whilst large enough to enable a genuine group dynamic (Krueger 1994). Group interviews followed the ethical procedures outlined by the British Research Association (2011). All participants were informed about the nature of the research and were asked to give consent to participation. Parents also gave consent for their children to be involved. The interviews were recorded and transcribed.

The interview schedule mostly consisted of open questions divided into four sections. Section one addressed the question of how young people experience and/or understand cyber-bullying in their everyday lives; section two explored the difference between face-to-face and online bullying; section three sought a better understanding of the motivation of cyber-bullies; and, section four contained questions aimed at determining effective educational strategies for reducing cyber-bullying. The group interview schedule was pre-piloted and piloted to ensure that it was fit for purpose.

The data collected during interviews was analysed thematically using a deductive approach of qualitative interpretation, since the themes informing the data had already been shaped by the prior literature review. Qualitative interviews permit access to unanticipated types of data, insofar as their purpose is to allow participants to recount their own narratives and to identify the themes that best reflect their own experiences of cyber-bullying. Thematic analysis is also a way of ensuring that the key issues are highlighted and addressed (Boyatzis 1998).

Contextual Details: The Participants and Schools

The participants were selected through cluster sampling, a method widely used by educational researchers working with schools (Robson 2011). The aim of cluster sampling is to identify a mixture of schools representing as far as possible the wider school population. The present research sites were selected on the basis that they contained a diverse range of participants within the 11–14 age bracket, in terms of gender, ethnicity, religion and rural and urban settings. Table 1 below provides details of the six schools involved.

Table 1: Group interview research sites

School	No. of pupils on roll	Age	Type M/F	Setting	% free school meals	Ethnicity of pupils	5 or more A*–C Grades at GCSE (in Maths and English) (2013)
School A	1074	11–18	Mixed	Urban	17.5	94 % White-British heritage Remainder: minority ethnic groups	64 %
School B	1195	4–19	Mixed	Urban	29.2	Proportion of ethnic minority groups is higher than national average.	46 %
School C	1607	11–18	Mixed	Urban	10	Majority White-British heritage; remainder being from ethnic backgrounds, mostly Polish	78 %
School D	482	9–13	Mixed	Urban	21.5	Most pupils White-British heritage.	n/a

School E	179	11–19	Mixed	Urban	12.3	Not Known	n/a
School F	1922	11–18	Mixed	Urban	26	Proportion from minority ethnic back-grounds: quarter of the national figure	71 %

The contact teachers in each school were asked to select a representative sample of young people to take part in the interviews. However, such selection may have been limited by availability of students at the time of the interviews, their willingness to participate, and also whether permission to participate had been granted by parents. Thus, it should be conceded that it is unlikely that representative samples were achieved in all interview groups. In addition, since participants were selected by the schools themselves, it is possible that more articulate students, and/or those of higher academic aptitude were selected to 'represent' their school. Insofar, the participants in this research might not be considered a probability sample. Still, though the selected groups cannot be said to be representative of all 11–14 year olds living in England, they may still provide useful indications of the attitudes of young people of this age group using the Internet. The results therefore need to be treated with caution, especially when attempting to draw more general conclusions from them.

The findings from the research are detailed in the section below. The quotations used in this article have been extracted from the group interviews and are generally representative of emerging themes. Genders of participants are indicated by an f (female) or m (male).

FINDINGS

Deontological Challenges

A deontological ethic regards moral conduct as the observance of rules or principles usually defined in terms of duties and/or obligations. In the group interviews questions were asked about how 'rules' and 'duties' on the Internet informs conduct, with particular regard to cyber-bullying. Two themes emerged from the data. The first was a perceived absence of clear rules online, leading to an increased sense of freedom. The second was that Internet users may easily conceal their identities, enabling them to bypass their ordinary duties.

some sound principles for moral behaviour on the Internet, it is not so easy to apply it in practice. The research findings show that calculating the consequences of any particular online interaction is difficult at best, and often impossible. Moreover, utilitarianism assumes empathy with the plight of other people, but the emotional identification underlying empathy seems to require (psychologically if not necessarily logically) the existence of particular rather than non-specific others. That said, utilitarianism and deontology might continue to provide useful frameworks for future research into morality and the Internet, in various partial and specifically targeted ways. However, the findings from this research show that virtue ethics has some advantages over the other two theories.

One distinct advantage of virtue ethics is that it places the onus on young people to make wise decisions on the Internet when it might not be obvious what the right thing is to do. As the Internet is described as 'free' and often involves new experiences, young users are often faced with situations where there is no categorical imperative, or right course of action based on rational principles. In these situations users are required to make judgements about the right course of action, based on previous experience as well as their effective emotions and feelings. Virtue ethics allows for young users of the Internet to become wiser over time through the development of online practical wisdom, or what we could call 'cyber-*phronesis*'. While a deontological approach might continue to be seen as helpful to bolster general rules and guidance governing what is good and bad online conduct, and a utilitarian one to draw greater attention to harmful online consequences, a virtue ethical perspective would prioritise the formation of wise and virtuous online citizens. Such an approach might provide young people with resources to negotiate the inevitable moral dangers and challenges of using the Internet.

Adopting a virtue ethical theoretical base for research into the impact of the Internet on young people requires us to ask different questions. Perhaps most importantly is to ask *how the character virtues of young people influence their use the Internet,* rather than simply to assume that because the technology exists, immoral behaviour will inevitably ensue. Unnecessarily deterministic accounts should be avoided. The interviews show that young people perceive their relationship with the Internet to be reciprocal, rather than unidirectional. They recognised that it was how agents used the Internet that largely determined the consequences of their online actions: that there was nothing about the technology as such that *made* people cruel, or dishonest. From a virtue ethical perspective, technological determinism is implausible insofar as it is the character virtues of the users of the technology, rather than the technology itself, that determines online behaviour. From this viewpoint, the technology is neither good nor bad (although it has features that might encourage good or bad behaviour): it is the user that determines whether it is put to good or bad use.

CONCLUSION

It would not be desirable to draw any simple picture of user experience from the data presented in this article. Given the limited nature of the present research, any attempt to make universal claims is not possible. However, the findings discussed above may provide a useful basis upon which to construct a moral theoretical framework for future research into cyber-bullying in particular as well as perhaps other moral issues found online. The new opportunities that the Internet has opened up for young people require them more than ever to 'do the right thing'; not so much motivated by rules, duties or consequences (since these may not always be explicit), but by having the character to choose wisely between alternatives. An important question to ask in future research is how best to educate digitally virtuous citizens to help them make good and wise decisions. On the basis of the present study, virtue ethics arguably offers not only a promising theoretical basis for researching the influence of the Internet on character virtues, but also provides a promising practical strategy for dealing with online moral concerns. The educational implications of this research will be returned to in a later paper.

23(6), 510–517.

27. Krueger, R. (1994). *Focus groups: A practical guide for applied research* (2nd ed.). London: Sage Publications.
28. Layard, R., & Dunn, J. (2009). *A good childhood, searching for values in a competitive age*. London: Penguin.
29. Lenhart, A. (2007). *Cyberbullying*. Washington, DC: Pew Research Center. Accessed November 20, 2013 from www.pewinternet.org/Reports/2007/Cyberbullying.aspx.
30. Lievens, E. (2011). Risk-reducing regulatory strategies for protecting minors in social networks. *Strategy for Telecommunications, Information and Media, 13*(6), 43–54.
31. Livingston, S. (2009). *Children and the Internet*. Cambridge: Polity Press.
32. Lyu, H. (2012). Internet policy in Korea: A preliminary framework for assigning moral and legal responsibility to agents in Internet activities. *Government Information Quarterly,29*(3), 394–402.
33. MacIntyre, A. (1981). *After virtue*. Notre Dame: University of Notre Dame Press.
34. Malti, T., Gasser, L., & Gutzwiller-Helfenfinger, E. (2010). Children's interpretive understanding, moral judgments, and emotion attributions: Relations to social behaviour. *British Journal of Developmental Psychology, 28*, 275–292.
35. McFall, M. T. (2012). Real character-friends: Aristotelian friendship, living together, and technology. *Ethics and Information Technology, 14*(3), 221–230.
36. Menesini, E., & Camodeca, M. (2008). Shame and guilt as behaviour regulators: Relationships with bullying, victimization and prosocial behaviour. *British Journal of Developmental Psychology, 26*(2), 183–196.
37. Menesini, E., Nocentini, A., & Calussi, P. (2011). The measurement of cyberbullying: Dimensional structure and relative item severity and discrimination. *Cyberpsychology, Behaviour and Social Networking, 14*(5), 267–274.
38. Menesini, E., Nocentini, A., & Camodeca, M. (2013). Morality, values, traditional bullying, and cyberbullying in adolescence. *The British Journal of Developmental Psychology,31*(1), 1–14.

39. Mishnan, F., Cook, C., Gadalla, T., Daciuk, J., & Solomon, S. (2010). Cyber-bullying behaviours among middle and high school students. *The American Journal of Orthopsychiatry, 80*(3), 362–374.
40. Mishnan, F., Michael, S., & Solomon, S. (2009). Ongoing and online: Children and youth's perceptions of cyberbullying. *Children and Youth Services Review, 3*(12), 1222–1228.
41. Ofcom. (2014). *Children and parents: Media use and attitudes report.* Accessed July 10, 2015 from http://stakeholders.ofcom.org.uk/binaries/research/media-literacy/media-use-attitudes-14/Childrens_2014_Report.pdf.
42. Perren, S., & Gutzwiller-Helfenfinger, E. (2012). Cyberbullying and traditional bullying in adolescence: Differential roles of moral disengagement, moral emotions, and moral values. *European Journal of Developmental Psychology, 9*, 195–209.
43. Plaisance, P. (2013). Virtue ethics and digital flourishing: An application of Philippa foot to life online. *Journal of Mass Media Ethics, 28*(3), 91–102.
44. Pozzoli, T., & Gini, G. (2010). Active defending and passive bystanding behavior in bullying: The role of personal characteristics and perceived peer pressure. *Journal of Abnormal Child Psychology, 38*, 815–827.
45. Robson, C. (2011). *Real world research.* Oxford: Blackwell Publishers.
46. Shariff, S. (2008). *Cyber-bullying: Issues and solutions for the school the classroom and the home.* Oxon: Routledge.
47. Shariff, S., & Hoff, D. L. (2007). Cyberbullying: Clarifying legal boundaries for school supervision in cyberspace. *International Journal of Cyber Criminology.* http://www.cybercrimjournal.co.nr. Accessed 12 Oct 2013.
48. Suler, J. (2004). The online disinhibition effect. *Cyberpsychology and Behaviour, 7*(3), 321–326.
49. Tokunaga, R. S. (2010). Following you home from school: A critical review and synthesis of research on cyberbullying victimisation. *Computers in Human Behaviour, 26*(3), 277–287.
50. Valkenburg, P. M., Peter, J. S., & Schouten, A. P. (2006). Friend networking sites and their relationship to adolescents' well-being and social self-esteem. *Cyberpsychology Behavior, 9*, 584–590.
51. Vallor, S. (2010). Social networking technology and the virtues. *Ethics and Information Technology, 12*(2), 157–170.

52. Weisband, S., & Kiesler, S. (1996). Self-disclosure on computer forms: Meta-analysis and implications. In *Proceedings of the SIGCHI conference on human factors in computing systems* (pp. 3–10).
53. Willard, N. (2002). *Computer ethics, etiquette, and safety for the 21st-century student*. Eugene, OR: ISTE.
54. Williams, B. (1985). *Ethics and the limitations of philosophy*. Cambridge: Harvard University Press.
55. Winter, R. E., & Leneway, R. J. (2008). *Cyberbullying—Terror in the classroom: What can be done?* Accessed January 15, 2013 from http://www.chaminade.org/cyberbullying.htm.
56. Zhang, X. (2010). Charging children with child pornography—Using the legal system to handle the problem of sexting. *Computer Law & Security Review, 26*(3), 251–259.

CHAPTER 8

CONSEQUENCES OF CYBER-BULLYING BEHAVIOUR IN WORKING LIFE: THE MEDIATING ROLES OF SOCIAL SUPPORT AND SOCIAL ORGANISATIONAL CLIMATE

Tuija Muhonen[1], Sandra Jönsson[1] and Martin Bäckström[2]

[1]Centre for Work Life and Evaluation Studies, Malmö University, Malmö, Sweden and Department of Urban Studies, Faculty of Culture and Society, Malmö University, Malmö, Sweden

[2]Department of Psychology, Lund University, Lund, Sweden

Citation: Tuija Muhonen, Sandra Jönsson, Martin Bäckström, (2017) "Consequences of cyberbullying behaviour in working life: The mediating roles of social support and social organisational climate", International Journal of Workplace Health Management, Vol. 10 Issue: 5, pp.376-390, https://doi.org/10.1108/IJWHM-10-2016-0075

ABSTRACT

Purpose

The purpose of this paper is to explore health- and work-related outcomes of cyberbullying behaviour and the potential mediating role of social organisational climate, social support from colleagues and social support from superiors.

Design/Methodology/Approach

Altogether 3,371 respondents participated in a questionnaire study.

Findings

The results of this study indicate that social organisational climate can have a mediating role in the relationship between cyberbullying behaviour and health, well-being, work engagement and intention to quit. Contrary to earlier face-to-face bullying research, the current study showed that cyberbullying behaviour had stronger indirect than direct relationships to health, well-being, work engagement and intention to quit.

Practical Implications

Communication through digital devices in work life is becoming more prevalent, which in turn increases the risk for cyberbullying behaviour. Organisations need therefore to develop occupational health and safety policies concerning the use of digital communication and social media in order to prevent cyberbullying behaviour and its negative consequences.

Originality/Value

Cyberbullying behaviour among working adults is a relatively unexplored phenomenon and therefore this study makes valuable contribution to the research field.

Keywords: Social support, Social organizational climate, Cyberbullying behaviour, Work life

Through the increasing use of digital media such as e-mails, text messages and social network sites, new forms of harassing behaviour in workplaces have emerged, referred to as cyberbullying or cyber-harassment (Borstorff *et al.*, 2007; Smith *et al.*, 2008). Research on cyberbullying and its consequences has mainly been conducted among adolescents and schoolchildren (Slonje and Smith, 2008; Dooley *et al.*, 2009), while the phenomenon among adults in working life has only recently started to attract researchers' attention (Brack and Caltabiano, 2014; Farley *et al.*, 2015; Forssell, 2016; Privitera and Campbell, 2009). Being a relatively new phenomenon, the pioneering studies investigating cyberbullying in working life have mainly focussed on determining its prevalence (Baruch, 2005; Brack and Caltabiano, 2014; Privitera and Campbell, 2009; Farley *et al.*, 2015; Forssell, 2016). These studies show varying prevalence rates from 9 to 21 per cent, but as in face-to-face bullying research the variation can be due to different ways of measuring and defining bullying. Since there is a paucity of research investigating cyberbullying in working life we refer to studies focussing on cyberbullying among youngsters/adolescents, as well studies on face-to-face bullying in work life.

There is an ongoing discussion among bullying researchers concerning what characterises cyberbullying compared to face-to-face bullying (Olweus, 2013; Runions *et al.*, 2013; Slonje and Smith, 2008). When it comes to face-to-face bullying, most researchers agree that the negative acts are conducted repeatedly and systematically over time, and that there is a power imbalance, i.e. the individuals who are exposed to the negative acts have difficulties defending themselves (Einarsen *et al.*, 2011). In a similar way, cyberbullying among youngsters has been defined as an aggressive intentional act carried out by a group or individual, using electronic forms of contact, repeatedly and over time against a victim who cannot easily defend him or herself (Smith *et al.*, 2008, p. 376). However, repetition of negative acts and power imbalance can have a different meaning in cyberbullying compared with face-to-face bullying (Dooley *et al.*, 2009; Runions *et al.*, 2013; Wang *et al.*, 2011).

Cyberbullying behaviours have a large potential audience as they are communicated through different digital media, which means that they can be easily stored, shared and viewed repeatedly. Therefore, the importance or meaning of repetition can be discussed as one act, e.g. sending a message or uploading a photo in social media can be viewed several times and easily distributed (Patchin and Hinduja, 2006; Slonje and Smith, 2008). From the targets' perspective every hit on the webpage where a picture or video clip is uploaded could be counted as repetition (Slonje and Smith, 2008). The concept of power imbalance is more complex in the cyberbullying context, as the formal power position can be challenged, e.g. by the invisibility of the actions and the perpetrators technological knowledge (Dooley *et al.*, 2009).

Other special characteristics of cyberbullying include high accessibility and to some extent even anonymity of the perpetrators (Kowalski *et al.*, 2014; Slonje and Smith, 2008). High accessibility implies that since we are more or less continuously connected to the internet, the victims of cyberbullying behaviour have few possibilities to escape the harassing behaviour (Patchin and Hinduja, 2006; Slonje and Smith, 2008; Tokunaga, 2010). The victims can be targeted whenever and wherever, even outside the workplace and after office hours. The harassment can continue, or even begin, when the workday is actually over. Thus, it is very difficult for the victims to avoid cyberbullying behaviour, which can result in feelings of powerlessness and power imbalance over time (Dooley *et al.*, 2009; Lutgen-Sandvik *et al.*, 2007).

As cyberbullying in working life is a relatively new phenomenon its consequences remain yet to be studied. Building upon earlier face-to-face bullying research based on occupational stress theory (cf. Hogh *et al.*, 2011), the aim of this study was to analyse how cyberbullying behaviour in working life was related to the following outcome variables: health, intention to quit, psychological well-being and work engagement. A further aim was to investigate whether social organisational climate, social support from colleagues and superior mediate the relationship between cyberbullying behaviour and the outcome variables.

HEALTH-RELATED OUTCOMES

Traumatic events such as bullying can have devastating effects on the victim's health and well-being (Hogh *et al.*, 2011). Earlier research has shown that victims of workplace face-to-face bullying report more health problems, more depressive symptoms, psychological stress, poorer well-being and are absent from work more often, compared with other employees (Dehue *et al.*, 2012; O'Driscoll *et al.*, 2011; Moayed *et al.*, 2006; Nielsen *et al.*, 2012; Vie *et al.*, 2010). These results are corroborated by a meta-analytic review (Nielsen and Einarsen, 2012) showing that exposure to bullying was associated with health- and well-being-related outcomes, such as mental and physical health problems, symptoms of post-traumatic stress and burnout. There are also indications that the negative health consequences of workplace bullying such as sick-listing, poor self-rated health and depressive symptoms may persist for a long time, even when the bullying no longer continues (Bonde *et al.*, 2016).

WORK-RELATED OUTCOMES

Earlier studies of face-to-face workplace bullying have shown that besides health and well-being, bullying is also related to several work-related outcomes such as lower job satisfaction, negative work attitudes and lower perceived job performance (Hoel *et al.*, 2011; O'Driscoll *et al.*, 2011). Further, bullying victims report lower work engagement and organisational commitment than non-victims (Nielsen and Einarsen, 2012). Several studies have shown that workplace bullying is related to higher intention to leave the organisation (Djurkovic *et al.*, 2004; Nielsen and Einarsen, 2012). It is understandable that the victims want to leave a workplace where they are bullied and, this is also what bullying victims often are advised to do in order to get away from a strenuous situation (Zapf and Gross, 2001).

Thus, several studies have indicated that face-to-face bullying has negative consequences for victims' health and well-being (Dehue *et al.*, 2012; O'Driscoll *et al.*, 2011; Moayed *et al.*, 2006; Nielsen *et al.*, 2012; Vie *et al.*, 2010). Further, there are indications that face-to-face bullying also results in lower work engagement and higher intention to leave their job (Djurkovic *et al.*, 2004; Nielsen and Einarsen, 2012). In line with these results from face-to-face workplace bullying, it could be expected that cyberbullying behaviour has similar consequences. We therefore hypothesise that:

Hypotheses

*H1.*Increasing cyberbullying behaviour is related to poorer health, higher intention to quit, lower well-being and lower work engagement.

MEDIATING FACTORS

In this study we view cyberbullying behaviour as a stress factor that can lead to different negative outcomes for the targeted individuals (Hauge *et al.*, 2010; Rodríguez-Muñoz *et al.*, 2009). Besides direct effects, cyberbullying behaviour can also have indirect effects on the outcome variables. Consequently, it is important to investigate factors that mediate in the relationship between cyberbullying and negative outcomes related to health and work. Social support from superiors and social support from colleagues are examples of these kinds of factors (Cassidy *et al.*, 2014; Zapf *et al.*, 1996).

Support from Colleagues and Superiors

Employees that have been exposed to bullying often report low support from their superiors (Hansen *et al.*, 2006; Zapf *et al.*, 1996), and as several authors have pointed out, the superiors can even be the perpetrators (Tepper, 2007; Vandekerckhove and Commers, 2003; Zapf *et al.*, 2011). Victims are often left with feelings of being ignored, minimised and not being believed when raising their concerns with the superior or human resources department (Keashly, 2001; Lewis and Orford, 2005). Also, support from colleagues is often rated as low by bullying targets (Zapf *et al.*, 1996). On the other hand, several studies indicate that support from colleagues can reduce the negative impact of bullying (Djurkovic *et al.*, 2004), e.g. perceived organisational support has been found to moderate the relationship between workplace bullying and victims' intention to leave (Djurkovic *et al.*, 2008).

Thus, as previous research has indicated that social support from colleagues and social support from superiors can be important factors in relation to the victims of face-to-face workplace bullying, we hypothesise that:

Hypotheses

*H2a.*Social support from colleagues mediates the relationship between cyberbullying behaviour and the outcomes: health, intention to quit, well-being and work engagement.*H2b.*

Social support from superiors mediates the relationship between cyberbullying behaviour and the outcomes: health, intention to quit, well-being and work engagement.

Social Organisational Climate

Earlier studies have pointed out the mediating role of social climate in the organisation in relation to employees' well-being, and even for their possibilities for learning and development at the workplace (Muhonen *et al.*, 2013; Jönsson *et al.*, 2015). Organisational culture and climate has also been shown to play an important role when it comes to face-to-face bullying (Powell *et al.*, 2015; Vartia, 1996). A negative organisational climate and culture can be directly related to face-to-face bullying (Bowling and

Beehr, 2006), or indirectly related through a stressful or competitive work environment, which triggers face-to-face bullying (Aquino and Lamertz, 2004; Salin, 2003). Workplace bullying has earlier been regarded as a consequence of organisational climate factors (Bowling and Beehr, 2006; Einarsen *et al.*, 2011), but this causality has been questioned (Hauge *et al.*, 2010). Giorgi (2012) maintains that workplace bullying can be a cause rather than a consequence of organisational climate. Furthermore, according to Giorgi (2012), workplace bullying can have an indirect effect, e.g. on health via organisational climate. As earlier face-to-face bullying research indicates that organisational climate can have an indirect mediating effect in the relationship between workplace bullying and different outcomes, we hypothesise that:

Hypotheses

*H3.*Social organisational climate mediates the relationship between cyberbullying behaviour and the outcomes: health, intention to quit, well-being and work engagement.

Furthermore, it can be postulated that cyberbullying may affect how social support from superior and social support from colleagues are experienced and that this in turn can have a detrimental effect on the experienced social organisational climate and thereby the different outcomes. In other words, if the bullying victims perceive less social support from superior and from colleagues, this could explain the relation to the perception of social organisational climate. In our model social climate can mediate the relation between support and outcomes, and therefore hide a possible influence of support from cyberbullying through support from superior and from colleagues.

Thus, we formulated following hypotheses:

Hypotheses

*H4.*Social support from colleagues, through its influence on the social climate mediates the relationship between cyberbullying behaviour and outcomes: health, intention to quit, well-being and work engagement.*H5.*

Social support from superior, through its influence on the social climate mediates the relationship between cyberbullying behaviour and outcomes: health, intention to quit, well-being and work engagement.

METHOD

Participants and Procedure

Data were collected between 17 April and 20 May 2014 by TNS Sifo, a public opinion poll and market research company. TNS Sifo has an online web panel consisting of a nationally representative random sample of 140,000 people aged 16 years or older. The questionnaire was distributed to a sample of individuals aged between 25 and 65 who were resident in Southern Sweden.

In total, 3,885 individuals responded the questionnaire, but as the aim of the study was to study cyberbullying in working life, those individuals who had not been employed during the last six months (n=514) were excluded from the study. The total number of participants was therefore 3,371, giving a response rate of 42 per cent.

Of the participants, 49 per cent were women, 32 per cent had a managerial position and the mean age was 50 years (SD=9.63). A majority (60 per cent) had university education and were working full-time (82 per cent). Also, a majority (73 per cent) reported that they used digital tools (computer, mobile phone, iPad, etc.) very often or always at their work.

Measures

Demographics

The demographic questions included age, gender, educational level (1=university degree or 2=not), organisational level (1=managerial position or 2=not).

Cyberbullying Behaviour

Cyberbullying behaviour was measured by a short version of Cyberbullying Behaviour Questionnaire (CBQ-S) developed by Jönsson *et al.* (2017). The reliability and validity of the questionnaire is reported and discussed in Jönsson *et al.* (2017). The CBQ-S consists of seven items; a sample item is: "Your work performance has been commented in negative terms on the internet" (α=0.88). Before they responded the following instruction was given to the participants "The following behaviours are often seen as examples of negative behaviour in the workplace that may occur via the use of technology. When responding consider every act in relation to these eight types of technologies: text messaging; pictures/photos or video clips, phone calls; e-mail; chat rooms; instant messaging; websites; and social networking websites (e.g. Facebook, Twitter, YouTube). Over the last six months, how often have you been subjected to the following negative acts related to your work through different forms of technology?"

The respondents rated the items on a five-point scale, 1=never, 2=now and then, 3=monthly, 4=weekly, 5=daily, in line with earlier bullying research (Einarsen *et al.*, 2009; Sprigg *et al.*, 2012). As the scale was very skewed the three highest rating categories (3-5) were collapsed into one and the whole rating scale was moved by one point for a new range from 0 to 2. This is a common procedure in several bullying studies (Einarsen *et al.*, 2009; Cassidy *et al.*, 2014), as the phenomenon assessed does not have a normal statistical distribution.

Social Organisational Climate

Social organisational climate was assessed by five items from QPSNordic (Dallner *et al.*, 2000). "What is the climate like in your work unit: (1) Competitive (2) Encouraging and supportive, (3) Distrustful and suspicious (4) Relaxed and comfortable (5) Rigid and rule-based?" The participants responded using a five-point scale ranging from 1=very little/not at all to 5=very much. Cronbach's α was 0.78.

Social Support from Superior and Support from Colleagues

Social support from superior was measured by two items from COPSOQ II (Pejtersen *et al.*, 2010; Berthelsen *et al.*, 2014). An example item is "How often is your nearest superior willing to listen to your problems at work?" Cronbach's α was 0.90.

Social support from colleagues was also measured by two items from COPSOQ II. A sample item is "How often do you get help and support from your colleagues?" Cronbach's α was 0.93. All the support items were rated on a five-point scale ranging from 1=very often to 5=very rarely. Before analyses the original values were reversed so that higher values indicate increasing support.

Psychological Well-being

Well-being was assessed by General Health Questionnaire-12, originally developed by Goldberg (1972); the Swedish version was developed by Sconfienza (1998). The scale consists of 12 items and a sample item is: "I have been able to face up my problems". The respondents rated the items on a four-point scale from 1 (=disagree very much) to 4 (=agree very much). Cronbach's α was 0.76. In the models we reduced the number of variables to six by creating random parcels.

Work Engagement

Work engagement was assessed by a short form of the Utrecht Work Engagement Scale (UWES-9; Schaufeli *et al.*, 2006). The scale consists of nine items and an example is: "I am enthusiastic about my job". The responses were rated on seven-point scale from 1 (=never) to 7 (=always). Cronbach's α was 0.95. In the models we reduced the number of variables to four by creating random parcels.

Intention to Quit

Intention to quit was measured by one item: "How often do you consider looking for work somewhere else?" (Pejtersen *et al.*, 2010; Berthelsen *et al.*, 2014). Ratings were made on a five-point scale from 1 (=very seldom) to 5 (=very often).

Health

Health was assessed by one item: "In general, would you say that your health is 1) Excellent, 2) Very good, 3) Good, 4) Not so good, 5) Poor?" Before analyses the original values were reversed so that higher values indicate better health. According to Lindberg *et al.* (2009), this single question has proven to be able to predict future sick leave and can therefore be used for identifying risk groups that are in need of preventive measures.

Statistical Analysis

The data were initially analysed by descriptive statistics, we report means, standard deviations and the correlations between the variables. Based on our hypotheses, we developed models shown in Figure 1 that were estimated with MPlus 7.1 (Muthén and Muthén, 1998/2012).

Random Parcels

Some of the scales used to create the latent variables of the models consisted of many items. To increase the reliability and validity of the observed variables in models, and to not have models that do not fit because of covariance between items on lower level, or collinearity between groups of items, for some of the scales, we created small random parcels, consisting of two or three items. Since all inventories had rather good homogeneity this should not influence the conclusions.

Measurement Models

The tested models included six latent variables of which four consisted of more than two observed variables. These four latent variables were tested separately to investigate whether their measurement models fitted the data. Table I displays the standardized loadings and the comparative fit indexes (CFI) of the measurement models. All models fitted data well with CFI on or above 0.950.

The starting model includes all paths and the hypotheses were tested by investigating to what extent the measurement fit was decreased when paths were deleted (set to zero). The mediation hypotheses were tested by investigating the indirect effects in the models (see Figure 1, which shows the paths tested and the models used to test thc paths). Cyberbullying is the sole exogenous independent variable in the model and its influence on the outcome variables work engagement, health, intention to leave and well-being are supposed to be indirect through social support from superior, social support from colleagues and social organisational climate. In the starting model there are also direct effects on the outcome variables. The influence of support from superior and support from colleagues is also supposed to influence the dependent variables through social organisational climate, but direct effects were included in the starting model. All outcome variables were defined to be correlated, and in addition, the two support latent variables were free to correlate. The models were estimated with the MPlus program with the observed variables of cyberbullying, social organisational climate, intention to quit and health defined as categorical. The weighted least square estimator (WLSMV) was used in all estimations. The α was set at 0.01 since the sample was very large.

between cyberbullying behaviour and the outcome variables were weak and the only significant one, work engagement, was found to be in the opposite direction (see Table III, Model 1). Based on the low correlations between cyberbullying behaviour and the outcome variables: health, intention to quit, psychological well-being and work engagement, direct relations were not supported, and hence the hypothesis (*H1*) was rejected. In the next model, we tested if indirect relations between cyberbullying behaviour and the outcome variables were more important.

Table III: Model results and β-coefficients from structural models

	Standardized coefficients	**Dependent variables**						
Model	**Independent variables**	**Social support superior**	**Social support colleagues**	**Social climate**	**Engagement**	**Well-being**	**Health**	**Intention to quit**
Model 1	Cyberbullying	–0.361**	–0.277**	–0.247*	0.077*	–0.057	–0.009	0.058
χ^2 (326): 1,950.3	Social support superior			0.358*	0.119**	0.012	0.014	–0.148**
CFI: 0.972	Social support colleagues			0.216*	–0.031	0.057	0.018	0.122**
RMSEA: 0.04	Social climate				0.501**	0.505**	0.251**	–0.479**
Model 2	Cyberbullying	–0.365**	–0.280**	–0.246**	0.079*			
χ^2 (333): 1,902.5	Social support superior			0.366**	0.080*			–0.153**
CFI: 0.974	Social support colleagues			0.222**				0.137**
RMSEA: 0.039	Social climate				0.510**	0.561**	0.282**	–0.521**
Model 3	Cyberbullying	–0.359**	–0.281**	–0.273**	0.081*			
χ^2 (336): 1,886	Social support superior			0.377**	0.077*			
CFI: 0.973	Social support colleagues			0.204**				
RMSEA: 0.039	Social climate				0.513**	0.591**	0.281**	–0.542**

Notes: $*p<0.01$; $**p<0.001$

The second hypothesis (Figure 1, panel 1B) tested if social support from colleagues (*H2a*) and social support from superior (*H2b*) could mediate the relationship between cyberbullying behaviour and the outcome variables (health, intention to quit, well-being and work engagement). The results showed that only work engagement had a direct relation to social support from superior (see Table III, Model 2); it was found that cyberbullying behaviour was indirectly related to work engagement over support from superior (β=–0.027, p=0.001). In general, however, there was no support that social support from colleagues (*H2a*) or social support from superior (*H2b*) mediate the relationship between cyberbullying behaviour and the outcome variables.

The third hypothesis (see Figure 1, panel 1C) tested whether social organisational climate could mediate the relationship between cyberbullying behaviour and the outcome variables (health, intention to quit, well-being and work engagement). The analyses showed that all four indirect relations were significant (see Table III, Model 3, and Table IV). This provides strong support for mediating relation (*H3*), suggesting that cyberbullying behaviour can have a negative influence on the social organisational climate and that this in turn can affect the outcome variables.

The fourth and fifth hypotheses (see Figure 1, panel 1D) tested, whether social support from colleagues and superior, through its influence on the social climate, mediates the relationship between cyberbullying behaviour and outcomes. These were tests of the significance of the indirect relations part of Model 3 shown in Table III. It was found that the indirect relation between cyberbullying bchaviour and the outcome variables in general was stronger for social support from superiors than for social support from colleagues, but all indirect effects were significant when they also went through social organisational climate (see Table IV). This verifies the hypotheses that social support from colleagues and social support from superiors mediate the effects of cyberbullying behaviour on the outcome variables. However, social support from superiors and social support from colleagues also influence the social organisational climate and this indirect relation appears to be the most important explanation for how cyberbullying behaviour can influence the outcome variables.

Table IV: Total effect, direct effects and indirect effects

Effect	**Health**	**Intention to quit**	**Well-being**	**Engagement**
Total effects	–0.116**	0.276**	–0.248**	–0.176**
Direct from CB		0.065		0.095**
Indirect SocClim	–0.077**	0.148**	–0.161**	–0.143**

Indirect SupSup and SocClim	–0.038**	0.073**	–0.080**	–0.071**
Indirect SupCol and SocClim	–0.016**	0.031**	–0.034**	–0.030**

Notes: CB, cyberbullying behaviour; SocClim, social climate; SupSup, social support from superior; SupCol, social support from colleagues. $^{**}p<0.001$

DISCUSSION

Cyberbullying behaviour among working adults is a relatively new and unexplored phenomenon (Brack and Caltabiano, 2014; Farley *et al.*, 2015), and therefore the current study makes a unique and timely contribution to the research field. Based on earlier studies of face-to-face bullying the purpose of the current study was to analyse how cyberbullying behaviour in working life was related to health, intention to quit, psychological well-being and work engagement. Further, the potential mediating relations of social organisational climate, social support from colleagues and superior between cyberbullying behaviour and the outcome variables were explored with SEM analyses.

The results showed that cyberbullying behaviour had only one significant direct relation to the outcome variables, namely, positive relationship to work engagement. Therefore, the first hypothesis (*H1*) postulating that increasing cyberbullying behaviour would be directly related to poorer health, higher intention to quit, lower well-being and lower work engagement was not supported. These findings suggest that cyberbullying behaviour does not have a direct and unique influence on intention to quit, well-being and work engagement (Dehue *et al.*, 2012; O'Driscoll *et al.*, 2011; Nielsen and Einarsen, 2012).

Likewise, the results did not support the hypotheses postulating that social support from colleagues (*H2a*) and social support from superior (*H2b*) would mediate between cyberbullying behaviour and the outcome variables (health, intention to quit, psychological well-being and work engagement). These findings differ from studies of face-to-face bullying pointing out colleagues' and supervisors' crucial role in the bullying situations (Djurkovic *et al.*, 2004; Hansen *et al.*, 2006; Zapf *et al.*, 2011).

When it comes to social organisational climate the results confirmed the hypothesis (*H3*) by showing a mediating relationship between cyberbullying behaviour and the outcome variables (health, intention to quit, psychological well-being and work engagement). This implies that cyberbullying behaviour may influence the experience of the social organisational climate and thereby can have negative consequences on health, well-being, engagement and intention to quit. This result is in line with earlier research of face-to-face bullying (Powell *et al.*, 2015; Vartia, 1996).

Further, the results supported the hypotheses that the social support from colleagues, and social support from superior mediates the relation between cyberbullying behaviour and the outcome variables through social organisational climate (*H4* and *H5*). The indirect relation between cyberbullying behaviour and the outcome variables was in general stronger for social support from superiors than for social support from colleagues, but all indirect effects were significant when they also went through social organisational climate. The results indicate that social support from superiors and social support from colleagues can influence the social organisational climate, and that this indirect relation is the most important explanation for how cyberbullying behaviour can influence the outcome variables.

In sum, the results showed both some similarities and some differences compared with face-to-face workplace bullying research. Rather than having a direct relationship with the outcome variables: health, intention to quit, psychological well-being and work engagement (Nielsen and Einarsen, 2012; O'Driscoll *et al.*, 2011), cyberbullying behaviour had stronger indirect relationships to the outcome variables through the other studied variables. Especially, social organisational climate seems to play a mediating role between cyberbullying behaviour and the outcome variables: health, intention to quit, psychological well-being and work engagement. The study shows that cyberbullying behaviour can influence both the amount of social support experienced from superiors and colleagues, and more generally can influence the social organisational climate. Another way of formulating this is that health-related (health and well-being) and work-related (intention to quit, work engagement) consequences of cyberbullying behaviour in working life, in general seem to be mediated by the experience of the social organisational climate, social support from colleagues and superior.

Further, it appeared that social support from superior had a somewhat stronger relationship than support from colleagues to the outcome variables. This is in accordance with face-to-face bullying studies (Djurkovic *et al.*, 2008), and can also have practical implications when dealing with cyberbullying behaviour.

The study has a limitation due to its cross-sectional design, which prevents us from making causal inferences. Earlier research (cf. Zapf, 1999) has also pointed out that there is a general problem in bullying research concerning the differentiation between causes and consequences of bullying behaviour. For example, a study by Rodríguez-Muñoz *et al.* (2009) showed that negative job-related well-being was the cause rather than a consequence of workplace face-to-face bullying. Likewise, negative working conditions can be either cause or a consequence of workplace bullying (Zapf, 1999). Stressful work environment can produce behavioural and affective reactions in certain individuals that in turn increase the risk of them being victimized (Bowling and Beehr, 2006). We have chosen to use the term consequences in this study, even though we are not claiming to prove causality between the study variables. The relationships between cyberbullying behaviour, social organisational climate and the outcome variables can be dynamic rather than unidirectional. Therefore, it can be discussed whether cyberbullying behaviour is caused by poor social organisational climate or the other way round, or if the relationship is reciprocal. In order to address the causality experimental and/or longitudinal design should be applied in future studies.

Another limitation is that some of the scales were measured with few items and both intention to leave and health were measured by only one item. However, earlier studies (Lindberg *et al.*, 2009; Tham, 2007) have indicated that these measures have good predictive validity. Further, the technological development and increasing digitalisation can give rise to new forms of cyberbullying behaviour that might not be assessed by the questionnaire used in this study.

The current study was conducted in Sweden where the prevalence of workplace bullying, like in the other Scandinavian countries, is lower compared with other European and non-European countries (Nielsen *et al.*, 2010; Forssell, 2016). As cyberbullying research is in its early stages yet there is need for further research in Sweden but also in other countries in order to contextualise the findings of the current study.

CONCLUSION

The results of this study indicate that social organisational climate can have a mediating role in the relationship between cyberbullying behaviour and health, well-being, work engagement and intention to quit. Contrary to earlier face-to-face bullying research, the current study showed that cyberbullying behaviour had stronger indirect rather than direct relationships to health, well-being, work engagement and intention to quit. As communication through digital devices and social media in work life increases, there is a danger that cyberbullying behaviour also might become more prevalent. Organisations need therefore to develop organisational health and safety policies concerning the use of digital communication and social media, as well as activities in order to prevent cyberbullying behaviour and its negative effects. As this study was conducted in the Swedish context, there is need for research in other countries concerning cyberbullying behaviour in working life, its causes and consequences, but also to develop evidence-based interventions.

REFERENCES

1. Aquino, K. and Lamertz, K. (2004), "A relational model of workplace victimization: social roles and patterns of victimization in dyadic relationships", Journal of Applied Psychology, Vol. 89 No. 6, pp. 1023-1034.
2. Baruch, Y. (2005), "Bullying on the net: adverse behavior on e-mail and its impact", Information & Management, Vol. 42 No. 2, pp. 361-371.
3. Berthelsen, H., Westerlund, H. and Kristensen, T.S. (2014), "COPSOQ II – en uppdatering och språklig validering av den svenska versionen av en enkät för kartläggning av den psykosociala arbetsmiljön på arbetsplatser", report, Stress Research Institute, Stockholm University, Stockholm.
4. Bonde, J.P., Gullander, M., Hansen, Å.M., Grynderup, M., Persson, R., Hogh, A. and Kolstad, H.A. (2016), "Health correlates of workplace bullying: a 3-wave prospective follow-up study", Scandinavian Journal of Work, Environment & Health, Vol. 42 No. 1, pp. 17-25.
5. Borstorff, P.C., Graham, G. and Marker, M.B. (2007), "E-harassment: employee perceptions of e-technology as a source of harassment", Journal of Applied Management and Entrepreneurship, Vol. 12 No. 2, pp. 44-60.
6. Bowling, N.A. and Beehr, T.A. (2006), "Workplace harassment from the victim's perspective: a theoretical model and meta-analysis", Journal of Applied Psychology, Vol. 91 No. 5, pp. 998-1012.
7. Brack, K. and Caltabiano, N. (2014), "Cyberbullying and self-esteem in Australian adults", Cyberpsychology, Vol. 8 No. 2, pp. 1-10.
8. Cassidy, T., McLaughlin, M. and McDowell, E. (2014), "Bullying and health at work: the mediating roles of psychological capital and social support", Work & Stress, Vol. 28 No. 3, pp. 255-269.
9. Dallner, M., Lindström, K., Elo, A.L., Skogstad, A., Gamberale, F., Hottinen, V., Knardahl, S. and Ørhede, E. (2000), Användarmanual för QPSNordic, Arbetslivsinstitutet, Stockholm.
10. Dehue, F., Bolman, C., Völlink, T. and Pouwelse, M. (2012), "Coping with bullying at work and health related problems", International Journal of Stress Management, Vol. 19 No. 3, pp. 175-197.
11. Djurkovic, N., McCormack, D. and Casimir, G. (2004), "The physical and psychological effects of workplace bullying and their relationship

to intention to leave: a test of the psychosomatic and disability hypotheses", International Journal of Organization Theory and Behavior, Vol. 7 No. 4, pp. 469-497.

12. Djurkovic, N., McCormack, D. and Casimir, G. (2008), "Workplace bullying and intention to leave: the moderating effect of perceived organisational support", Human Resource Management Journal, Vol. 18 No. 4, pp. 405-422.
13. Dooley, J.J., Pyżalski, J. and Cross, D. (2009), "Cyberbullying versus face-to-face bullying: a theoretical and conceptual review", Zeitschrift für Psychologie/Journal of Psychology, Vol. 217 No. 4, pp. 182-188.
14. Einarsen, S., Hoel, H. and Notelaers, G. (2009), "Measuring exposure to bullying and harassment at work: validity, factor structure and psychometric properties of the negative acts questionnaire – revised", Work & Stress, Vol. 23 No. 1, pp. 24-44.
15. Einarsen, S., Hoel, H., Zapf, D. and Cooper, C.L. (2011), "The concept of bullying and harassment at work: the European tradition", in Einarsen, S., Hoel, H., Zapf, D. and Cooper, C.L. (Eds), Bullying and Harassment in the Workplace: Developments in Theory, Research, and Practice, 2nd ed., CRC Press, Boca Raton, FL, pp. 3-39.
16. Farley, S., Coyne, I., Sprigg, C., Axtell, C. and Subramanian, G. (2015), "Exploring the impact of workplace cyberbullying on trainee doctors", Medical Education, Vol. 49 No. 4, pp. 436-443.
17. Forssell, R. (2016), "Exploring cyberbullying and face-to-face bullying in working life – prevalence, targets and expressions", Computers in Human Behavior, Vol. 58, pp. 454-460.
18. Giorgi, G. (2012), "Workplace bullying in academia creates a negative work environment: an Italian study", Employee Responsibilities and Rights Journal, Vol. 24 No. 4, pp. 261-275.
19. Goldberg, D.P. (1972), The Detection of Psychiatric Illness by Questionnaire, Oxford University Press, London.
20. Hansen, Å.M., Hogh, A., Persson, R., Karlson, B., Garde, A.H. and Ørbæk, P. (2006), "Bullying at work, health outcomes, and physiological stress response", Journal of Psychosomatic Research, Vol. 60 No. 1, pp. 63-72.
21. Hauge, L.J., Skogstad, A. and Einarsen, S. (2010), "The relative impact of workplace bullying as a social stressor at work", Scandinavian Journal of Psychology, Vol. 51 No. 5, pp. 426-433.

CHAPTER 9

A STUDY ON CYBERBULLYING: ITS FORMS, AWARENESS AND MORAL REASONING AMONG YOUTH

Zsa Zsa Tajol Asanan, Ibiwani Alisa Hussain, Nooraneda Mutalip Laidey

Faculty of Business and Management, Asia Pacific University of Technology and Innovation, Kuala Lumpur, Malaysia

ABSTRACT

This purpose of the study is to investigate forms, awareness and moral reasoning against cyberbullying among youth. The study used primary data which was obtained through self-administered survey questionnaire. A total of 120 questionnaires were distributed to three different universities to examine the behaviour of youth towards cyberbullying pattern. Descriptive,

Citation: Zsa Zsa Tajol Asanan, Ibiwani Alisa Hussain, Nooraneda Mutalip Laidey, A Study on Cyberbullying: Its Forms, Awareness and Moral Reasoning Among Youth, *International Journal of Information and Communication Sciences*. Vol. 2, No. 5, 2017, pp. 54-58. doi: 10.11648/j.ijics.20170205.11

frequency and correlation analysis were carried out on the primary data gathered. Findings showed that the three independent variables have close relationship towards the activities of cyberbullying among youth.

Keywords: Awareness, Cyber Bullying, Forms, Moral Reasoning, Youth

INTRODUCTION

The modern technology which creates a borderless world had upgraded bullying into cyberbullying [1] and it is a prevalent issue that happens everywhere regardless of schools or the working world [2]. The word cyberbullying did not even exist before, yet it has becoming as one of a major issue nowadays. Cyberbullying can be defined as adolescent aggression through electronic communication [2]. It can also be defined as a repeated intentional aggression carried out by an individual or group of people using electronic forms such as chat rooms towards victim who does not have the ability to defend themselves [3, 4]. Cyberbullying is also defined as wilful and repeated harm inflicted through the use of computers, cells phones and other electronic devices [5] meanwhile [6] explained cyberbullying as a repetition of insult, hurt or harassing others using information technology. It is a systematic abuse of power which occurs through the use of information and communication technologies [7]. Many studies had been conducted among school children in the United States, however, similar study had not been conducted among university students. Therefore, this study is intended to investigate the level of awareness, the forms as well as moral reasoning of university students (hereinafter after known as youth) in Malaysia.

Forms

Cyberbullying is a build-up problem that has expanded with the growth of social hierarchy [8]. It can be traced back to normal bullying and now with the advancement of technology, bullying takes a new form which is cyberbullying. The forms cyberbullying are flaming, harassment, cyberstalking, impersonation, cyber threats and online harassment [9, 10]. Through these forms, the bullies reach their victim through social media site, text messages and phone calls. Cyberbullying takes such forms because of the users' addictiveness towards the internet [11]. These people can only live with the internet because it is the only time they feel alive [12]. Going online gives them the feel of being in control and safer because the identity remains anonymous and they are in their comfort zone. Cyberbullying activities can be subcategorized into text messages bullying, pictures or video clips, phone call bullying, email bullying, chat-room bullying, bullying through instant messages or via websites [13]. Breakdown of cyberbullying helps people to understand which forms are most prevalent [13].

Awareness

Awareness of cyberbullying is faint among the society and cyberbullying is on the rise caused by the lack of knowledge and awareness in this issue. Awareness is an important factor for prevention sake as society are more aware of traditional bullying compared to cyberbullying [14]. The only difference is that it does not inflict physical injury but rather emotional disturbance which can do worse damages compare to physical wound. However, cyberbullying has been taking over the reign [15, 16]. Awareness is still at minimal level and it had been confirmed by previous research [14, 17]. Hence, it is believed that it needs to be understood by society including parents and teachers the potential of cyberbullying happening to their children. Merely installing filters on computers does not help in protecting them from unwanted contacts [18]. Most importantly, parents need to be aware that this unhealthy activity is happening around them. Hence, it is important for them to be aware of each subtype of cyberbullying [14]. The higher the awareness level among public is, the lower the statistics of cyberbullying case happening globally.

Moral Reasoning

Moral reasoning can be referred to as common sense and judgment. Kohlberg stated that there are six stages of moral development [19]. The theory of moral reason that was adopted back then was further classified into two new typologies [20]. The first is up-standers and the second is bystander. However, it was stated that the moral reasoning of a bystander and the up stander clouded upon only at the scenarios, the role play by the users, gender, emotion and contextual factors [20]. In contrast, another researcher [21] commented that moral reasoning means the public tolerance level towards cyberbullying activities, as well as how acceptive the public are towards the rules that regulate cyberbullying. Moral reasoning also depends on individuals' thoughts on how much can they accept and up to what extend do they consider cyberbullying as an unhealthy practice [21]. Moral judgement is made purely on emotion or affection rather than reason [20, 22, 23]. An interesting development in the theory of moral development

[19] was the argument put forth by reference [20]. He argued that the stage of moral judgement can only be achieved by certain individual in a certain context based on their own ethical thoughts. The author suggested that moral reasoning is a dependent concept whereby different individuals express their morality differently than their personal needs and ability.

METHODOLOGY

The objective of this study is to study youths' responsiveness on cyberbullying predicted by forms, awareness and moral reasoning. The study adopts quantitative method using primary data gathered through self-administered survey questionnaire. The population for the data respondent are youth living in Malaysia. These youth were from three private universities in Malaysia of the age of 18-25. In terms of research design, this study used quota sampling methodology. Hence out of 120 questionnaires, 40 questionnaires were distributed at each university. Items used to measure the predictors of cyberbullying (i.e.: forms, awareness and moral reasoning) which were used in the survey questionnaires were adopted from 'An investigation into cyberbullying, its forms, awareness and impact, and the relationship between age and gender in cyberbullying' [13].

FINDINGS

Table 1 shows a higher percentage of female respondent compared to male respondent which is denoted by 53% and 47% respectively. Out of the 120 respondents, 73% were Malaysian while the remaining were foreigners. Since cyberbullying happen through social media, there were a few general items used to measure the preference of social network, time spend on browsing through their social network account and most common platform utilized by youth.

Table 1. Gender & Nationality

Gender	
Male	47%
Female	53%
Nationality	
Malaysian	73%
Foreigner	27%

The results shows the most popular social network is Facebook. 112 respondents have an account with Facebook and 87 respondents mentioned that they have YouTube account. While the least favourable social network is blog and only 7 respondents mentioned they are using it. Based on the popularity of social media among youth in this modern era, the research shows that, 39.2% of youth spend around 3 to 4 hours browsing through their social media account such as Facebook, YouTube and others per day. Internet browsing activities mostly happen via smartphone (81.7%) compared to laptop and tablets.

Few predictors were used in the awareness section and level of awareness of cyber bullying among youth are summarised as: posting mean and hurtful pictures of others (27.5%); mean and hurtful comments (26.7%); spreading rumours about others (24.2%); hacking into someone else account and pretending to be them (15.8%); and threat to hurt someone (5%). The level of awareness is worrying as many respondents are not aware that a threat to hurt someone is considered as cyber bullying as it can be seen that only 5% respondents agreed to this predictor and only one respondent (0.83%) is fully aware that all of the predictors are considered as cyber bullying.

Table 2. Most Aware Forms of Cyberbullying

	Frequency	Percent
Mean or hurtful comments	32	26.7
Spreading rumours about someone	30	25.0
Threats to hurt someone	5	4.2
Hacking into my account and pretending to be someone	20	16.7
Posting mean and hurtful pictures or videos of someone	31	25.8
Other: In any form that hurt someone is cyber bullying. All type. None excluded.	1	.8
10.00	1	.8
Total	120	100.0

In terms of awareness, 55% respondents agreed and 30.8% strongly agreed that they are aware of cyberbullying incidents/activities on the internet. 11.7% respondents were neutral about cyberbullying activities and a small, percentage (2.5%) are not at all aware of cyber bullying activities.

Table 3. Awareness of Cyberbullying

	Frequency	**Percent**
Strongly Agree	37	30.8
Agree	66	55.0
Neutral	14	11.7
Disagree	2	1.7
Strongly Disagree	1	.8
Total	120	100.0

Despite the respondents' awareness about cyberbullying activities, 50.8% of the respondents are a bystander (a person who sees something happens, without being involved in it) and the remaining 49.2% are an up stander (a person who sees a person bullied and stand up against bullies).

Table 4. Up stander/ Bystander

	Frequency	**Percent**
Up stander	59	49.2
Bystander	61	50.8
Total	120	100.0

A correlation analysis was conducted to examine the relationship between the forms of cyberbullying, the awareness of cyberbullying and moral reasoning of cyberbullying and cyberbullying [24] and to achieve this purpose, reference [25] guideline on correlation score was adopted. The guideline is described in this manner: the scale of small is r=.10 to.29, medium is r=.30 to.49, and large is r=.50 to 1.0.

Table 5. Correlation Test

		Cyberbullying	**Forms**	**Awareness**	**Moral Reasoning**
Cyberbullying	Pearson Correlation	1	.640**	.809**	.793**
	Sig. (2-tailed)		.000	.000	.000
	N	120	120	120	120
Forms	Pearson Correlation	.640**	1	.685**	.706**
	Sig. (2-tailed)	.000		.000	.000
	N	120	120	120	120
Awareness	Pearson Correlation	.809**	.685**	1	.841**
	Sig. (2-tailed)	.000	.000		.000
	N	120	120	120	120
Moral Reasoning	Pearson Correlation	.793**	.706**	.841**	1
	Sig. (2-tailed)	.000	.000	.000	
	N	120	120	120	120

**Correlation is significant at the 0.01 level (2-tailed).

The correlation table above illustrates the relationship between the predictors and dependent variables. The first correlation: cyberbullying and the forms of cyberbullying shows a strong relationship where 0.64 was denoted. Next is the relationship between awareness on cyberbullying and cyberbullying activity and it was denoted at 0.809. Here it can be revealed that there is a there is a significant level of relationship between the awareness of cyberbullying and cyberbullying compared to the first predictor. On the moral reasoning predictor, findings revealed that, it has significant relationship, valued at 0.793. The value is higher compared to forms of cyberbullying but lower than the value of awareness on cyberbullying activity. The value of 0.793 indicated that there is a high significant level of relationship between moral reasoning of cyberbullying against cyberbullying activity.

DISCUSSION

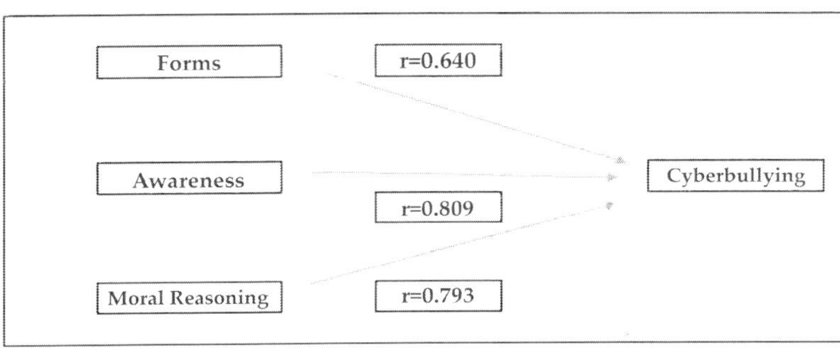

Figure 1. Correlation Test Findings.

Based on the results obtained from correlation analysis, it can be described that there is a significant relationship between cyberbullying and the forms of cyber bullying. 64% respondents are familiar with the forms of cyberbullying. A study on cyberbullying conducted by other researcher also revealed similar results [13]. However, the previous studies were focusing more towards teenagers, between the ages of 12 to 20 years old. Findings from previous studies revealed that most of the students at a younger age know the pattern and forms of cyberbullying and picture and video clips were the highest form of cyberbullying performed by teenage respondents [26]. On a different note, a study by reference [27] found the opposite whereby there are many forms of cyberbullying that are actively going on among youth. The form of cyberbullying applied on their victims differs, depending on the reason as well as gender. In most of the cases, the victim of cyberbullying activities revolves among the youth who are within the younger generation [2]. Therefore it can be concluded that youth these days are familiar with the forms of cyberbullying.

Result from the correlation analysis shows that awareness of cyberbullying has a positive significant relationship towards cyberbullying activity among the youth. The findings showed the relationship is at 0.809. This means that 80.9% of the respondents has the awareness of cyberbullying among youth in the cyber space. It is also found that those who have more awareness of cyberbullying activities appeared to be more supportive in helping the victim to voice out their distress [28]. Adults are becoming more aware of the signs of cyberbullying as to understand and prevent their children from becoming a victim of cyberbullying [29]. Results from survey showed that 47% of the sample size had witnessed cyberbullying activities while 11% admitted to being the bully and 29% stated that they were a victim of cyberbullying. In total, out of 100%, 87% knows what is cyberbullying and cyberbullying activity and hence, there is a high level of awareness of cyberbullying activities among the sample size.

Moral reasoning has a positive significant relation with cyberbullying activities among youth (79.3%). A study conducted by reference [30] found that age and gender are among the important factors for cyberbullies in choosing the victim. However, what is worrying is that youth who are involved in cyberbullying activities does not even morally aware that they are the bully [31]. Therefore, one way to increase the moral reasoning level among youth and encourage them to reduce cyberbullying activities is to educate them on many types of cyberbullying characteristics. Additionally, moral values can be instilled by creating cognizance amongst the public on the moral reasoning behind the activities of cyberbullying [32]. With the establishment of moral reasoning in a person, cyberbullying activities can be minimized [33]. The findings in this study revealed that victims of cyberbullying will usually experience high negative impact psychologically and most of the time caused the victim to lower their self-esteem [34, 35] and this activity is prevalent and has gaining its popularity amongst youth.

CONCLUSION

Cyberbullying is proven to be prevalent among youth and all of the predictors have a significant level of correlation with the independent variable. Even when it was proven that most youth have either witnessed cyberbullying or admitted to being the bully themselves, cyberbullying is still a predominant issue among youth. Then, we must go back to basics in which awareness is the key. However, individual self-concepts evaluate one's perception, moral believes, personal attributes, family life and social dimensions which can be powerfully affected by the judgement made by others. Finally, as recommendation, the sample size in this research cannot represent the total population. Therefore, it is recommended that the study is to be continued in a large scale. Another dimension can also be added to make this research more meaningful.

greater access than the group who are not in power. Therefore, those in power have a greater chance to have access to media, and greater opportunities to influence public awareness. With their access to influence the discourse on Instagram, making them more free to express all forms of resentment and hatred.

CONCLUSION

'Manual' bullying requires face to face interaction between the offender and the victim, but now it moved to the virtual world which is then referred to as cyberbullying. Perpetrators do cyberbullying to the figures which are considered to have the identity out of the ordinary, in this case is transgender. They give negative comments and tend to be rough on transgender's Instagram account. The logic of truth raised by the commentators on Instagram is already become their mindset because it has been institutionalized in everyday life through education, social life, and state regulations. They feel threatened with something outside the 'normality'.

One thing we should understand is technology will continue to develop and it is very possible that LGBTQ people will express theirselves in other social media when people restrict their expression in Instagram. I concluded that the public itself is still overlap between accepting the existence of LGBT as a reality that must be faced or support their existence. Here, I hope the community, not stuck on the logic of normative truth, and although not yet to accept the existence of LGBT people, but at least they do not do rejection and attacks against LGBT.

REFERENCES

1. R. Nasrullah, Teori dan Riset Media Siber (Cybermedia), (Kencana Prenadamedia Group, Jakarta, 2014)
2. Mulia, Siti Musdah, Islam dan Homoseksualitas: Membaca Ulang Pemahaman Islam, (Jurnal Gandrung 1(1): 9-31, 2010)
3. J. Butler, Gender Trouble, (Routledge, New York, 1990)
4. Julia I Suryakusuma, Konstruksi Sosial Seksualitas: Sebuah Pengantar Teoritis, (Prisma: 3-14, 1991)
5. T. A. van Dijk, Discourse, Power and Access, (Routledge, London, 1996)
6. T. A. van Dijk, Principles of Discourse Analysis. Discourse & Society, J. E **4**, 2 (1993)
7. T. A. van Dijk, Power and The News Media, (Hampton Press, New Jersey, 1995)

CHAPTER 12

CYBER BULLYING PREVENTION: INTERVENTION IN TAIWAN

Ming-Shinn Lee[1], Wu Zi-Pei[1], Leif Svanstrom[2], Koustuv Dalal[3]

[1] Department of Curriculum Design and Human Potentials Development, National Dong Hwa University, Hualien, Taiwan

[2]Department of Public Health Science, Karolinska Institutet, Stockholm, Sweden

[3] Centre for Injury Prevention and Safety Promotion (CIPSP), School of Health and Medical Sciences, O¨ rebro University, O¨ rebro, Sweden

ABSTRACT

Background

This study aimed to explore the effectiveness of the cyber bullying prevention WebQuest course implementation.

Citation: Lee M-S, Zi-Pei W, Svanström L, Dalal K (2013) Cyber Bullying Prevention: Intervention in Taiwan. PLoS ONE 8(5): e64031. https://doi.org/10.1371/journal.pone.0064031

Methodology/Findings

The study adopted the quasi-experimental design with two classes made up of a total of 61 junior high school students of seventh grade. The study subjects comprised of 30 students from the experimental group and 31 students from the control group. The experimental group received eight sessions (total 360 minutes) of the teaching intervention for four consecutive weeks, while the control group did not engage in any related courses. The self-compiled questionnaire for the student's knowledge, attitudes, and intentions toward cyber bullying prevention was adopted. Data were analysed through generalized estimating equations to understand the immediate results on the student's knowledge, attitudes, and intentions after the intervention. The results show that the WebQuest course immediately and effectively enhanced the knowledge of cyber bullying, reduced the intentions, and retained the effects after the learning. But it produced no significant impact on the attitude toward cyber bullying.

Conclusions/Significance

The intervention through this pilot study was effective and positive for cyber bulling prevention. It was with small number of students. Therefore, studies with large number of students and long experimental times, in different areas and countries are warranted.

INTRODUCTION

Bullying is one of the most significant school health problems among children and adolescents. Literature indicated that bullying is a "systematic abuse of power" in an asymmetric power relation between the victim and the bully [1]. The victim belongs to a physically or psychologically weaker minority group than the aggressor (bully). Bullying is a set of repeated actions of bully against the bullied (victim) [2].

Depending on the means and ways, bullying can generally be divided into six types: verbal-bullying, physical-bullying, sexual-bullying, social-bullying, defensive-bullying, and cyber bullying. Cyber bullying takes place in cyber space. Cyber bullying is arising from the popularization of the computer network and communication technology in recent years is also known as electronic bullying, SMS bullying, digital bullying, or online bullying.

Bullying has several social, emotional, mental health and academic effects [3]–[10]. It results with depression, anxiety (individual and social), aggression, hyperactivity, academic discomfort and conduct problems at school [3], [9], [10]. However, cyber victims demonstrated a higher level of depression than other forms of bullying [11].

Cyber bullying has been increasing rapidly for the last few decades with the intense use of internet, sms, mms and other electronic media. It has been emerged as a major concern for the teachers, academicians and school authorities. Hence, the growing prevalence of cyber-bullying demands adequate research for prevention including mainly teachers and academicians. Teaching young students the correct knowledge and attitude toward cyber bullying control has become an important issue.

WebQuest is a theme-based teaching activity that has been widely accepted by scholars and teachers [12]. This teaching strategy aims to assist students engaging in exploratory learning activities through network resources. Teachers design the targets of tasks to help learners concentrate more effectively on information use rather than the search for information and assist them to engage in higher levels of analysis, integration, and assessment-based thinking activities.

Cyber bullying media varies with the different habits of the technology-use in different regions, including use of email, blogs, websites, chat rooms, mobile phones, instant messaging, web pages, text messages, online voting websites, and online games. Cyber bullying comes in quite diverse forms such as online debates of mutual accusations, harassment, slander, imitation, disclosure, fraud, exclusion, and network tracking [13]. In Taiwan, cyber bullying is one of the major school health problems [14]. WebQuest is a teaching activity that assists students, engaging in online (cyber) exploratory-oriented teaching activities. Cyber bullying problems encompass within cyber world. In the current study, an effort was mead in Taiwan school to use the WebQuest course, designed to determine if the course does indeed contribute to the student's correct knowledge and attitude toward cyber bullying, as well as their intentions to reduce cyber bullying.

Table 4. The generalized estimating equation analyses of the *attitude aspect* of the cyber bullying prevention WebQuest course (n=61)

Variable	Coefficient estimate	Standard error	Wald	*P* value
Score of the attitude scale				
Group	2.87	2.97	.98	.334
Pretest	.86	.08	3.41	.000
Post-test T_1	13.20	8.34	1.26	.114
Post-follow up test T_2	10.07	8.38	1.10	.229
Group × time	.40	2.01	.45	.844

doi:10.1371/journal.pone.0064031.t004

WebQuest Course in the Intention Aspect for Cyber-bullying Prevention

As shown in Table 5, the results of the analyses on the cyber-bulling intention aspect of the WebQuest course for cyber-bulling prevention showed that the scores of the pretest for the two groups were significantly different, i.e. the cyber-bulling intentions of the two groups were significantly different before course teaching. With controlling the scores of the pretest, the post-test, the post-posttest, and the interaction of group and time, the mean difference in the intention score between the experimental and control groups was −2.49, which was not significant. With controlling pretest, group, the interaction of group and time, there was a significant difference for the post-test and the post-posttest. The score for the post-test decreased by 5.39, which was significant ($p=.005$); and the score for the follow-up posttest decreased by 5.81, which was significant ($p=.002$). Apparently, there was a significant difference between the experimental and the control groups at the post-test and after learning retention. The interaction of group and time was not significant ($p=.962$). In other words, the intention scores for the experimental and control groups were not affected by the test time.

Table 5. The generalized estimating equation analyses of the *intention aspect* of the cyber bullying prevention WebQuest course (n=61)

Variable	Coefficient estimate	Standard error	Wald	*P* value
The intention score				
Group	−2.49	1.95	1.13	.201
Pretest	.63	.15	2.02	.000
Post-test T_1	−5.39	1.93	1.67	.005
Post-follow up test T_2	−5.81	1.89	1.75	.002
Group × time	−.05	1.09	.20	.962

doi:10.1371/journal.pone.0064031.t005

DISCUSSION

Cyber bullying prevention program using WebQuest is successful. Cyber-bulling prevention WebQuest course can immediately enhance the knowledge and reduce the intention of cyber-bulling and is successful for retaining learning effects. To the best authors knowledge, first time an effort was made to utilize WebQuest course to educate school students for cyber-bulling prevention. However considering the small-scale study the current effort can be seen as a pilot study, warranting large-scale studies for further generalization.

The results have indicated that the course can immediately and effectively enhance the knowledge of cyber-bulling and has after learning retention effects. These findings are same as the results of the research by Hsing-Fang [31], but different from that by Hsing-Kuo [16]. Study by Hsing-Kuo found that the core values of the WebQuest were to improve students' capacities for analysis, synthesis, and evaluation, but schools' mid-term tests could not measure these capacities [16]. According to our observations on teaching, the WebQuest course designed for our research is mainly task-oriented learning, in which students can develop a peer support system in the processes of problem solving or completing learning tasks. The level of cooperation among peers combined with the WebQuest design framework has a great influence on the effectiveness of learning knowledge.

The results of our research have failed to find evidence of the effectiveness of the intervention on improving the attitude towards cyber-bulling. These findings are same as the results of Yen-Yu's study [19], but different from the results of Wen-Cheh's study [32]. Yen-Yu's study found that the course content had less emphasis on developing a concept but had emphases on the learning of knowledge and behavior change [19]. The researcher believes that the small sample size and short experimental sessions are the reasons why our experiment does not have a significant effect. It takes a long time to change the attitude towards cyber-bulling; therefore, it is not easy to change students' attitudes toward cyber-bullying after only a four-week course. Considering the study as a pilot one, further long experimental sessions with large number of students are warranted which may have different results.

The course for the present study can immediately and effectively reduce the cyber-bullying intention and has after learning retention effects. These results are in line of Kuo-Chin's study [33]. This is because the course content makes students be aware of the formal rules of the internet usage, enhances the self-protection prevention measures from an internet security viewpoint, and finally guides students to learn responsibilities and justice through the internet law. These have a great influence on the cyber-bulling intention.

Experience of the current study indicates that the teaching methods of the WebQuest course can be vivid and vigorous. The course content can primarily be on a daily-life basis. It is better to give a number of examples to increase students' awareness and sympathy. Other teachers in the teaching team may be invited to join a discussion and work together on the resources provided by the resource web pages. Students of similar age to the subjects of the research can be invited to provide their views of WebQuest web pages. Other teachers in the team can be invited to come to the classroom to help the researcher keep a record of observations on the classroom. In addition to keeping a record of what happens in the classroom, peer teachers can also give objective advices about the teaching and can support and encourage one another. Information literacy and internet ethics can be added to the course. Other course contents in information field can also be explored. It is warranted that for the related research in the future, the sample sizes of the experimental and the control groups can be increased.

The current study has tested a new intervention with a newly designed scale. The study is a pilot designed as a preliminary test of the measure and the intervention. Based on pilot study purposes and results following conclusions can be drawn. The cyber-bulling prevention WebQuest course can immediately enhance the knowledge of cyber-bulling and has after learning retention effects. The cyber-bulling prevention WebQuest course does not have significant effects upon improving the attitude towards cyber-bulling. The cyber-bulling prevention WebQuest course can immediately and effectively reduce the cyber-bulling intention and has after learning retention effects. However, we need a large-scale study before it's universal implementation.

AUTHOR CONTRIBUTIONS

Conceived and designed the experiments: MSL KD. Performed the experiments: MSL WZP. Analyzed the data: MSL WZP. Contributed reagents/materials/analysis tools: MSL. Wrote the paper: MSL WZP LS KD.

REFERENCES

1. Smith PK, Sharp S (2006) The problem of school bullying. In P. K. Smith & S. Sharp (Eds.), School bullying: Insights and perspectives (1–19). London: Routledge.
2. Ma X, Stewin LL, Mah D (2001) Bullying in school: Nature, effects and remedies. Research Papers in Education 6(3): 247–270.
3. Merrell KW, Gueldner BA, Ross SW, Isava DM (2008) How effective are school bullying intervention programs? A meta-analysis of intervention research. School Psychology Quarterly 23: 26–42.
4. Sourander A, Jensen P, Rönning JA, Niemalä S, Hlenius H, et al. (2007) What is the early adulthood outcome of boys who bully or are bullied in childhood? The Finnish "From a boy to a man" Study. Pediatrics 120: 397–404.
5. Beaty LA, Alexeyev EB (2008) The problem of school bullies: what the research tells us. Adolescence 43: 1–11.
6. Ttofi MM, Farrington DP (2008) Bullying: short-term and long-term effects, and the importance of defiance theory in explanation and prevention. Victims and Offenders 3: 289–312.
7. Srabstein J, Piazza T (2008) Public health, safety and educational risks associated with bullying behaviors in American adolescents. International J of Adolescent Med and Health 20: 223–233.
8. Bosacki S, Marini Z, Dane A (2006) Voices from the classroom: pictorial and narrative representations of children's bullying experiences. J of Moral Edu 35: 231–45.
9. Klomek AB, Sourander A, Kumpulainen K, Piha J, Tamminen T, et al. (2008) Childhood bullying as a risk for later depression and suicidal ideation among Finnish males. J of Affective Disorders 109: 47–55.
10. Bacchini D, Affuso G, Trotta T (2008) Temperament, ADHD and peer relations among schoolchildren: the mediating role of school bullying. Aggressive Behavior34: 447–59.
11. Wang J, Nansel TR, Iannotti RJ (2011) Cyber and Traditional Bullying: Differential Association With Depression. Journal of Adolescent Health 48: 415–417.
12. WebQuest. http://webquest.sdsu.edu/index.html. Accessed 2010 February 22.
13. Kowalski RM, Limber SP, Agatston PW (2008) Cyber Bully: Bullying

in the Digital Age. Australia: Blackwell.

14. Ministry of Education's Investigation of the Status of School Bullying and Report of the Research Project of Improvement strategies. Ministry of Education, Department of Military Training Education, 2009.
15. Johnson D, Zufall L (2004) Web watch not just for kids anymore: WebQuests for professional development. Reading Online 2: 26–30.
16. Kang HK (2007) A Study of WebQuest Life Education Curriculum's Impacts on Elementary School Students's Self-concept. Unpublished master's thesis, Fo Guang University, Yilan City, Taiwan.
17. Wu WC (2007) The study of learning effects of WebQuest on students' attitude and achievement:example by the science and technology of upper grades of the elementary school. Unpublished master's thesis, National Hualien University of Education, Hulien City, Taiwan.
18. Chang AL (2007) Effects of WebQuest Learning Activities on Social Studies' Learning Attitudes and Academic Achievement of Sixth Graders. Unpublished master's thesis, National PingTung University of Education, PingTung City, Taiwan.
19. Lin YY (2009) Effect of WebQuest curriculum on self healthy management for 6th graders of elementary school. Unpublished master's thesis, National Hualien University of Education, Hulien City, Taiwan.
20. Hou CJ (2009) The study of learning effects of WebQuest on sixth graders' resilience. Unpublished master's thesis, National Hualien University of Education, Hulien City, Taiwan.
21. Cheng CF (2004) High School thematic inquiry learning in the implementation of design and application of the Internet. Unpublished master's thesis, National Central University, Taoyuan City, Taiwan.
22. Li Q (2007) New bottle but old wine: A research of cyberbullying in schools. Computers in Human Behavior 23(4): 1777–1791.
23. Lin WM (2009) A Study of Elementary School High-grade Students' Attitude and Behavior Intention towards Information Ethics: An Example of An Elementary School in Taipei. Unpublished master's thesis, Department of Mathematics, Taipei Municipal University of Education, Taipei City, Taiwan.
24. Wu HL (2009) Investigation of Adults' Awareness of Cyber-bulling. Unpublished master's thesis, Department of Information Management, Chung Hua University, Hsinchu City, Taiwan.

25. Hsu PF (2005) A Study of the Relation of Elementary School Students' Internet Literacy and Internet Ethics. Unpublished master's thesis, Graduate Institute of Educational Entrepreneurship and Management (majored in Curriculum and Instruction), National University of Tainan, Tainan City, Taiwan.
26. Batsche GM, Knoff HM (1994). Bullies and their victims: Understanding a pervasive problem in the school. School Psychology Review, 23, 165–174.
27. Dodge KA (1991) The structure and function of reactive and proactive aggression. In I. Rubin & D. Pepler (Eds.), The development and treatment of childhood aggression (201–216).Hillsdale, NJ: Erlbaum.
28. Cheng HF (2001) A Study on the Effects of "Cognitive-Behavioral Approach Group Counseling" for the Aggressive Students in Elementary School. Unpublished master's thesis, National Hsinchu University of Education, Hsinchu City, Taiwan.
29. Jung SH, Ahn CW (2005) Sample size for a two-group comparison of repeated binary measurements using GEE. Statistics in Medicine 24(17): 2583–2596.
30. Donner A, Klar N (2000) Design and Analysis of Cluster Randomization Trials in Health Research. Arnold: London.
31. Lee HF (2008) The Effectiveness of WebQuest on Elementary School Students' Problem Solving, English Learning Achievement, and Learning Motivation. Unpublished master's thesis, National Cheng Kung University, Tainan City, Taiwan.
32. Hsueh WC (2008) The study of learning effects of WebQuest on fifth graders' resilience. Unpublished master's thesis, National Hualien University of Education, Hulien City, Taiwan.
33. Chen KC (2010) The Study on Learning Effectiveness of Applying WebQuest in The Teaching of Shihmen Reservoir Related Water Resources Environmental Education for The Fifth-grade Students. Unpublished master's thesis, National Taiwan Normal University of Education, Taipei City, Taiwan.

CHAPTER 13

MEDIA USE AND BRAIN DEVELOPMENT DURING ADOLESCENCE

Eveline A. Crone[1] & Elly A. Konijn[2]

[1]Department of Psychology, Faculty of Social Sciences, Leiden University, Wassenaarseweg 52, 2333AK Leiden, Netherlands

[2]Department of Communication Science, Media Psychology, Vrije Universiteit Amsterdam, De Boelelaan 1105, 1081 HV Amsterdam, Netherlands

ABSTRACT

The current generation of adolescents grows up in a media-saturated world. However, it is unclear how media influences the maturational trajectories of brain regions involved in social interactions. Here we review the neural

Citation: Eveline A. Crone & Elly A. Konijn, "Media use and brain development during adolescence," DOI: 10.1038/s41467-018-03126-x.

development in adolescence and show how neuroscience can provide a deeper understanding of developmental sensitivities related to adolescents' media use. We argue that adolescents are highly sensitive to acceptance and rejection through social media, and that their heightened emotional sensitivity and protracted development of reflective processing and cognitive control may make them specifically reactive to emotion-arousing media. This review illustrates how neuroscience may help understand the mutual influence of media and peers on adolescents' well-being and opinion formation.

INTRODUCTION

Media play a tremendously important role in the lives of today's youth, who grow up with tablets and smartphones, and do not remember a time before the internet, and are hence called 'digital natives'1·2. The current generation of the adolescents lives in a media-saturated world, where media is used not only for entertainment purposes, such as listening to music or watching movies, but is also used increasingly for communicating with peers via WhatsApp, Instagram, SnapChat, Facebook, etc. Taken together, these media-related activities comprise roughly 6–9 h of an American youth's day, excluding home- and schoolwork (https://www.commonsensemedia.org/the-common-sense-census-media-use-by-tweens-and-teens-infographic)3·4. Social media enable people to share information, ideas or opinions, messages, images and videos. Today, all kinds of media formats are constantly available through portable mobile devices such as smartphones and have become an integrated part of adolescents' social life5.

Adolescence, which is defined as the transition period between childhood and adulthood (approximately ages 10–22 years, although age bins differ between cultures), is a developmental stage in which parental influence decreases and peers become more important6. Being accepted or rejected by peers is highly salient in adolescence, also there is a strong need to fit into the peer group and they are highly influenced by their peers7. Therefore, it is imperative that we understand how adolescents process media content and peers' feedback provided on such platforms. Adolescents' social lives in particular seem to occur for a large part through smartphones that are filled with friends with whom they are constantly connected (cf. "A day not wired is a day not lived"5·8). This is where they monitor their peer status, check peers' feedback, rejection and acceptance messages, and encounter peers as (idealized) images[9] on screens[5,8,10]. Likely, this plays an important role in adolescent development, and we therefore focus primarily on adolescents' social media use[11]. Most media research to date is based on correlational and self-report data, and would be strengthened by integrating experimental paradigms and more objectively assessed behavioral, emotional, and neural consequences of experimentally induced media use.

Recently, cognitive neuroscience studies have used structural and functional magnetic resonance imaging (fMRI) to examine how the adolescent brain changes over the course of the adolescent years[6]. The results of several studies demonstrate that cognitive and socio-affective development in adolescence is accompanied by extensive changes in the structure and function of the adolescent brain[6]. Structurally, white matter connections increase, allowing for more successful communication between different areas of the brain[12]. The maturation of these connections is related to behavioral control, for example, connections between the prefrontal cortex and the subcortical striatum mediate age-related improvements in the ability to wait for a reward[13]. In addition to these changes in white matter connections, neurons in the brain grow in number between conception and childhood, with greatest synaptic density in early childhood. This increase in synaptic density co-occurs with synaptic pruning, and pruning rates increase in adolescence, resulting in a decrease in synaptic density in late childhood and adolescence[14]. Structural MRI research revealed that the peak in grey matter volume probably occurs before the age of 10 years, but dynamic non-linear changes in grey matter volume continue over the whole period of adolescence, and the timing is region-specific[15]. Interestingly, changes in grey matter volume are observed most extensively in brain regions that are important for social understanding and communication such as the medial prefrontal cortex, superior temporal cortex and temporal parietal junction[16]. Figure 1 displays the extensive changes in the human cortex during adolescence.

adolescent brain is more sensitive to, or more likely to be shaped by these changing patterns of media usage.1

Box 1 Multiple perspectives on adolescent risk-taking

Adolescence is often defined as a period of increased risk taking and sensation-seeking, this is observed across cultures101 and across species102. However, the way risk-taking is expressed differs across generations. In middle ages, risk-taking in adolescence took place through reckless fights and wars. In contrast, in the late 20th century and early 21st century, adolescents were more prone towards risk-taking in context of alcohol, sex, and drug experimentation103. Recently, through social media, new forms of risk-taking are expressed, such as excessive or unlimited self-disclosure or sexting104. These observations suggest that social media may be the new way in which sensation-seeking behavior is expressed, which is possibly an adolescent-specific tendency to explore and learn to adapt to new social environments.

ACKNOWLEDGEMENTS

We thank the reviewers for their detailed and insightful comments on the manuscript, and Lara Wierenga for providing helpful comments on previous versions of the manuscript. This work was supported by The Netherlands Organization for Scientific Research (NWO-VICI 453-14-001 E.A.C.) and by an innovative ideas grant of the European Research Council (ERC CoG PROSOCIAL 681632 to E.A.C.). Both authors were supported by the Netherlands Institute for Advanced Study in the Humanities and Social Sciences (NIAS: September 2013–September 2014).

REFERENCES

1. Prensky, M. Digital natives, digital immigrants part 1. Horizon 9, 1–6 (2001).
2. Ståhl, T. How ICT savvy are digital natives actually? Nord. J. Digit. Lit. 12, 89–108 (2017).
3. Rideout, V. The Common Sense Census: Media Use by Tweens and Teens (Common Sense Media, San Francisco, 2015).
4. Livingstone, S., Mascheroni, G., Ólafsson, K. & Haddon, L. Children's online risks and opportunities: Comparative findings from EU Kids Online and Net Children Go Mobile http://eprints.lse.ac.uk/60513/. (2014).
5. Konijn, E. A., Veldhuis, J., Plaisier, X. S., Spekman, M. & den Hamer, A. H. in The Handbook of Psychology of Communication Technology (ed. Sundar. S.) (Wiley-Blackwell, Hoboken, NJ, 2015).
6. Blakemore, S. J. & Mills, K. L. Is adolescence a sensitive period for sociocultural processing? Annu. Rev. Psychol. 65, 187–207 (2014).
7. Sebastian, C. L. et al. Developmental influences on the neural bases of responses to social rejection: implications of social neuroscience for education. Neuroimage 57, 686–694 (2011).
8. Valkenburg, P. M. & Taylor Piotrowski, J. How Media Attract and Affect Youth (Yale University Press., Yale, 2017).
9. Ma, J. & Yang, Y. What can we know from selfies - An exploratory study on selfie and the implication for marketers. In Global Marketing Conference at Hong Kong Proceedings 597–601 (Global Alliance of Marketing & Management Associations, 2016).
10. Nesi, J. & Prinstein, M. J. Using social media for social comparison and feedback-seeking: gender and popularity moderate associations with depressive symptoms. J. Abnorm. Child. Psychol. 43, 1427–1438 (2015).
11. Wartella, E. et al. What kind of adults will our children become? the impact of growing up in a media-saturated world. J. Child. Media 10, 13–20 (2016).
12. Ladouceur, C. D., Peper, J. S., Crone, E. A. & Dahl, R. E. White matter development in adolescence: the influence of puberty and implications for affective disorders. Dev. Cogn. Neurosci. 2, 36–54 (2012).
13. Achterberg, M., Peper, J. S., Van Duijvenvoorde, A. C., Mandl,

symptoms. Games Health J. 5, 258–269 (2016).

87. Schoneveld, E. A. et al. A neurofeedback video game (mindlight) to prevent anxiety in children: a randomized controlled trial. Comput. Human. Behav. 63, 321–333 (2016).

88. van Duijvenvoorde, A. C., Peters, S., Braams, B. R. & Crone, E. A. What motivates adolescents? Neural responses to rewards and their influence on adolescents' risk taking, learning, and cognitive control. Neurosci. Biobehav. Rev. 70, 135–147 (2016).

89. Konijn, E. A., Veldhuis, J. & Plaisier, X. S. YouTube as a research tool: three approaches. Cyber. Behav. Soc. Netw. 16, 695–701 (2013).

90. Sundar, S. S. Handbook of the Psychology of Communication Technology (Wiley-Blackwell., Hoboken, NJ:, 2015).

91. Huang, C. Time Spent on social network sites and psychological well-being: a meta-analysis. Cyber. Behav. Soc. Netw. 20, 346–354 (2017).

92. Baker, D. A. & Algorta, G. P. The relationship between online social networking and depression: a systematic review of quantitative studies. Cyber. Behav. Soc. Netw. 19, 638–648 (2016).

93. Przybylski, A. K. & Weinstein, N. A large-scale test of the goldilocks hypothesis. Psychol. Sci. 28, 204–215 (2017).

94. Wilmer, H. H. & Chein, J. M. Mobile technology habits: patterns of association among device usage, intertemporal preference, impulse control, and reward sensitivity. Psychon. Bull. Rev. 23, 1607–1614 (2016).

95. Wilmer, H. H., Sherman, L. E. & Chein, J. M. Smartphones and Cognition: a review of research exploring the links between mobile technology habits and cognitive functioning. Front. Psychol. 8, 605 (2017).

96. Reich, S. M., Subrahmanyam, K. & Espinoza, G. Friending, IMing, and hanging out face-to-face: overlap in adolescents' online and offline social networks. Dev. Psychol. 48, 356–368 (2012).

97. Lemola, S., Perkinson-Gloor, N., Brand, S., Dewald-Kaufmann, J. F. & Grob, A. Adolescents' electronic media use at night, sleep disturbance, and depressive symptoms in the smartphone age. J. Youth Adolesc. 44, 405–418 (2015).

98. Meshi, D., Tamir, D. I. & Heekeren, H. R. The emerging neuroscience of social media. Trends Cogn. Sci. 19, 771–782 (2015).

99. Chein, J., Albert, D., O'Brien, L., Uckert, K. & Steinberg, L. Peers increase adolescent risk taking by enhancing activity in the brain's reward circuitry. Dev. Sci. 14, F1–F10 (2011).
100. Van Hoorn, J., Crone, E. A. & Van Leijenhorst, L. Hanging out with the right crowd: peer influence on risk-taking behavior in adolescence. J. Res Adolesc. 27, 189–200 (2017).
101. Duell, N. et al. Interaction of reward seeking and self-regulation in the prediction of risk taking: a cross-national test of the dual systems model. Dev. Psychol. 52, 1593–1605 (2016).
102. Sisk, C. L. & Foster, D. L. The neural basis of puberty and adolescence. Nat. Neurosci. 7, 1040–1047 (2004).
103. Gladwin, T. E., Figner, B., Crone, E. A. & Wiers, R. W. Addiction, adolescence, and the integration of control and motivation. Dev. Cogn. Neurosci. 1, 364–376 (2011).
104. van Oosten, J. M. & Vandenbosch, L. Sexy online self-presentation on social network sites and the willingness to engage in sexting: a comparison of gender and age. J. Adolesc. 54, 42–50 (2017).
105. Mills, K. L. et al. Structural brain development between childhood and adulthood: convergence across four longitudinal samples. Neuroimage 141, 273–281 (2016).

CHAPTER 14

CYBER BULLYING: CHILD AND YOUTH SPIRITUALITY

Anastasia Apostolides

Department of Christian Spirituality, Church History and Missiology, University of South Africa, South Africa

ABSTRACT

Digital culture is part of children's and adolescents' everyday lives. Digital culture has both positive and negative consequences. One such negative consequence is cyber violence that has been termed cyber bullying. Cyber bullying can cause serious emotional, behavioural and academic problems for both the victim and the bully. Although there is ongoing research on the effects of cyber bullying on children and youth in South Africa, no research has been carried out on how children's and youth's spirituality may be affected when they are cyber bullied. This article discusses the accumulative results from different South African institutes that have researched the cyber bullying effects on children and adolescents. These results point to the spiritual effects that children and youth may experience as a result of cyber

Citation: Apostolides, Anastasia. (2017). Cyber bullying: Child and youth spirituality. *HTS Theological Studies*, *73*(3), 1-7. https://dx.doi.org/10.4102/hts.v73i3.4692

children and youth who participate in religious activities or have a spiritual way of leading their lives cope better with cyber bullying than those who do not. More specific research needs to be done on how the trauma caused by cyber bullying may ultimately affect child and youth spirituality. More research will put the phenomenon of cyber bullying into perspective.

ACKNOWLEDGEMENTS

Competing interests

The author declares that she has no financial or personal relationships which may have inappropriately influenced her in writing this article.

REFERENCES

1. Apostolides, A., 2017, 'Adolescent spirituality with the support of adults', *HTS Teologiese Studies/Theological Studies* 73(4), 4332, 1-6, viewed 20 July 2017, fromhttps://www.hts.org.za/index.php/HTS/article/view/4332/html
2. Badenhorst, C., 2011, *Legal responses to cyber bullying and sexting in South Africa*, Centre for Justice and Crime Prevention, CJCP Issue Paper No. 10, pp. 1-20, viewed 3 May 2017, from http://www.cjcp.org.za/uploads/2/7/8/4/27845461/issuepaper13-cyberbullying-sa-impact_responses.pdf
3. Berger, P.L., 1969, *The sacred canopy: Elements of a sociological theory of religion*, Anchor Books, New York.
4. Berger, P.L. & Luckman, T., 1976, *The social construction of reality: A treatise in the sociology of knowledge*, Penguin Books, London.
5. Burton, P. & Mutongwizo, T., 2009, *Inescapable violence: Cyber bullying and electronic violence against young people in South Africa*, Centre for Justice and Crime Prevention, CJCP Issue Paper No. 8, pp. 1-11, viewed 3 May 2017, from http://www.cjcp.org.za/uploads/2/7/8/4/27845461/issue_paper_8.pdf
6. Coles, R., 1998, *The moral intelligence of children: How to raise a moral child*, Plume, New York.
7. Eaude, T., 2006, *Children's spiritual, moral, social and cultural development: Primary and early years*, Bell & Bain Ltd, Glasgow.
8. Englander, E.K., 2008, *Research brief: Cyber bullying & bullying in Massachusetts: Frequency & motivations*, pp. 1-15, viewed 17 May 2015, from http://vc.bridgew.edu/cgi/viewcontent.cgi?article=1009&context=marc_pubs
9. Finnegan, J., 2008, *The audacity of spirit. The meaning and shaping of spirituality today*, Veritas, Dublin.
10. Fowler, J.W., 1981, *Stages of faith*, Harper & Row, San Francisco, CA.
11. Good, M. & Willoughby, T., 2008, 'Adolescence as a sensitive period for spiritual development', *Child Development Perspectives* 2(1), 32-37. https://doi.org/10.1111/j.1750-8606.2008.00038.x
12. Harris, K.I., 2007, 'Re-conceptualizing spirituality in the light of educating young Children', *International Journal of Children's Spirituality* 12(3), 263-275. https://doi.org/10.1080/13644360701714936

prevention over a life Span', *Journal of Counseling & Development* 71, 140-148. https://doi.org/10.1002/j.1556-6676.1992.tb02189.x

38. Yust, K.M., 2014, 'Digital power: Exploring the effects of social media on children's spirituality', *International Journal of Children's Spirituality*19(2), 133-143. https://doi.org/10.1080/1364436X.2014.924908
39. Yust, K.M., 2015, 'Digital play as a spiritually formative activity', *International Journal of Children's Spirituality*20(2), 129-138. https://doi.org/10.1080/1364436X.2015.1055459
40. Yust, K.M., Johnson, A.N., Sasso, S.E. & Roehlkepartain, E.C., 2006, 'Traditional wisdom: Creating space for religious reflection on child and adolescent spirituality', in K. Yust, A.N. Johnson, S.E. Sasso & E.C. Roehlkepartain (eds.), *Nurturing child and adolescent spirituality: Perspectives from the world's religious traditions*, pp. 253-263, Rowman & Littlefield Publishing Group, Inc, MD.
41. Zulu, G. & Tustin, D.H., 2012, *Nature, extent, and impact of bullying among secondary school learners in Gauteng*, viewed 12 April 2017, from http://www.gauteng.gov.za/government/departments/education/Specialised%20Do cuments/Bureau%20of%20Market%20Research.pdf.

CHAPTER 15

THE IMPACT OF SOCIAL MEDIA ON SOCIETY

Jacob Amedie

Santa Clara University

INTRODUCTION

Knowledge is power. We all recognize this saying but few understand the empowering role social media has played. Through social media, anyone online is empowered by an unrestricted flow of information to add to their knowledge bank. In today's world, it is undeniable that social media plays an important role in impacting our culture, our economy and our overall view of the world. Social media is a new forum that brings people to exchange idea, connect with, relate to, and mobilize for a cause, seek advice, and offer guidance. Social media has removed communication barriers and created decentralized communication channel and open the door for all to have a voice and participate in a democratic fashion including people in repressive countries. This media outlet accommodates a wide variety spontaneous, formal, informal, scholarly and unscholarly writings to flourish. It enables

Citation: Amedie, Jacob, "The Impact of Social Media on Society" (2015). Advanced Writing : Pop Culture Intersections. 2. http://scholarcommons.scu.edu/engl_176/2

REFERENCE

1. Brockman, John. *Is the Internet Changing the Way You Think?: The Net's Impact on Our Minds and Future*. 2011 ed. New York: Harper Perennial, 2011. 451.
2. Bannink, Rienke; Broeren, Suzanne; van de Looij – Jansen, Petra M; *Cyber and Traditional Bullying Victimization as a Risk Factor for Mental Health Problems and Suicidal Ideation in Adolescents*. PLoS ONE. Apr2014, Vol. 9 Issue 4, p1-7. 7p. http://eds.b.ebscohost.com.libproxy.scu.edu/ehost/detail/
3. Bhui, Kamaldeep, Brian Everitt, and Edgar Jones. "Might Depression, Psychosocial Adversity, and Limited Social Assets Explain Vulnerability to and Resistance against Violent Radicalisation*?" PLoS ONE, 2014.*
4. Bryfonski, Dedria. *The Global Impact of Social Media*. 2011 ed. Detroit, MI: Greenhaven Press, 2012.
5. Campbell, Marilyn (2005) *Cyber bullying: An old problem in a new guise?* Australian Journal of Guidance and Counseling, Australian Academic Press, 2005, 76.
6. Deen, Hana S., and John A. Hendricks. *Social Media: Usage and Impact*. 2012 ed. Lanham, Md.: Lexington Books, 2012. 307.
7. Jacobs, Tom; *The Link Between Depression and Terrorism*; SEP 29, 2014 http://books-and-culture/antidepressants-depression-terrorism-weapon
8. O'keeffe, G. S., and K. Clarke-Pearson. "The Impact of Social Media on Children, Adolescents, and Families." Pediatrics, 2011, 800-04
9. Saedi, Auzeen, Ph.D., (2012) Psychology Today; Millennial Media; The media saturated generation Y; "Catfish" and the Perils of Online Dating. http://www.psychologytoday.com/blog/millennial-media/201212/catfish-and-the-perils-online-dating
10. Spears, Barbara ; Campbell, Marilyn; Slee, Phillip T.2Butler; Cyberbullies' perceptions of the harm they cause to others and to their own mental health School Psychology International. Dec2013, Vol. 34 Issue 6, p613-629. 17p. http://www.protectachild.com.au/latest_news.php#article80
11. Weimann, Gabriel; *The Psychology of Mass-Mediated Terrorism*; American Behavioral Scientist. Sep2008, Vol. 52 Issue 1, p69-86. 18p http://eds.a.ebscohost.com.libproxy.scu.edu/ehost/detail/

12. Mark W. Becker, Reem Alzahabi, and Christopher J. Hopwood. Cyberpsychology, Behavior, and Social Networking. February 2013
13. Becker, Mark W., Reem Alzahabi, and Christopher J. Hopwood. *Media Multitasking Is Associated with Symptoms of Depression and Social Anxiety*. Cyberpsychology, Behavior, and Social Networking 16, no. 2 (2013): 132-35. Accessed August 27, 2015
14. Starr, Lisa; Davilla, Joanne Dr. ; *Excessive Discussion Of Problems Between Adolescent Friends May Lead To Depression And Anxiety.* Stony Brook University . January 27, 2009.

CHAPTER 16

SYSTEM TO DETECT RACIAL-BASED BULLYING THROUGH GAMIFICATION

José A. Álvarez-Bermejo[1], Luis J. Belmonte-Ureña[2], Africa Martos-Martínez[3], Ana B. Barragán-Martín[3] and María del Mar Simón-Marquez[3]

[1]Department of Informatics, Universidad de Almería, Almería, Spain

[2]Department of Economy and Business, Universidad de Almería, Almería, Spain

[3]Department of Psychology, Universidad de Almería, Almería, Spain

Prevention and detection of bullying due to racial stigma was studied in school contexts using a system designed following "gamification" principles and integrating less usual elements, such as social interaction, augmented reality and cell phones in educational scenarios. "Grounded Theory" and

Citation: Álvarez-Bermejo JA, Belmonte-Ureña LJ, Martos-Martínez A, Barragán-Martín AB and del Mar Simón-Marquez M (2016) System to Detect Racial-Based Bullying through Gamification. *Front. Psychol.* 7:1791. doi: 10.3389/fpsyg.2016.01791

"User Centered Design" were employed to explore coexistence inside and outside the classroom in terms of preferences and distrust in several areas of action and social frameworks of activity, and to direct the development of a cell phone app for early detection of school bullying scenarios. One hundred and fifty-one interviews were given at five schools selected for their high multiracial percentage and conflict. The most outstanding results were structural, that is the distribution of the classroom group by type of activity and subject being dealt with. Furthermore, in groups over 12 years of age, the relational structures in the classroom in the digital settings in which they participated with their cell phones did not reoccur, because face-to-face and virtual interaction between students with the supervision and involvement of the teacher combined to detect bullying caused by racial discrimination.

Keywords: bullying, cell phone apps, discrimination, gamification, sociogram

INTRODUCTION

Bullying and cyberbullying, which are formally defined as is the act of harming or harassing, also via IT networks, in a repeated and deliberate manner against an individual who is unable to defend him, are a serious social problem among youth (Olweus, 1993). In addition, the individual and collective repercussions to adolescents known as victimization (Craig et al., 2009) lead to such injury to minors as psychological imbalance (Cook et al., 2010), suicide, health problems (Klomek et al., 2007) and high-risk social behavior (Carmona-Torres et al., 2015). Minors have to be protected from bullying/cyberbullying and the consequences of this type of aggression, as research in Europe, America, and Spain shows the prevalence of victimization of bullying and cyberbullying among students, suggesting that policies for improving the school environment are necessary (Caravaca et al., 2016). This idea is reinforced by the exhaustive work done in 33 countries from 2002 to 2010 with students aged 10–15, which concluded that countries which have made decisions concerning the social problem of bullying and have carried out specific actions in school contexts have reduced both occasional and chronic victimization (Chester et al., 2015). Another recent study included the family along with the school in the bullying/cyberbullying prevention measures (Ortega et al., 2016). Beyond that, even the need to talk about citizenship is suggested, as the relationship between bullying and cyberbullying with homophobia, sexism, racism and other discriminatory situations, which are reinforced and modeled by the adult society, has been demonstrated, and structured action leading to the prevention of this phenomenon must start when schooling begins (Cabra and Marciales, 2015).

It has been attempted to analyze the causes generating bullying (Kim et al., 2006) and its consequences to its student victims (Bender and Lösel, 2011), and an important number of studies have analyzed its prevention (Ttofi and Farrington, 2010). The main purpose of these studies was to design preventive, analytical and intervention instruments for bullying/cyberbullying (Del Rey et al., 2012; Allison and Kirsten, 2015).

Recent research has concentrated more on a type of bullying called social stigma, that is, because of individual characteristics, such as race, weight, gender, social class or sexual orientation (Rosenthal et al., 2015). This type of bullying shares many characteristics with discrimination (Piña and Callejas, 2005), since the abuse originates from the victim pertaining to a deprecated social group. Research on bullying because of racial stigma has been mainly directed at adults, and the problem of bullying at school due to racial stigma has not been well enough studied in academic literature (Rosenthal et al., 2015). In this study, we concentrated on this type of bullying, because Spain is one of the main host countries for immigrants (Pajares, 2009). In this context, many immigrant students in Spain are bullied because of racial discrimination (Ávila, 2013) with disastrous consequences for their development, such as anxiety, or development of aggressive behavior (Smith et al., 2014).

In view of the above, that is the interest in preventing bullying/cyberbullying in schools, including social stigma, and minimizing later victimization in educational environments, the results of antibullying and bullying prevention programs have had only moderate success in changing intimidating behavior and conduct (Ansary et al., 2015). A review of prevention programs in Europe and the United States showed that interventions for bullying were only effective for a week (Pepler et al., 2004), while another concluded that about 20% of interventions did either not cause any change at all or caused changes that were negative (Craig et al., 2010). Recent reviews have suggested that anti-intimidation programs with the best results are the multidisciplinary or "whole-school" approach, which first, accentuates a good social and emotional climate in the school based on solid antibullying philosophy principles (Thornberg, 2011). Second, those maintaining a long-term program extend it to the community and it is externally supervised. And finally, they are constant and firm in applying the strategies when bullying appears (Ansary et al., 2015). Of the main antibullying programs considered effective, the one most used worldwide, is the "Olweus Bullying Prevention Program," which originated in Norway in 1983, and has been applied in other countries with some variations, such as the "Toronto Project" in Canada in 1991–1993 (Fekkes et al., 2006), and the "South Carolina Project" in 1995 (Limber, 2004) and the "Seattle Project" in 2003–2005 (Bauer et al., 2007) in the United States.

Another widely used program is the "Sheffield Project" which originated in England in 1991–1993 (Smith and Sharp, 1994). These two programs have been jointly implemented in Belgium since 1995–1997 (Smith et al., 2003), and in Spain, "SAVE (*Sevilla Anti Violencia Escolar*)" since 1996–96 (Ortega, 1997) and "ANDAVE (Andalucía Antiviolencia Escolar)" since 1999–2000 (Ortega and Mora-Merchán, 1998). Another two more recent programs, also from an integral perspective, are the "ViSC Program" started in Austria in 2008 (Trip et al., 2015), and also implemented in Turkey in 2012–2014 (Solomontos-Kauntouri et al., 2016) and the KiVA Project from Finlandia in 2006–2009 (Salmivalli and Poskiparta, 2012), which has been used in Estonia (Ginter and Tropp, 2012), Italy, the Netherlands and Whales (Clarkson et al., 2016). One characteristic which makes this project unique is the use of a virtual working environment with games simulating daily life, for constant team monitoring of the project (Kärnä et al., 2013).

But in the last few years, these "whole-school" programs are being enriched by research on preventing bullying which seeks the answers in students, teachers and families (Patton et al., 2015), (Cabra and Marciales, 2015), as bullying prevention programs should be adapted to the cultural context (Olweus, 2010), make use of ICTs related to social sciences and integrate prevention procedures close to adolescent experience (Huitsing and Veenstra, 2012), such as of cell phones (Ruiz and Belmonte, 2014) and gamification strategies (Bishop, 2014; Richter et al., 2015) in school environments (Hanewinkel, 2004; Middaugh and Kahne, 2013).

The term "gamified" refers to the use of videogame design elements in non-game contexts to improve user experience and the ability to hook and motivate (Schoech et al., 2013). A review of the scientific literature on the use of gamification in educational contexts, that is, the use of game design elements, such as including prizes, reward, score charts, credentials, levels, trophies, and so forth (Kapp, 2013), shows widely extended production spanning from studies on their effects on education (Hakulinen and Auvinen, 2014), improved educational quality (Kuo and Chuang, 2016), simulated activities (Rojas et al., 2014), student attention using mobile devices (Su and Cheng, 2015), motivation of different types of students (Hakulinen and Auvinen, 2014), academic scenarios for gamification (Laskowski, 2015), gamification in the search for educational innovation (González and Area, 2013), learning materials for gamification, and evaluation of gamification for motivating students to learn (Ibanez et al., 2014).

In the specific area of bullying, three applications should be highlighted, FearNot (Vannini et al., 2011), a videogame in third person which promotes learning antibullying strategies and which has had good results in detecting bullying by minors (Sapouna et al., 2010), Mii School (Carmona et al., 2011), a 3D videogame for youths in third person which helps detect bullying in schools based on five scenes in which the adolescent has to make choices from different roles (aggressor, victim), and ARBAX-School Bullying (Raminhos et al., 2015), which is a first-person 3D videogame for 16-year-old students, promoting awareness of racial intimidation, but no research at all has been done on this development.

Context

In recent years, as a result of a multitude of complex causes, the immigration role Spain has undergone a radical change since Spain has become one of the main recipients of immigrants, unlike what happened in the 50s and 60s (Pajares, 2009). In the last decade the growth rate of foreigners has been vertiginous, from 1,60% of the population in 1998 to the 12.22% of the population as of January 2012. While from 2012 to 2015 the foreign contingent has been reduced by more than one million people (see Figure 1). As a direct consequence of these important migratory movements, many immigrant adolescents under 16 are in the schools.

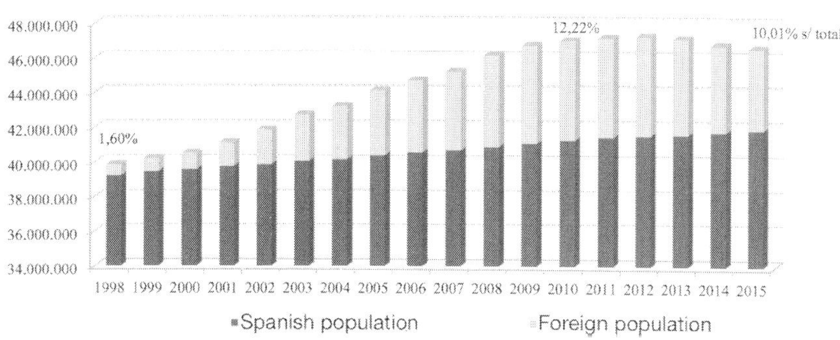

Figure 1. Evolution of the population: Spaniards and foreigners (1998–2015). *Source*: INE.

Over the past decade, Spain has experienced a remarkable influx of immigrants, especially sourcing from Africa and from Eastern Europe. In this scenario, Almeria is a priority destination for a bunch of nationalities that, in many cases, are emerging as outsiders with limited financial resources who come to this province in search of a job opportunity, in the sector of the intensive agriculture and sometimes they are discriminated against, relegating them to the last positions of the value chain. More specifically, it is noted that the province of Almeria has shown a tendency of growth of foreign population very pronounced since the mid-nineties, rising from 13,260 in 1998 to 142,810 in 2014 (see Figure 2). In this period the foreign population in the province has grown by 977% in simple variation rate, representing an average annual growth rate of 16%. Nationally, the growth of the foreign population between 1998 and 2014, amounted to 689%, in simple variation rate, and 13.8% in cumulative average rate variation. This significance of the contingent of foreigners in the province of Almeria is the highest across the country, behind only of Alicante, which has a percentage of 20.62% of foreigners. In turn, this percentage of significance is almost double the weight that has the group of foreigners in national average (10.74%).

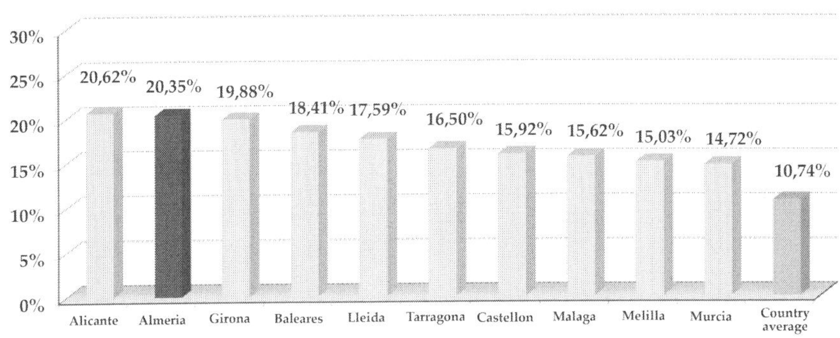

Figure 2. Provinces with greater weight of foreigners on the total population (2014). *Source*: INE.

If we consider the age group of less than 16 years, it is that the province of Almeria is in third place in the ranking of Spanish provinces with the highest number of adolescent foreigners, on the total population, with 19.69% (Figure 3).

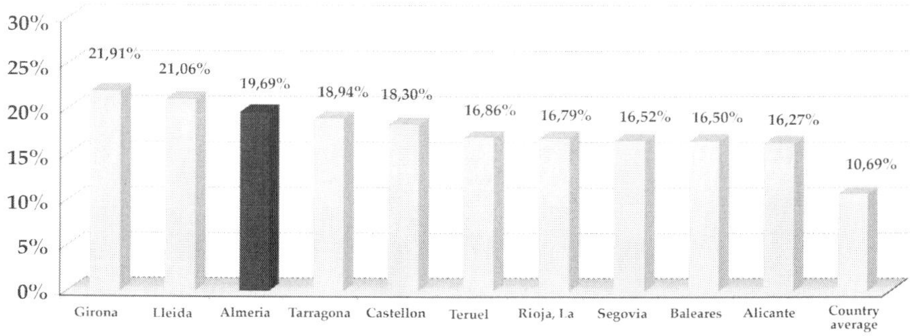

Figure 3. Provinces with greater weight of under 16 foreigners on the total population of that age group (2014). *Source*: INE.

In this regard, at the municipal level, the largest population, under 16, are concentrated around the capital of Almeria, Roquetas de Mar, El Ejido, Níjar and Vícar. These five municipalities account for 64% of young people fewer than 16, of the province (Figure 4). Also, in these five territories a large number of young foreigners that, in the case of Nijar, accounts for almost half of the population in this age group. Therefore, under the context depicted, it seems appropriated to analyze the causes of racial harassment stigma among young people under 16 years. That severely affects school life.

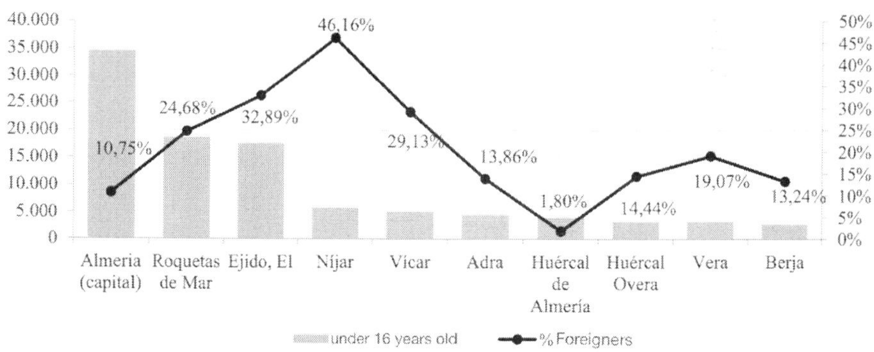

Figure 4. Municipalities in Almeria with more young people under 16 years (main axis) weight of foreigners on total (secondary axis). Año 2014. *Source*: INE. (A) Database server. Stores the interactions. (B)How the interaction works: QR codes identify students. (C) All the students are equipped with QR and smartphones. (D) Screenshot of the game representing the interaction depicted in (B).

METHODOLOGY AND PROCEDURE

The review of publications and analysis of antibullying videogames oriented the focus of our research and the methodological design which would best respond to the purpose of developing an application preventing bullying for social stigma. In brief, it showed the need to adapt antibullying action culturally and socially and develop new instruments for social mediation in realistic situations. That is, it should be based on the expressions and experiences of the social actors to find out what preventive/intervention actions, means and measures they prefer. It should also surpass the design of scenarios in which an attempt has been made to monitor the activity of students through the use of traditional videogames (Serrano et al., 2012), which does not provide realistic results since the students are unaware of the real context of their class (i.e., although it is a videogame, it should not detach them completely from their setting). Furthermore, it is understood that it is not appropriate to measure violence using videogames which reinforce it and in which the players do not receive feedback on the consequences of the decisions they make during the game. Therefore, the use of cell phone games based on gamification principles and supported by augmented reality enabling classroom bullying to be detected was the option chosen for this study.

Its methodological design follows the principles of Grounded Theory (Strauss and Corbin, 1998; Charmaz, 2006), as its purpose is to identify basic social processes related to behavior in organizations, groups or social structures such as the school (Glaser, 1992). The grounded theory is very well-established in educational research. Let the work on inclusion in higher education (Givon and Court, 2010), on teaching staff in particular cultural settings (Cherubini et al., 2010), on new teachers during their first year (Smart and Brent, 2010) and in the field of bullying or cyberbullying (Mishna et al., 2009) suffice as examples.

In harmony with the above, User-Centered Design (Norman and Draper, 1986) principles, and specifically for education, Designed Based Research (Luckin et al., 2013), are also followed by incorporating the value of the user in the design of applications and/or tools. However, this subject value does not reside in the traditional view of the user as archetype, client or final user (Maguire, 2001), but in actors, who in this study are bully victims, bullies, witnesses, teachers, families, etc., are not investigated or directed (Sin, 2003; Penuel et al., 2007).

These references help understand the path taken in this study. To explain the methodology more clearly, it is described in two parts. The first part collected information from 151 students at five schools in Almeria province (Spain) with multiracial populations and coexistence problems. As this information is sensitive, it is not available nor has it been published by the schools. Thus their specific selection was based on information acquired from the school direction teams when discussing access with them. Also for reasons of confidentiality, the names of the five schools chosen from among 20 met with are not revealed either. However, Table 1 shows details on the student population at each school and the characteristics of each group.

Table 1. Group characteristics

Group	School location	Grade	Age	N◦ of students[1]	% Foreign	Main nationality
A	Almería	1st year high schoo	12–13	40	8%	Morocco
B	Roquetas de Mar	4th year high schoo	15–16	27	22%	Rumania
C	El Ejido	5th grade primary	10–11	28	43%	Morocco
D	Níjar	3rd grade primary	8–9	31	39%	Morocco
E	Vícar	2nd grade primary	7–8	25	24%	Morocco

In addition to the meetings held with the direction teams, informal conversations were held with teachers, students and tutors, some at the school itself, in parents and teachers associations, immigrant associations, parks and plazas. When these were analyzed with the grounded theory (Strauss and Corbin, 1998), categories emerged and by theoretical triangulation (Denzin, 1989), specifically reviewing other questionnaires on school coexistence (Avilés, 2002, un published; Ortega and Del Rey, 2003), an ad hoc questionnaire was designed which was given to 151 students at five selected schools, with items for detecting the existence of discrimination by students, both in the classroom and outside of it (see Table 2). All of the items on the questionnaire were measured on a three-point Likert-type response scale where 1 was native student, 2 foreign student and 2 any student. The questionnaires were given a convenience sample of five Spanish students selected from each of the groups.

has connections with the real environment, which is an important aspect to consider. Everyone, from the student as the individual to the whole class as the collective, are aware that the other colleagues are real, as the environment. Thus they understand that their actions with others even if they are not real-, can trigger consequences in the real context.

The architecture of the game is based on each student carrying two elements (see Figure 5B) a Smartphone with the application and a QR code that identifies him/her in the game (each student is put a tag with two QR codes, one in the chest and another in the back). When a child plays with the application, she sees the classroom environment through their mobile device with augmented information (see Figures 5C,D). This augmented information comes from the query that the student's device performs to the terminal server (see Figure 5A) using the QR code of the person being pointed by. The server, then, sends interactive information on the student being pointed to the device which it interacts with. The system also recognizes the context in which students (e.g., class, patio) are and whether the interaction is performed through the front QR or through the rear QR code that the student is wearing. The whole class (Figure 5C) has these elements and interact freely among them.

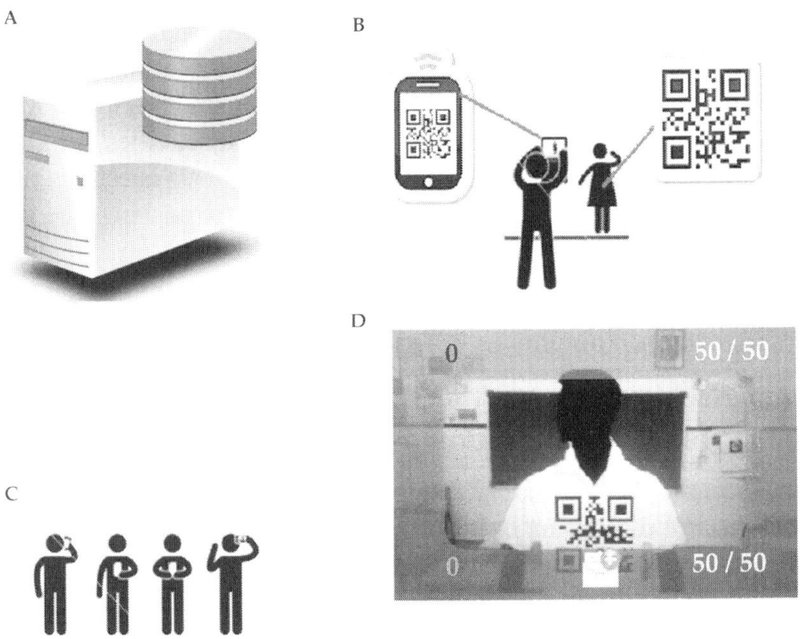

Figure 5. Proposed architecture.

The server gathers the data in a csv file (comma-separated values; it is a document type in simple open format to represent data in tabular form) relating to all students to be examined by a sociogram (graphical representation of the different relationships between subjects that make up a group). So the interaction analysis can be performed.

The proposed model forces that both parties affected by an interaction are notified of the event. Participants have information notified to them when they are involved in an interaction, so that whoever starts it can not take any action without a supposed and probable consequence in the real environment. Likewise, interactions are catalyzed by the fact that it is a game in which they are motivated to participate.

Figure 6 refers to the starting screen of the game on the student's smartphone (see Figure 6A) and how it connects to the server (see Figure 6B) to register the student with his QR codes and data.

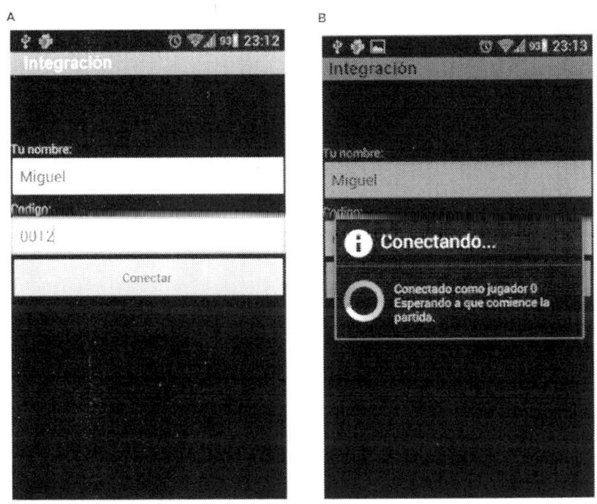

Figure 6. Smartphone screenshots related to the game. (A) The student is assigned a numeric Id to avoid identity association. (B) The screen shows how, now, student 0012 is connecting. From now, the student will be tagged as 0012 instead of Miguel.

Following, an example of interaction in which a certain student is required to bringing together his friends in order to perform a task, namely the organization of a football. In interactions it is allowed to exclude fellow students from groups with a movement of the smartphone (smartphones incorporate sensors like accelerometers, which indicates how the phone is moved and how vehemently). Thus the rejection of one person to another who wants to join the team is registered. Understanding that, in this case, the reaction means not only segregation but a violent reaction. It is intended to relate this segregation reaction to the difficulty of integrating immigrant children in schools. Figure 7shows the smartphone screen of a student who is not being selected by any partner to perform a specific activity and that is not selecting any other student, he is simply using the game it to observe the classroom. In the top left of the screen you can see the score of the student (depending on the number of people in your group).

Figure 7. Mobile screen without selecting a fellow student.

Figure 8 shows an example of interaction where you can add components to your group once launched a group activity.

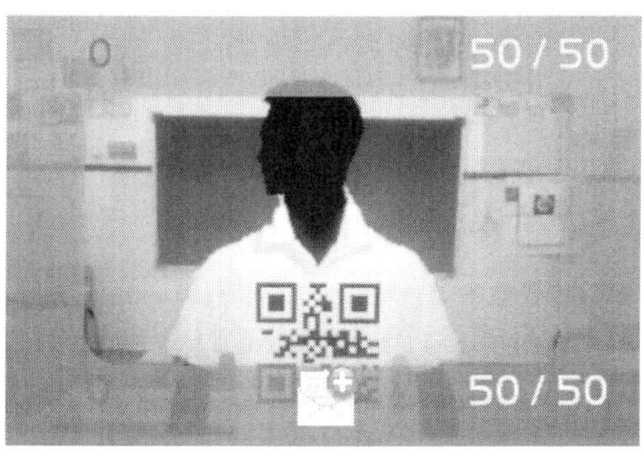

Figure 8. Mobile screen selecting a fellow student.

The interaction model is not only limited to directly selecting partners for activities, and in addition it can be controlled in the sense that for every action you want to perform, a question must be correctly answered. In this case, if the question posed at the partner is not resolved, the opponent wins. On the contrary, if resolved who starts the interaction wins (and therefore the action is performed). Figures 9 and 10 show this feature.

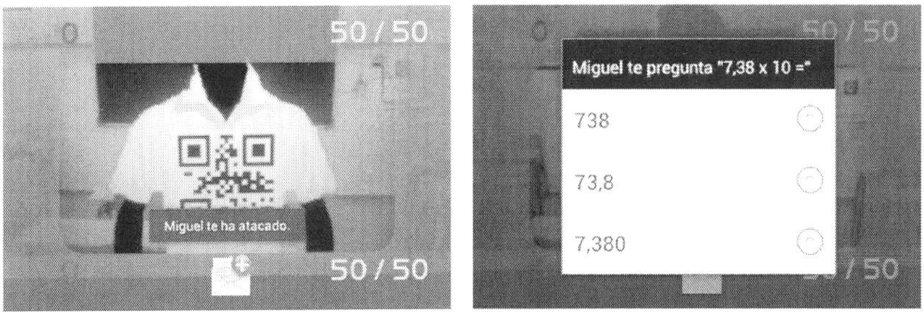

Figure 9. Validation of an expulsion by the student #0012.

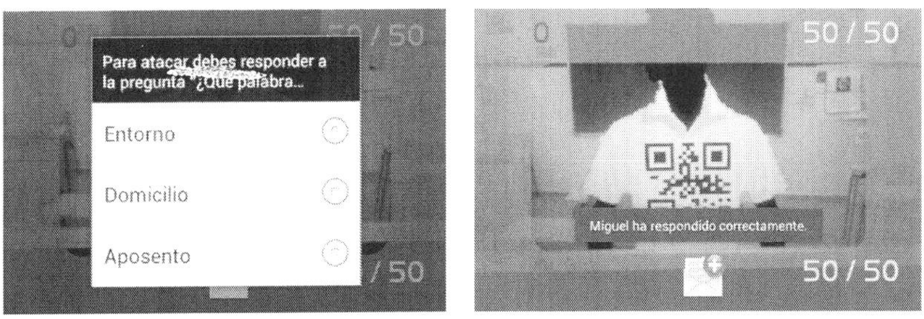

Figure 10. Cancelation of an expulsion by the student #0012.

As noted above, the application server (see Figure 5A) records all interactions between students, so the teacher can access this server to download this information and to control what happens (i.e., what kind of interaction it is generated) among students in the class through a sociogram or x-ray interactions that occur in the group. See Figure 11, this is an example of the visual data that the application generates.

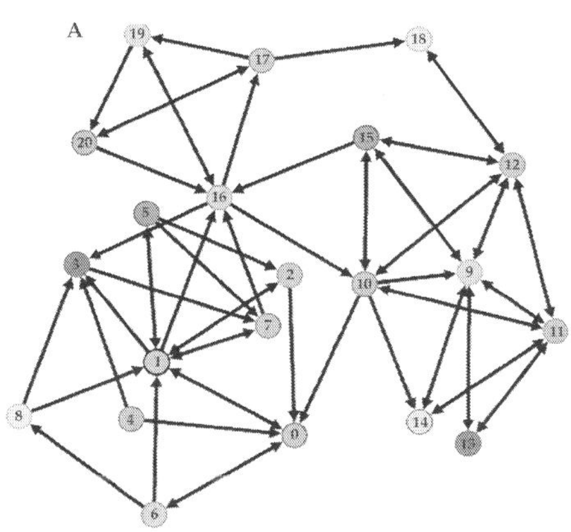

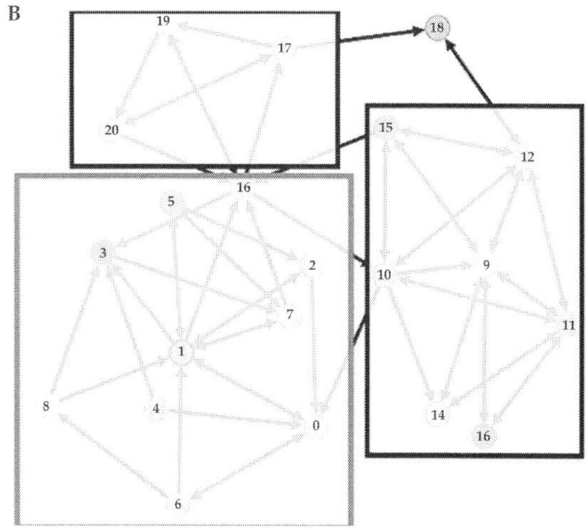

Figure 11. Sociogram of the interaction. (A) The complete sociogram of the interaction. (B) The sociogram after the racial analysis. We can see how students group by nationality.

RESULTS

Concerning coexistence in the classroom, it should be mentioned that in four of the five classrooms analyzed, none of the foreign students sat at desks in the front row, that is, they were rather near the back of the class, except in the group of second-graders (Vicar), who were from seven to 8 years old. This agrees with studies done on discrimination in classrooms (i.e., they tend to "hide" in the last rows of the classroom) except in second-grade. Even though descriptive analyses of the data collected from the five schools shows that most of the students prefer to work or share a table with a native classmate (72% of the sample), distrust was not associated to any greater extent with foreign students (60% of the sample said they distrusted any classmate of whatever nationality). With respect to coexistence outside of the classroom, it should be mentioned that discrimination for racial stigma does not seem to be present in sports as clearly as in other cases mentioned above (only 20% of the sample said they would not invite an immigrant classmate). When organizing other non-sport activities (a birthday party), the percentage of rejection of foreign students rises slightly to 24% (64% of the sample said they might not invite "any classmate"). Finally, outside of the classroom in matters leading to closer involvement in their relations (go on vacation with a classmate), the results show that in this case in particular the majority of students prefer to go with foreign students (56% of the sample).

The PREVER app records all the interactions among students as described above, so the teacher can access the server and download this information to monitor what is happening (i.e., what type of interaction is being generated) among the students in the class on a sociogram of interactions going on in the group. Figure 10 below shows an example of interaction in a class of students in the last year of primary school (to help understand the graphic, unimportant interactions have been omitted and only the more significant are kept in). It may be seen that three differentiated groups are joined by hubs common to them: (1) the group of Spaniards (numbered 0–8) has little interaction with the rest of the students who belong to other groups, (2) groups 9–15 are made up of Moroccans who have also established strong hubs basically among themselves (perhaps due to family interaction and the language, but they refuse to enlarge their groups), and (3) the Romanian students (groups 17, 18, 19, and 20) and one Eastern European student (Russian). This sociogram shows how the students in a class relate to each other. Some strong cores of students and others not as strong are observed. The clusters detected are by origin. It is assumed that as they have the same origin and share the same language, relations among their parents are quite probably closer and this generates stronger bonds.

DISCUSSION AND CONCLUSION

It is a fact that the discriminatory and excluding behavior in society should be detected early for better coexistence among the various nationalities that make up the population of a territory. However, acceptance of interculturality in the classroom is a problem that arises and affects immigrant students who are discriminated because of their origin and their appearance, which stigmatizes their future personal and professional development (Baysu et al., 2013). Gradual general awareness of the importance of human rights and repercussion in communications media of aggression in schools demand that the parties involved in education intervene in both prevention and treatment of bullying when it occurs. In this sense, the subject of bullying has awakened growing interest in developing prevention and intervention programs for its reduction (Breakstone et al., 2009) which have had ambiguous results. This study has therefore attempted to advance in this matter by offering a gamified cell phone app which assists teachers in finding out the extent of interaction among students in a class and for early detection of possible bullying or discrimination based on the data stored in the proposed system's server.

The data analyzed demonstrate that the main problems of discrimination affecting the foreign population under 16 years of age in their compulsory education and which could potentially generate bullying are related more to their relations within the classroom itself. In spite of this, the app guides those students who install it on their devices through a series of stages dominated by situations in which they have to choose classmates which will lead them to select those with whom they prefer to interact and relate in each case. Thus it provides a useful dynamic tool for finding out the interactions taking place among students and for detecting cases of discrimination and even extreme cases of bullying.

The main implication of the study is possible decrease in cases of abuse derived from their early detection and consequent intervention/treatment by the teacher (and other parties involved), who can periodically consult data on student interaction stored on the system's server. It is an application mainly for implementation in classrooms to be used in student leisure periods (e.g., recess) and even outside of the classroom because of its gamified design. However, one of the main lines of future research is integration of the app in the learning setting itself, proposing this new context for interaction among students which could provide more clues to their relationships in the classroom and outside it. Finally, the first thing that should be pointed out concerning the main limitations for using this type of technologies in the classroom is the need for the students to have access to a cell phone in which to install the app developed and interact with their classmates, as well as the different degrees of involvement developed by the students in their use of the applications. Other limitations related to the performance of the teacher's work should also be mentioned, since the introduction of this type of technology in the classroom means that more time would have to be devoted to periodic control of the interactions among students with the data stored on the server.

AUTHOR CONTRIBUTIONS

JA-B: He has developed and designed the software application for detecting the discrimination in the educational context. LB-U: He has been responsible for design the questionnaire that was passed to students in schools, as well as the study of the number of immigrants in Spain and Almeria. AM-M: She has participated in the field study, as pollster. Also, she has participated in the methodological support. AB-M: She has participated in the field study, as pollster. Also, she has participated in the methodological support. MdMS-M: She has participated in the field study, as pollster. Also, she has participated in the methodological support.

CONFLICT OF INTEREST STATEMENT

The authors declare that the research was conducted in the absence of any commercial or financial relationships that could be construed as a potential conflict of interest.

REFERENCES

1. Allison, A. P., and Kirsten, L. H. (2015). Old wine, new bottle? Comparing interpersonal bullying and cyberbullying victimization. *Youth Soc.* 47, 30. doi: 10.1177/0044118X15617401
2. Ansary, N. S., Elias, M. J., Greene, M. B., and Green, S. (2015). Best practices to address (or reduce) bullying in schools. *Phi Delta Kappan* 97, 30–35. doi: 10.1177/0031721715610088
3. Ávila, J. A. (2013). *El acoso escolar en Educación Primaria en la provincia de Huelva. [Bullying in Primary Education in the. province of Huelva.* Doctoral thesis, University of Huelva, Huelva.
4. Bauer, N. S., Lozano, P., and Rivara, F. P. (2007). The effectiveness of the olweus bullying prevention program in public middle schools: a controlled trial. *J. Adolesc. Health* 40, 266–274. doi: 10.1016/j.jadohealth.2006.10.005
5. Baysu, G., Phalet, K., and Brown, R. (2013). Relative group size and minority school success: the role of intergroup friendship and discrimination experiences. *Br. J. Soc. Psychol.* 53, 328–349. doi: 10.1111/bjso.12035
6. Bender, D., and Lösel, F. (2011). Bullying at school as a predictor of delinquency, violence and other anti-social behaviour in adulthood. *Crim. Behav. Ment. Health* 21, 99–106. doi: 10.1002/cbm.799
7. Bishop, J. (2014). *Gamification for Human Factors Integration: Social. Education, and Psychological Issues.* Hershey, PA: IGI Global.
8. Breakstone, S., Dreiblatt, M., and Dreiblatt, K. (2009). *How to Stop Bullying and Social Aggression?* Thousand Oak, CA: Corwin Press.
9. Cabra, F., and Marciales, G. (2015). "Cyberbullying and education: a review of emergent issues in Latin America research," in *Cyberbullying Across the Globe: Gender, Family, and Mental Health*, eds R. Navarro and S. Yubero (New York, NY: Springer), 131–147.
10. Caravaca, F., Falcón, M., Navarro-Zaragoza, J., Luna, A., Rodriges, O., and Luna, A. (2016). Prevalence and patterns of traditional bullying victimization and cyber-teasing among college population in Spain. *BMC Public Health* 16:176. doi: 10.1186/s12889-016-2857-8
11. Carmona, J. A., Espínola, M., Cangas, A. J., and Iribarne, L. (2011). MII-School: a 3d videogame for the early detection of abuse of substances, bullying, and mental disorders in adolescents. *Eur. J. Psychol.* 4, 75–84.

12. Carmona-Torres, J. A., Cangas, A. J., Langer, A. I., Aguilar-Parra, J. M., and Gallego, J. (2015). Acoso escolar y su relación con el consumo de drogas y trastornos alimentarios: comparación entre adolescentes de Chile y España [Bullying and its relation to drug abuse and eating disorders: a comparison between Chile and Spain teenagers]. *Psicol. Conduct* 23, 507–552.
13. Charmaz, K. (2006). *Constructing Grounded Theory: A Practical Guide through Qualitative Analysis*. London: Sage.
14. Cherubini, L., Niemczyk, E., Hodson, J., and McGean, S. (2010). A grounded theory of new aboriginal teachers' perceptions: the cultural attributions of medicine wheel teachings. *Teach. Teach. Theory Pract.* 16, 545–557. doi: 10.1080/13540602.2010.507965
15. Chester, K., Callaghan, M., Cosma, A., Donnelly, P., Craig, W., Walsh, S., et al. (2015). Cross-national time trends in bullying victimization in 33 countries among children aged 11, 13 and 15 from 2002 to 2010. *Eur. J. Public Health* 25, 61–64. doi: 10.1093/eurpub/ckv029
16. Clarkson, S., Axford, N., Berry, V., Edwards, R. T., Bjornstad, G., Wrigley, Z., et al. (2016). Effectiveness and micro-costing of the KiVa school-based bullying prevention programme in wales: study protocol for a pragmatic definitive parallel group cluster randomised controlled trial. *BMC Public Health*16:1. doi: 10.1186/s12889-016-2746-1
17. Cook, C. R., Williams, K. R., Guerra, N. G., Kim, T. E., and Sadek, S. (2010). Predictors of bullying and victimization in childhood and adolescence: a meta-analytic investigation (PDF). *Sch. Psychol. Q.* 25, 65–83. doi: 10.1037/a0020149
18. Craig, W., Harel-Fisch, Y., Fogel-Grinvald, H., Dostaler, S., Hetland, J., Simons-Morton, B., et al. (2009). A cross-national profile of bullying and victimization among adolescents in 40 countries. *Int. J. Public Health* 54, 216–224. doi: 10.1007/s00038-009-5413-9
19. Craig, W. M., Pepler, D. J., Murphy, A., and McCuaig-Edge, H. (2010). "What works in bullying prevention?," in *Preventing and Treating Bullying and Victimization*, eds E. M. Vernberg and B. K. Biggs (New York, NY: Oxford University Press), 215–242.
20. Dedousis, A., Shute, R., Varlow, M., Murrihy, R., and Kidman, T. (2014). Predictors of teacher intervention in indirect bullying at school and outcome of a professional development presentation for teachers. *Educ. Psychol.* 34, 862–875. doi: 10.1080/01443410.2013.785385

21. Del Rey, R., Casas, J. A., and Ortega, R. (2012). El programa ConRed, una práctica basada en la evidencia [The ConRed program, an evidence-based practice]. *Commun. Rev.* 39, 129–138.

22. Denzin, N. K. (1989). *The Research Act.* Englewood Cliffs, NJ: Prentice Hall.

23. Fekkes, M., Pijpers, F. I., and Verloove-Vanhorick, S. P. (2006). Effects of antibullying school program on bullying and health complaints. *Arch. Pediatr. Adolesc. Med.* 160, 638–644. doi: 10.1001/archpedi.160.6.638

24. Ginter, J., and Tropp, K. (2012). Questionnaire on violence in education: Estonia. *Int. J. Educ. L. Pol'y* 8:183. doi: 10.1186/s12884-015-0558-4

25. Givon, S., and Court, D. (2010). Coping strategies of high school students with learning disabilities: a longitudinal qualitative study and grounded theory. *Int. J. Qual. Stud. Educ.* 23, 283–303. doi: 10.1080/09518390903352343

26. Glaser, B. G. (1992). *Basics of Grounded Theory Analysis: Emerge vs. Forcing.* Mill Valley, CA: Sociology Press.

27. González, C., and Area, M. (2013). "Breaking the rules: gamification of learning and educational materials," in *Proceedings of the 2nd International Workshop on Interaction Design in Educational Environments*, Angers, 47–53.

28. Hakulinen, L., and Auvinen, T. (2014). "The effect of gamification on students with different achievement goal orientations," in *Proceedings of Conference on Learning and Teaching in Computing and Engineering (LaTiCE 2014)*, eds B. Aris and A. Selamat (Rome: IEEE), 47–54. doi: 10.1109/LaTiCE.2014.1

29. Hanewinkel, R. (2004). "Prevention of bullying in German schools: an evaluation of an anti-bullying approach," in *Bullying in schools: How Successful Can Interventions Be?*, eds P. K. Smith, D. Pepler, and K. Rigby (Cambridge: Cambridge University Press), 81–97.

30. Huitsing, G., and Veenstra, R. (2012). Bullying in classrooms: participant roles from a social network perspective. *Aggress. Behav.* 38, 494–509. doi: 10.1002/ab.21438

31. Ibanez, M., Di-Serio, A., and Delgado-Kloos, C. (2014). Gamification for engaging computer science students in learning activities: a case study. Learning Technologies. *IEEE Trans.* 7, 291–301. doi: 10.1109/TLT.2014.2329293

32. Kapp, K. M. (2013). *The Gamification of Learning and Instruction*

Fieldbook: Ideas into Practice. Hoboken, NJ: John Wiley & Sons.

33. Kärnä, A., Voeten, M., Little, T., Alanen, E., Poskiparta, E., and Salmivalli, C. (2013). Effectiveness of the KiVa antibullying program: grades 1-3 and 7-9. *J. Educ. Psychol.* 105, 535–551. doi: 10.1037/a0031120
34. Kim, Y. S., Leventhal, B. L., Koh, Y. J., Hubbard, A., and Boyce, W. T. (2006). School bullying and youth violence: causes or consequences of psychopathologic behavior? *Arch. Gen. Psychiatr.* 63, 1035–1041. doi: 10.1001/archpsyc.63.9.1035
35. Klomek, A., Marrocco, F., Kleinman, M., Schonfeld, I. S., and Gould, M. S. (2007). Bullying, depression, and suicidality in adolescents. *J. Am. Acad. Child Adolesc. Psychiatry* 46, 40–49. doi: 10.1097/01.chi.0000242237.84925.18
36. Kuo, M. S., and Chuang, T. Y. (2016). How gamification motivates visits and engagement for online academic dissemination. An empirical study. *Comput. Hum. Behav.* 55, 16–27. doi: 10.1016/j.chb.2015.08.025
37. Laskowski, M. (2015). "Implementing gamification techniques into university study path. A case study," in *Proceedings of the IEEE Global Engineering Education Conference (EDUCON), 2015*, (Rome: IEEE), 582–586.
38. Limber, S. P. (2004). "Implemetation of the olweus bullying prevention program in American schools: lessons learned in the field," in *Bullying in American Schools: A Social-ecological Perspective on Prevention and Intervention*, eds D. L. Espelage and S. M. Swearer (Mahwah, NJ: Erlbaum), 351–363.
39. Luckin, R., Puntambekat, S., Goodyear, P., Grabowski, B. L., Underwood, J., and Winters, N. (2013). *Handbook of Design in Educational Technology.* London: Routledge.
40. Maguire, M. (2001). Methods to support human-centred design. *Int. J. Hum. Comput. Stud.* 55, 587–634. doi: 10.1006/ijhc.2001.0503
41. Middaugh, E., and Kahne, J. (2013). Nuevos medios como herramienta para el aprendizaje cívico. [New media as a tool for civic learning]. *Commun. Rev.*40, 99–108. doi: 10.3916/C40-2013-02-10
42. Mishna, F., Saini, M., and Solomon, S. (2009). Ongoing and online: children and youth's perceptions of cyber bullying. *Child. Youth Serv. Rev.* 31, 1222–1228. doi: 10.1016/j.childyouth.2009.05.004
43. Norman, D. A., and Draper, S. W. (1986). *User Centered System*

Design. London: Erlbaum.

44. Olweus, D. (1993). *Bullying at School: What We Know and What We Can Do*. Malden, MA: Willey-Black-Well.
45. Olweus, D. (2010). "Understanding and researching bullying: some critical issues," in *Handbook of Bullying in Schools: An International Perspective*, eds S. R. Jimerson, S. M. Swearer, and D. L. Espelage (New York, NY: Routledge), 9–33.
46. Ortega, J., Buelga, S., and Cava, M. J. (2016). Influencia del clima escolar y familiar en adolescentes, víctimas de ciberacoso [The influence of school climate and family climate among adolescents victims of cyberbullying]. *Commun. Rev.* 46, 57–65. doi: 10.3916/C46-2016-06
47. Ortega, R. (1997). El proyecto Sevilla anti-violencia escolar. Un modelo de intervención preventiva contra los malos tratos entre iguales [Sevilla school anti-violence project. A model of preventive intervention against abuse among equals]. *Rev. Educ.* 313, 143–158.
48. Ortega, R., and Del Rey, R. (2003). *Cuestionario Sobre Convivencia, Violencia y Experiencias de Riesgo-COVER. [Questionnaire on Coexistence, Violence and Risk Experiences-COVER]*. Córdoba: Universidad de Córdoba.
49. Ortega, R., and Mora-Merchán, J. (1998). *La convivencia Escolar: Qué es y Cómo Abordarla. Programa Educativo de Prevención de Maltrato Entre Compañeros y Compañeras [School life: What It is and How to Address It. Educational Abuse Prevention Program among Colleagues]*. Seville: Consejería de Educación y Ciencia. Junta de Andalucía.
50. Pajares, M. (2009). *Inmigración y mercado de trabajo. Informe 2009. [Immigration and labor market. report 2009]*. Madrid: Observatorio Permanente de la Inmigración, Secretaría de Estado de Inmigración y Emigración del Ministerio de Trabajo e Inmigración.
51. Patton, D. U., Hong, J. S., Patel, S., and Kral, M. J. (2015). A Systematic review of research strategies used in qualitative studies on school bullying and victimization. *Trauma Violence Abuse* doi: 10.1177/1524838015588502 [Epub ahead of print].
52. Penuel, W. R., Roschelle, J., and Shechtman, N. (2007). The WHIRL co-design process: participant experiences. *Res. Pract. Technol. Enhanc. Learn.* 2, 51–74. doi: 10.1142/S1793206807000300

53. Pepler, D., Smith, P. K., and Rigby, K. (2004). "Looking back and looking forward: implications for making interventions work effectively," in *Bullying in Schools: How Successful Can Interventions be?*, eds P. K. Smith, D. Pepler, and K. Rigby (New York, NY: Cambridge University Press), 307–324.

54. Piña Mendoza, C., and Callejas Fonseca, L. (2005). La estigmatización social como factor fundamental de la discriminación juvenil. [Social stigmatization as a fundamental factor in juvenile discrimination]. *El Cotidiano* 134, 64–70. Available at: http://www.redalyc.org/articulo.oa?id=32513409

55. Raminhos, C. S., Claudio, A. P., Carmo, M. B., Carvalhosa, S., de Jesus Candeias, M., and Gaspar, A. (2015). "A serious game to prevent bullying and promote empathy," in *Proceedings of the 10th Iberian Conference on Information Systems and Technologies (CISTI), 2015*, (Rome: IEEE), 1–6.

56. Richter, G., Raban, D. R., and Rafaeli, S. (2015). "Studying gamification: the effect of rewards and incentives on motivation," in *Gamification in Education and Business*, eds T. Reiners and L. C. Wood (London: Springer International Publishing), 21–46.

57. Rojas, D., Cowan, B., Kapralos, B., and Dubrowski, A. (2014). "Gamification and health professions education," in *Proceedings of the IEEE Games Media Entertainment (GEM)*, (Rome: IEEE), 1–2.

58. Rosenthal, L., Earnshaw, V., Carroll-Scott, A., Henderson, K., Peters, S., McCaslin, C., et al. (2015). Weight and race based bullying: health associations among urban adolescents. *J. Health Psychol.* 20, 401–412. doi: 10.1177/1359105313502567

59. Ruiz, F. J., and Belmonte, A. M. (2014). Los jóvenes como usuarios de aplicaciones de marca en dispositivos móviles. [Young people as users of branded applications on mobile devices]. *Commun. Rev.* 22, 73–81. doi: 10.3916/C43-2014-07

60. Salmivalli, C., and Poskiparta, E. (2012). Making bullying prevention a priority in finnish schools: the KiVa antibullying program. *New Dir. Youth Dev.*2012, 41–53. doi: 10.1002/yd.20006

61. Sapouna, M., Wolke, D., Vannini, N., Watson, S., Woods, S., Schneider, W., et al. (2010). Virtual learning intervention to reduce bullying victimization in primary school: a controlled trial. *J. Child Psychol. Psychiatry* 51, 104–112. doi: 10.1111/j.1469-7610.2009.02137.x

62. Schoech, D., Boyas, J. F., Black, B. M., and Elias, N. (2013). Gamification for behavior change: lessons from developing a social, multiuser, web-tablet based prevention game for youths. *J. Technol. Hum. Serv.* 31, 197–217. doi: 10.1080/15228835.2013.812512

63. Serrano, A., Torrente, J., Moreno, P., and Fernández, B. (2012). Tracing a little for big improvements: application of learning analytics and videogames for student assessment. *Proc. Comput. Sci.* 15, 203–209. doi: 10.1016/j.procs.2012.10.072

64. Sin, K. W. M. (2003). Users' creative response and designers' roles. *Des. Issues* 19, 64–73. doi: 10.1136/bmjspcare-2015-000906.39

65. Smart, J. B., and Brent, I. L. (2010). A grounded theory of behavior management strategy selection, implementation, and perceived effectiveness reported by first-year elementary teachers. *Elem. Sch. J.* 110, 567–584.

66. Smith, M. A., Lambert, S. F., English, D., and Ialongo, N. S. (2014). Associations between trajectories of perceived racial discrimination and psychological symptoms among African American adolescents. *Dev. Psychopathol.* 26, 1049–1065. doi: 10.1017/S0954579414000571

67. Smith, P. K., Ananiadou, K., and Cowie, H. (2003). Interventions to reduce school bullying. *Can. J. Psychiatry* 48, 591–599.

68. Smith, P. K., and Sharp, S. (1994). "The problem of school bullying," in *School Bullying: Insights and Perspectives*, eds P. K. Smith and S. Sharp (London: Routledge), 1–19.

69. Solomontos-Kauntouri, O., Gradinger, P., Yanagigida, T., and Strohmeier, D. (2016). The implementation and evaluation of the ViSC program in cyprus: challenges of cross-national dissemination and evaluation results. *Eur. J. Dev. Psychol.* 13, 737–755. doi: 10.1080/17405629.2015.1136618

70. Strauss, A. L., and Corbin, J. (1998). *Basics of Qualitative Research. Techniques and Procedures for Developing Grounded Theory.* Thousand Oaks, CA: Sage.

71. Su, C. H., and Cheng, C. H. (2015). A mobile gamification learning system for improving the learning motivation and achievements. *J. Comp. Assist. Learn.* 31, 268–286. doi: 10.1111/jcal.12088

72. Thornberg, R. (2011). "She's Weird!" the social construction of bullying in school: a review of qualitative research. *Child Soc.* 25, 258–267. doi: 10.1111/j.1099-0860.2011.00374.x

73. Trip, S., Sipos-Gug, S., Tocai, I., Gradinger, P., Yanagida, T., and Strohmeier, D. (2015). Bullying prevention in schools by targeting cognitions, emotions and behavior: evaluating the Effectiveness of the REBE-ViSC Program. *J. Couns. Psychol.* 62, 732–740. doi: 10.1037/cou0000084
74. Ttofi, M. M., and Farrington, D. P. (2010). "School bullying: risk factors, theories and interventions," in *Handbook of Crime*, eds F. Brookman, M. Maguire, H. Pierpoint, and T. Bennett (Cullompton: Willan), 427–457.
75. Vannini, N., Enz, S., Sapouna, M., Wolke, D., Watson, S., Woods, S., et al. (2011). "FearNot!": a computer-based anti-bullying-programme designed to foster peer intervention. *Eur. J. Psychol. Educ.* 26, 21–44. doi: 10.1007/s10212-010-0035-4

CHAPTER 17

HATE SPEECH, CYBERBULLYING AND ONLINE ANONYMITY

César Arroyo López[1] and Roberto Moreno López[2]

[1]Asociación Socioeducativa Llere, Toledo, Spain

[2]University of Castilla—La Mancha, Talavera de la Reina, Spain

ICTs and internet access are a defining element in the lives of young people. In Spain alone, daily internet use among young people aged 16–35 is above 90% (INE 2016). The online experience, however, is not always positive, and as some recent studies indicate, traditional school bullying has taken a leap into the digital world, to the point that the number of incidents in both settings is practically the same (Calmaestra et al. 2016).

Citation: César Arroyo López and Roberto Moreno López, "Hate Speech, Cyberbullying and Online Anonymity," https://link.springer.com/content/pdf/10.1007/978-3-319-72604-5.pdf#page=88

While it is true that cyberhate, the online variety of hate speech, and cyberbullying are not the same thing, as the former targets certain groups on the basis of a common characteristic and the latter targets individuals usually in the setting of a particularly community (like a school or a workplace), the two concepts are definitely intertwined in the mind of young people. Bullying can be defined as "a type of behaviour aimed at doing harm, repeated over time and occurring in the midst of an interpersonal relationship characterised by an imbalance of power" (Olweus 1999: 25). Cyberbullying resembles bullying in that it, too, is intentional, aggressive and repeated over time, but with the particularity that those who engage in it do so through the use of electronic means. As Del Río et al. (2010) note, cyberbullying, as a mode of harassment, has characteristics that make it particularly intense, like the absence of temporal limits, the imperishability of online content, its capacity to be instantaneously witnessed by a vast audience and the perceived anonymity of its instigator. What is more, the consequences of cyberbullying have been analysed in several studies (cf. Garaigordobil 2011), and their connection with the effects that hate speech has on its victims is clear (cf. Ayto. Barcelona 2017). During the C.O.N.T.A.C.T. interviews in Spain,19 as many as six interviewees directly linked their experiences of hate speech to (cyber)bullying:

(124) *Interviewer* *Have you had any experience with hate speech?*
Interviewee 2 *Yes, what I said about bullying in the first years of high school with my nose problem, adenoids, they harassed me about my tone of voice and such things.*

Although in the particular case in (124) the motivation for the incident was not some protected characteristic of the victim, as is typically the case in instances of hate speech, in other reported cases, the cause of the harassment was precisely that:

(125) *Interviewer* *Maybe it was done to people around you?*
Interviewee 4 *Yes (...)*
Interviewer *Did they harass them about something particular or just because (...)?*
Interviewee 4 *No, it was with me and another girl, no, and also with a guy who was disabled.*
Interviewer *Was it because of his disability?*
Interviewee 4 *Yes*

In this respect, our interviewees' perceptions coincide with research that has shown that racial and sexual prejudice often appear as causes of cyberbullying (cf. Hoff and Mitchell 2009).

(126) *Interviewer* *What other reasons do you find being used on the Internet that lead to such comments?*

Interviewee 5 *Physical appearance, race, homosexuality, culture, there are so many issues that people are always (...) disability, they chase those groups a lot, so to speak in quotes, to crush them, and, really, there is no reason.*

A further analysis of the interviews revealed that most interviewees believed that the main pretext behind both cyberbullying and online hate speech was that perpetrators take advantage of the perceived anonymity of the internet and therefore feel free to utter and spread insults, vexations and extreme opinions; things that might not be as easy to do in the offline world. In the words of one of the interviewees,

(127) *Because they do not really show their face, they are through a screen they do not give the face and put the first thing that occurs to them. When they are facing you, maybe if you are going to say it, to a friend of you by WhatsApp or by social networks, you put a thing and if then if you had to say it to the face, you would not say the same thing or you wouldn't say it in the same way.*

(Interviewee 1)

So, what is the role that anonymity plays in the spread of intolerance and hate speech in social networks? In the case that concerns us, that is, of young users who communicate through the Internet, the perception among our interviewees was that, simply because it is not face-to-face, much of the communication that takes place on the Internet is not as 'filtered' as it would otherwise be:

(128) *For the anonymity or shame of saying it face-to-face and you do it for social networks then it's like, I do not know, that we hide, it's like we put on a mask and as a carnival you wear a mask and you can do everything you want. This is the same but over the Internet.*

(Interviewee 1)

Indeed, several of the young people interviewed believe that posting anonymous comments online allows people to openly express intolerance, reject difference and embrace racism without the social limitations that exist in offline communication. For example:

(129) *There is less [hate speech] on the street, but I think that this is because of shame, because he does not like to show his face. However, through a social network I put it [the comment] on and that's it. Saying things behind*

[other people's backs] is much easier.

(Interviewee 2)

Current research has shown that there is no single profile of a hater or cyberbully who is concealed under the cloak of anonymity. Even though there are organised groups that seek to promote hatred online, in most cases the people that hide behind hateful or discriminatory trolling messages are not linked to openly intolerant ideological movements (cf. Isasi and Juanatey 2016), but are instead users who just do not realise the potential impact of their digital activity, and the effects that it can have in the offline world (cf. Stein 2016):

(130) *Because on the Internet it seems that the thing is diluted, people feel shielded behind their computer, and I am here in my house in Toledo, no matter who reads this. The one who reads it will be far away, so nothing will happen.*

(Interviewee 14)

Our interviewees also discussed the impact of hate speech and cyberbullying on the victim:

(131) *Interviewer*	*But in the event that it (hate speech online) takes place how you think it affects the people who are targeted by it?*
Interviewee 3	*Well, I suppose that it is bad. Evidently you won't like anyone who speaks badly about you. Surely then that, as we are in the society that we are, will affect your private life. I don't know, I imagine, I don't know what measures should be taken: closing Facebook or changing names or changing friends on Facebook. I want to say, I don't know, or don't see it in some way or, I know, I guess it will affect and I don't know, your security will not be the same if you are being insulted.*

(132) *I think so, because they already make comments that can affect the other person psychologically and physically (...).*

(Interviewee 17)

Hatred towards certain groups, which underlies both online and offline hate speech, can also manifest itself in other modes of expression of violence and intolerance, such as that of (cyber)bullying. Through their personal experiences, some of our interviewees showed that the expression of hate is intimately linked to the experience of (cyber)bullying, and more specifically, that a person's identity is often used by perpetrators as a weapon to exercise (cyber)bullying. Keeping in mind that (cyber)bullying is typically tied to the school context and considering at the same time that the educational context should be the primary place where the causes of violence, intolerance and hatred against those who are perceived to be different are dealt with, it just seems sensible to us to propose that more focus is placed on embracing diversity, implementing a human rights approach and carrying out activities within the realm of citizenship and intercultural education.

REFERENCES

1. Amnesty International. 2017. Tackling hate crime in the UK. Amnesty International UK briefing paper. http://www.amnesty.org.uk/files/Against-Hate-Briefing-AIUK.pdf. Accessed August 12, 2017.
2. Baider, Fabienne H. 2013. The saliency hypothesis: Affects and emotions. In Research trends in intercultural pragmatics, ed. Istvan Kecskes, and Jesús Romero-Trillo, 7–25. Berlin: Mouton de Gruyter.
3. Bednarek, Monika. 2008. Semantic preference and semantic prosody re-examined. Corpus Linguistics and Linguistic Theory 4: 119–139. https://doi.org/10.1515/CLLT.2008.006.
4. Berger, Peter, and Thomas Luckmann. 1966/1991. The social construction of reality: A treatise in the sociology of knowledge. London: Penguin Books.
5. Bleich, Erik. 2011. The rise of hate speech and hate crime laws in liberal democracies. Journal of Ethnic and Migration Studies 37: 917–934. https://doi.org/10.1080/1369183X.2011.576195.
6. Boromisza-Habashi, David. 2013. Speaking hatefully: Culture, communication, and political action in Hungary. Philadelphia: Pennsylvania State University Press.
7. Brown, Alexander. 2017. What is hate speech? Part 2. Family resemblances. Law and Philosophy. https://doi.org/10.1007/s10982-017-9300-x.
8. Calmaestra, Juan, Almudena Escorial, Paloma García, Carmela del Moral, Catalina Perazzo, and Thomas Ubrich. 2016Yo a eso no juego: Bullying y ciberbullying en la infancia. Save the Children Spain report. http://www.savethechildren.es/sites/default/files/imce/docs/yo_a_eso_no_juego.pdf. Accessed August 12, 2017.
9. Del Río, Jorge, Charo Sádaba, and Xavier Bringué. 2010. Menores y redes ¿sociales? De la amistad al cyberbullying. Revista de Estudios de Juventud 88: 115–129. http://www.injuve.es/ sites/default/files/RJ88-09.pdf. Accessed August 12, 2017.
10. Duffy, Margaret E. 2003. Web of hate: A fantasy theme analysis of the rhetorical vision of hate groups online. Journal of Communication Inquiry 27: 291–312. https://doi.org/10.1177/ 0196859903252850.
11. Fairclough, Norman, and Ruth Wodak. 1997. Critical discourse analysis. In Discourse studies—a multidisciplinary introduction: Discourse as social interaction, ed. Teun A. van Dijk, 258– 284. London: Sage

Publications.

12. Galtung, Johan. 1969. Violence, peace, and peace research. Journal of Peace Research 6: 167–191.
13. Garaigordobil, Maite. 2011. Prevalencia y consecuencias del cyberbullying: Una revisión. International Journal of Psychology and Psychological Therapy 11: 233–254.
14. Giora, Rachel. 1997. Understanding figurative and literal language: The graded salience hypothesis. Cognitive Linguistics 7: 183–206. https://doi.org/10.1515/cogl.1997.8.3.183.
15. Giora, Rachel. 2003. On our mind: Salience, context and figurative language. Oxford: Oxford University Press.
16. Habermas, Jürgen. 1989. The structural transformation of the public sphere: An inquiry into a category of Bourgeois society. Cambridge, MA: MIT Press.
17. Herz, Michael, and Peter Molnar (eds.). 2012. The content and context of hate speech: Rethinking regulation and responses. Cambridge: Cambridge University Press.
18. Hess, Amanda. 2016. Earning the 'Woke' Badge. New York Times Magazine, April 19. http:// www.nytimes.com/2016/04/24/magazine/earning-the-woke-badge.html. Accessed August 12, 2017.
19. Hoff, Diane L., and Sidney N. Mitchell. 2009. Cyberbullying: Causes, effects and remedies. Journal of Educational Administration 47: 652–665. https://doi.org/10.1108/ 09578230910981107.
20. Houlston, Michelle. 2017. Reverse racism does not exist. Galdem magazine. http://www.gal-dem. com/reverse-racism-not-exist/. Accessed August 12, 2017.
21. Hughes, Laura. 2016. Theresa May hits out at universities 'safe spaces' for stifling free speech. The Telegraph, September 14. http://www.telegraph.co.uk/news/2016/09/14/theresa-may-hitsout-at-universities-safe-spaces-for-stifling-fr/. Accessed August 12, 2017. INE. 2016.
22. Encuesta sobre equipamiento y uso de tecnologías de información y comunicación en los hogares. Instituto Nacional de Estadística report. http://www.ine.es/jaxi/Datos.htm?path=/ t25/p%20450/base_2011/a2016/l0/&file=04005.px. Accessed August 12, 2017. Isasi, Alex Cabo, and Ana García Juanatey. 2016.
23. El discurso del odio en las redes sociales: Un estado de la cuestión. Ajuntament de Barcelona progress report. http://ajuntament.barcelona.

cat/bcnvsodi/wp-content/uploads/2017/02/Informe_discurso-del-odio_ES.pdf. Accessed August 12, 2017.

24. Kopytowska, Monika. 2013. Blogging as the mediatization of politics and a new form of social interaction. In Analyzing genres in political communication, ed. Piotr Cap, and Urszula Okulska, 379–421. Amsterdam/Philadelphia: John Benjamins.
25. Kopytowska, Monika (ed). 2015a. 'Contemporary discourses of hate and radicalism across space and genres.' Special issue, Journal of Language Aggression and Conflict 3:1.
26. Kopytowska, Monika. 2015b. Covering conflict: Between universality and cultural specificity in news discourse genre and journalistic style. International Review of Pragmatics 7: 308–339. https://doi.org/10.1163/18773109-00702007.
27. Kopytowska, Monika. 2015c. Mediating identity, ideology and values in the public sphere: Towards a new model of (constructed) social reality. Lodz Papers in Pragmatics 11: 133–156. https://doi.org/10.1515/lpp-2015-0008.
28. Leezenberg, Michiel. 2015. Discursive violence and responsibility: Notes on the pragmatics of Dutch populism. Journal of Language Aggression and Conflict 3: 200–227. https://doi.org/10. 1075/jlac.3.1.09lee.
29. Loewenstein, Karl. 1937. Militant democracy and fundamental rights II. American Political Science Review 31: 638–658. https://doi.org/10.2307/1948103.
30. Main, Douglas. 2013. Who are the millennials? Live Science. http://www.livescience.com/38061- millennials-generation-y.html. Accessed August 12, 2017.
31. McIntosh, Peggy. 1989. White privilege: Unpacking the invisible knapsack. Peace and Freedom Magazine, July/August issue.
32. McLuhan, Marshall. 1964. The medium is the message. In Understanding media: The extensions of man, ed. Marshall McLuhan, 22–35. New York: McGraw Hill.
33. National Police Chief's Council. 2016. Tackling hate crime remains a priority.
34. National Police Chief's Council Online, National Police Chief's Council press release. http://news.npcc.police. uk/releases/tackling-hate-crime-remains-a-priority. Accessed August 12, 2017.

35. Nicholson, Rebecca. 2016. 'Poor little snowflake'—the defining insult of 2015. Guardian, November 28. http://www.theguardian.com/science/2016/nov/28/snowflake-insult-disdainyoung-people. Accessed August 12, 2017.
36. Olweus, Dan. 1999. Conductas de acoso y amenaza entre escolares. Madrid: Morata.
37. Oxford Living Dictionaries. 2017a. "snowflake". http://en.oxforddictionaries.com/definition/us/ snowflake. Accessed August 12, 2017.
38. Oxford Living Dictionaries. 2017b. "keyboard warrior". http://en.oxforddictionaries.com/ definition/keyboard_warrior. Accessed August 12, 2017.
39. Perry, Barbara, and Patrick Olsson. 2009. Cyberhate: The globalization of hate. Information and Communications Technology Law 18: 185–199. https://doi.org/10.1080/13600830902814984.
40. Roy, Jessica. 2016. 'Cuck,' 'snowflake,' 'masculinist': A guide to the language of the 'alt right'. LA Times, November 11. http://www.latimes.com/nation/la-na-pol-alt-right-terminology20161115-story.html. Accessed August 12, 2017.
41. Said, Edward W. 1978. Orientalism. London/New York: Routledge & Kegan Paul. Searle, John. 1995. The construction of social reality. London: Penguin books.
42. Searle, John. 2010. Making the social world: The structure of human civilization. Oxford: Oxford University Press.
43. Stein Joel. 2016. How trolls are ruining the internet. Times, August 18. http://time.com/4457110/ internet-trolls/. Accessed August 12, 2017.
44. Santana, Arthur D. 2014. Virtuous or vitriolic: The effect of anonymity on civility in online newspaper reader comment boards. Journalism Practice 8: 18–33. https://doi.org/10.1080/ 17512786.2013.813194.
45. Steinmetz, Katy. 2017. The Oxford English Dictionary just added 'woke'. It's older than you might think. Time, June 25. http://time.com/4830959/oxford-english-dictionary-woke/. Accessed August 12, 2017.
46. Stromme, Lizzie. 2016. MP demands people stop saying Remoaners despite calling Brexit a TERRIBLE mistake. Express, December 7. http://www.express.co.uk/news/uk/741081/AnnaSoubry-stop-saying-Remoaners-Brexit-terrible-mistake. Accessed August 12, 2017.

47. Telegraph. 2015. University union officer who wrote 'kill all white men' tweet will remain in post. The Telegraph, May 27. http://www.telegraph.co.uk/news/uknews/11633305/Universityunion-officer-who-wrote-kill-all-white-men-tweet-will-remain-in-post.html. Accessed August 12, 2017.

48. Tetlock, Philip E. 1983. Accountability and judgment processes in a personality prediction task. Journal of Personality and Social Psychology 45: 74–83. http://doi.org/10.1037/0022-3514.52. 4.700.

49. Travis, Alan. 2017. Anti-Muslim hate crime surges after Manchester and London Bridge attacks. Guardian, June 20 Online. http://www.theguardian.com/society/2017/jun/20/anti-muslim-hatesurges-after-manchester-and-london-bridge-attacks. Accessed August 12, 2017.

50. van Hooren, David. 2015. Outsiders as invaders: On the attitudes of Maltese citizens toward irregular immigrants. In Contributions from European symbolic interactionists: Conflict and cooperation, ed. Thaddeus Müller, 75–98. Emerald: Bingley.

51. van Houtum, Henk, and T. Ton van Naerssen. 2002. Bordering, Ordering and Othering. Tijdschrift voor economische en sociale geografie 93: 125–136. https://doi.org/10.1111/1467-9663.00189.

52. Waldron, Jeremy. 2012. The harm in hate speech. Cambridge, MA: Harvard University Press.

53. Waugh, Paul. 2017. Michael Gove calls Boris Johnson's critics 'snowflakes' after he compares French President to WW2 guard. Huffington Post, January 18. http://www.huffingtonpost.co. uk/entry/jeremy-corbyn-wild-and-inappropriate-downing-street-defends-boris-johnsonstheatrical-comparison-of-francois-hollande-to-ww2-prison-camp-guard-fawlty-towers-dontmention-the-war_uk_587f7c97e4b0831b7c6e6948. Accessed August 12, 2017.

54. Youngs, Gillian. 2009. Blogging and globalization: The blurring of the public/private spheres. Aslib Proceedings 61: 127–138. https://doi.org/10.1108/00012530910946884.

CHAPTER 18

ONLINE PESTKOPPENSTOPPEN: SYSTEMATIC AND THEORY-BASED DEVELOPMENT OF A WEB-BASED TAILORED INTERVENTION FOR ADOLESCENT CYBERBULLY VICTIMS TO COMBAT AND PREVENT CYBERBULLYING

Niels CL Jacobs, Trijntje Völlink, Francine Dehue and Lilian Lechner

Faculty of Psychology, Open University, Valkenburgerweg 177, 6419 AT Heerlen, The Netherlands

Citation: Jacobs et al.: Online Pestkoppenstoppen: systematic and theory-based development of a web-based tailored intervention for adolescent cyberbully victims to combat and prevent cyberbullying. BMC Public Health 2014 14:396. doi:10.1186/1471-2458-14-396.

ABSTRACT

Background

The purpose of this article is to give an integrative insight into the theoretical and empirical-based development of the *Online Pestkoppenstoppen* (Stop Bullies Online/Stop Online Bullies). This intervention aims to reduce the number of cyberbully victims and their symptoms of depression and anxiety (program goal), by teaching cyberbully victims how to cope in an adequate and effective manner with cyberbully incidents (program's outcomes).

Method/Design

In developing the program the different steps of the Intervention Mapping protocol are systematically used. In this article we describe each step of Intervention Mapping. Sources used for the development were a literature review, a Delphi study among experts, focus group interviews with the target group, and elements from a proven effective anti-bullying program. The result is a fully automated web-based tailored intervention for cyberbully victims (12-15 years) consisting of three web-based advice sessions delivered over three months. The first advice aims to teach participants how behavior is influenced by the thoughts they have, how to recognize and dispute irrational thoughts and how to form rational thoughts. In the second advice, participants will learn about the way bullying emerges, how their behavior influences bullying and how they can use effective coping strategies in order to stop (online) bullying. In the third advice, participants receive feedback and will learn how to use the Internet and mobile phones in a safe manner. Each advice is tailored to the participant's personal characteristics (e.g., personality, self-efficacy, coping strategies used and (ir)rational thoughts). To ensure implementation of the program after testing it for effectiveness, the intervention was pretested in the target-population and an implementation plan was designed. Finally, we will elaborate on the planned randomized controlled trial in which the intervention will be compared to a general information group and waiting list control group. This evaluation will provide insight into the intervention's efficacy to reduce cyberbullying and its negative effects.

Discussion

Intervention Mapping is a time consuming but profound way to ensure that each step of developing an intervention is taken, and resulted in three web-based tailored pieces of advices that teach adolescents how to cope more effectively with cyberbullying experiences.

Keywords: (Cyber) bullying, Intervention, Web-based, E-health, Computer tailoring, Behavior change, Intervention Mapping

BACKGROUND

The growing popularity of social media (e.g. Facebook, Twitter) and instant messenger services (e.g. IMchat, Twitter) [1] does not always lead to positive experiences. Cyberbullying is defined as a repeated aggressive and intentional act, carried out by a group or an individual, using electronic forms of contact. This act is directed towards a victim who cannot easily defend him or herself [2]. Between 20% and 40% of the adolescents worldwide report being a cyberbully victim [3]. Research has indicated that cybervictimization is associated with serious internalizing difficulties such as depression [4, 5], anxiety [6], emotional distress [5] and suicidality [7, 8]. Cyberbully victims also more often have experienced drugs, alcohol, physical or sexual abuse, have displayed delinquent and aggressive behavior, have problems at school and have dropped out of school [9, 10, 11, 12, 13, 14, 15, 16]. The more adolescents engage in cyber aggression, the more loneliness they feel, the lower their global self-worth is, the fewer mutual friendships they have and the lower their ratings of social acceptance and popularity by peers are [17]. Cyberbullies as well as cyberbully/victims (i.e. both victim and bully) have worse subjective health than those who are not involved [18], and victims of both traditional and cyberbullying are four times more likely to experience depressive symptoms and are five times more likely to attempt suicide compared to non-victims [8].

Unfortunately, intervention programs that deal specifically with cyberbullying are scarce [19]. Moreover, students perceive that methods used in traditional bullying incidents are not equally effective in cyberbullying incidents [20]. Therefore, there is an urgent need for effective cyberbullying interventions. Ideally, these interventions should: (1) do more than increase awareness of potential threats of the Internet by offering victims intensive intervention strategies on the basis of individual needs of the student [21]; (2) offer health education and teach emotional self-management competencies [22]; (3) increase victims′ knowledge of reactive (e.g. deleting, blocking

69]. To increase knowledge about coping strategies used in cyberbullying, it is useful to look at coping strategies employed in cyberbullying and in daily life. These coping strategies appear to not differ significantly, and knowledge about traditional bullying can, to some extent, be applied to cyberbullying [60]. Furthermore, coping strategies used in response to daily stressors are good predictors for coping strategies used in response to cyberbullying [68]. To reduce victimization and its negative effects, it thus appears that adolescents need to improve their current coping strategies. They need to employ effective coping strategies that not only help them to mentally deal with (cyber)bullying, but also contribute to the prevention and discontinuation of (cyber)bullying. Therefore, the primary program goals were reducing the number of: (1) cyberbully victims; and (2) depressive and anxious victims as a consequence of cyberbullying. Secondary goals were a decrease in: (3) victims truanting from school; (4) victims with suicidal thoughts; and (5) an increase in determinants related to cyberbully victims' behavior, such as self-esteem, self-efficacy, rational helpful beliefs, and effective coping.

Step 2: Matrices of Change Objectives

Next, the focus shifts from the needs assessment to the formation of a change model (Figure 1). In this step intended change in behavior is be further delineated into specific sub-behaviors: the performance objectives (POs). The POs are crossed with relevant determinants in order to create a matrix of change objectives (COs) [44].

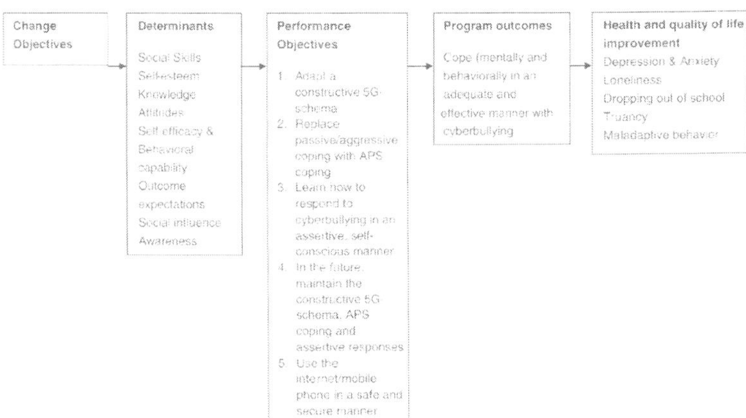

Figure 1: Change model *Online Pestkoppenstoppen* . Read figure from right to left to see which steps were taken for the development of the program. Read

figure from left to right to see how the program influences behavior and determinants in order to improve health and quality of life.

Performance Objectives

First, we translated the risk behavior ineffective coping into a program outcome: after the intervention, cyberbully victims will cope in an adequate and effective manner with (cyber)bullying experiences. This program outcome is a broad conceptualization of what a participant has to do in order to reach the program's goals. Therefore, participants have to perform specific sub-behaviors, called performance objectives (POs). The POs, and accordingly the content of the intervention, were based on a literature search, focus group interviews with the target group and the linkage group (including the research team, a healthcare coordinator of a school community, a trainer who works with bullied children, and a project leader and director of a website addressing bullied children) formed for this project, a review of relevant (cyber)bullying websites, discussions in an online group about cyberbullying and cybersafety (YouthRiskOnline/Embracecivilty) and a Delphi study among 70 international experts in the field of cyberbullying and coping [70]. In total, eleven performance objectives were formed for this intervention. For an overview of all POs see the first column of Additional file 1.

Based on discussions with the linkage group, it was decided to develop an online translation of the "Pleasure at school" training (PaS) [50]. Victims apparently have negative self-related attitudes, thoughts [71], and self-blaming attributions [72] after a bully experience. PaS is partly based on principles of Rational Emotive (Behavioral) Therapy (RE(B)T) [73, 74], and uses the 5G-schema [75] (see Figure 2) to raise awareness in the relation between a thought, feeling and behavior, and to replace irrational thoughts with more rational thoughts. According to RE(B)T, evaluative thoughts mediate the view people have about events that happen and the emotional, behavioral, and inferential reactions to these events [74, 76, 77]. PaS has proven effective in reducing bullying behavior, anxiety and psychological problems [50] in adolescents. Similarly, RE(B)T has proven effective in the treatment of problems related to cyberbullying [59, 78, 79] and bullying [4, 80], such as anxiety, depression and behavioral problems in adolescents [81, 82]. Adolescents therefore learn how to recognize (PO 1), dispute (PO 2) and replace (PO 3) irrational thoughts with rational thoughts.

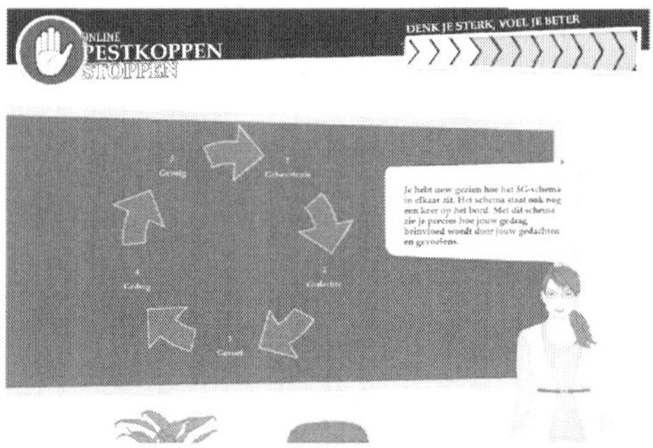

Figure 2: The 5G-schema in *Online Pestkoppenstoppen.* The 5G-schema gives insight into the relation between an event (*Gebeurtenis*), a thought (*Gedachte*), a feeling (*Gevoel*), a behavior (*Gedrag*) and a consequence (*Gevolg*).

After thoughts, the 5G-schema focuses on emotions. Relational bullyvictims often have problems with the correct encoding and interpretation of emotions [83]. It is important for an adolescent's social and cognitive development to correctly perceive and attribute emotions [84]. The understanding and experiencing of emotions of others seems to inhibit antisocial behavior [85], and adolescents who are able to perceive, handle, understand and express their emotions tend to experience better social relationships and are more socially accepted [86]. Furthermore, despite bullyvictims probably being afraid, their most common reactions to victimization are interest and joy [54]. Emotional displays of joy and interest can provide the bully with positive social reinforcement, leading to continued victimization. Therefore, (cyber)bullyvictims need to learn more about emotions and emotion regulation and need to receive health education and emotional self-management competencies [22] (PO 4).

The next aspect the 5G-schema focuses on is behavior. As explained before, whether an adolescent becomes a long-term victim of (cyber) bullying seems to depend on how (s)he copes with (cyber)bullying attempts. Sometimes, the coping strategies employed reduce stress, but the victim fails to confront the bully [70] leading to possible continuation of the bullying. Victims of cyberbullying therefore should become increasingly aware of the ineffectiveness of their current coping style (PO 5). They need knowledge of reactive and preventive strategies (PO 6) and should change their ineffective coping strategies into effective coping strategies (PO 7) [23]. In this paper, all effective coping strategies are named Active Problem Solving (APS) strategies. APS strategies appear to resolve the bullying situation and allows the victim to act assertively [54]. For example, cyberbully victims should try to get help from bystanders, because one quarter of cyberbullying occurs in the presence of witnesses [87]. They should also block or ignore the cyberbully [88], or seek social support [3]. Seeking social support from family is likely to help [89]. Therefore adolescents need information regarding who to ask for help, how to seek help and the benefits of seeking help [88]. Furthermore, having social skills is associated with reductions in victimization and fewer internalizing problems [90]. Cross et al. [91] for example suggested that students should develop their social skills and learn effective ways of addressing relational difficulties online and offline, in order to prevent and reduce cyberbullying. Additionally, interventions should also focus on improving peer relationships in general [88], because social acceptance [92] and integration [93] moderate the impact and consequences of different forms of cyberbullying. Moreover, victims and adolescents not involved in bullying most frequently indicated assertiveness as an intervention strategy [94]. Therefore, interventions should also teach (cyber) bullyvictims non-aggressive responses, and how to cope in an assertive and prosocial manner (PO 8 and 9).

A specific risk factor for cyberbullying is the little control exerted over personal information [27]. A lot of cyberbully victims frequently use the Internet, most of the time in a risky manner [2, 78, 95]. They share passwords, openly display personal information (e.g. addresses, phone numbers) and communicate with strangers [96, 97]. Adolescents should therefore receive cyber safety education, learn to treat each other with respect (both online and offline), and become aware of the importance to regularly change their passwords and never sharing personal information [28] (PO 11).

Determinants

The next step in IM is an analysis of the most relevant (i.e. important, changeable) determinants [44] of each PO, by asking what factors determine whether a victim would or is able to perform each PO. The methods used to obtain these determinants were the above mentioned literature review, focus group interviews, a Delphi study on the determinants of ineffective and improved coping with cyberbullying [70], and a study of protocols of (cyber) bullying interventions. Further, several behavior-oriented theories were applied, such as social cognitive theory, theory of planned behavior, transtheoretical model and goal-setting theory. This resulted in a large list of determinants (see the second column of Additional file 1). The aims of this intervention did not include environmental levels (e.g. parents, teachers or schools). Therefore only determinants on the individual level were identified.

Change Objectives

A matrix was developed to combine performance objectives and their hypothesized determinants into change objectives (COs) [44]. In total, we formed 50 COs. Examples of COs are 'Individual describes characteristics of irrational and rational thoughts' and 'Individual becomes aware of current ineffective (aggressive/passive) coping style' (see third column Additional file 1). All COs were used in the selection of theoretical methods and applications (step 3) that will change the determinants.

Step 3: Theory-based Methods and Practical Strategies

A theoretical method is a general process that is supposed to influence change in behavioral determinants, based on theories. A practical application is a specific technique for practical use of theoretical methods, in ways that are applicable to the intervention population and context in which the intervention will be used [44]. When a method is translated into a practical application, sufficient understanding of the theory behind the method and its theoretical parameters that determine the effectiveness is needed [98]. For example, to influence determinants such as self-efficacy, modeling [99, 100] can be used as a theoretical method. A practical strategy would be to use a role model demonstrating how to react assertively to a difficult situation (see Figure 3a and b). Theoretical parameters for modeling state that modeling is effective when the individual is able to identify with the model, the model demonstrates adequate skills and is reinforced for the behavior displayed [98].

a

b

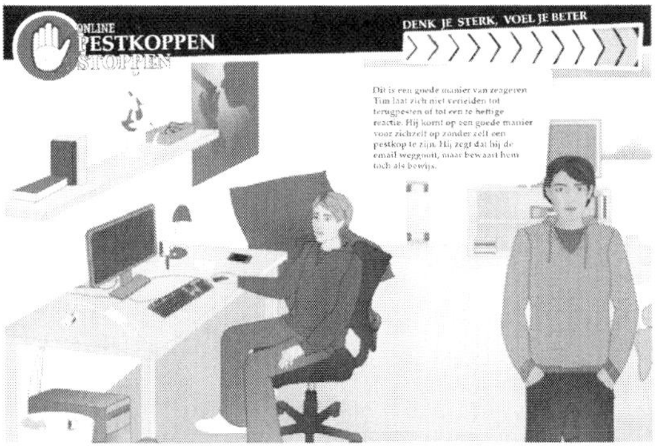

Figure 3: Example of a model demonstrating behavior. a. Noa and Linda demonstrating how to act assertively online, and explaining that cyberbullying events (in this case an email) should be saved as evidence. Female participants receive this environment and these digital guides. **b**. Levi and Tim demonstrating how to act assertively online, and explaining that cyberbullying events (in this case an email) should be saved as evidence. Male participants receive this environment and these digital guides.

To identify theoretical methods, parameters and practical strategies: (1) the literature was searched for behavior change techniques [44]: (2) the IM book was used to find theoretical methods that influence specific determinant; (3) existing (cyber)bullying interventions were compared; (4) the PaS training [50] was used; and (5) focus group interviews were held, asking the members of the target group what they believed were effective strategies. An overview of theoretical methods and practical applications used in the *Online Pestkoppenstoppen* intervention is shown in the fifth column of Additional file 1. An elucidation of the most important methods follows next.

Computer Tailoring

As mentioned before, tailoring appears to be a successful health promotion technique [38, 39]. Tailoring is the combination of strategies and information intended to reach one specific person by providing personalized feedback based on unique characteristics of a person. These characteristics are assessed individually and are related to the outcome of interest [101]. The use of tailored information results in more improvement in behavior over time compared to the use of generic information [38, 102]. Tailored messages are better read, saved and remembered than non-tailored messages [103]. There are two types of tailoring; dynamic tailoring (DT), assessing intervention variables prior to each feedback; and static tailoring (ST), assessing intervention variables at one baseline moment. Although research indicates that DT interventions outperform ST interventions [39], this intervention mostly tailors statical, because several variables used for tailoring are also used for the measurement of effectiveness, and thus need to be assessed prior to each advice. Tailoring is a general technique used throughout the complete intervention and is also combined with the other methods used. Prior to each advice several variables are assessed to enable tailoring. The intervention is for example tailored to personality (ST) as measured by the Big 5 Questionnaire –Short form [104]. Personality may determine a participant's behavior within a specific context, and this behavior (e.g. reactions, interpretations) can influence the reoccurrence of that event [105]. Other variables on which the intervention provides tailored feedback are for example coping strategies (ST), irrational (ST) and rational (DT) thoughts, self-efficacy (DT), (cyber)bullying experiences (ST) and progress (ST).

Consciousness Raising

Consciousness raising is used to increase a participant's awareness about: (1) the thoughts (s)he has after a (cyber)bullying event; (2) his/her own negative 5G-schemas; (3) ineffective coping styles and negative outcomes; and (4) effective coping styles and positive outcomes. Based on answers about irrational thoughts and coping styles, the participant receives tailored feedback concerning his/her irrational thoughts, 5G-schemas, and current coping responses. This feedback may increase awareness, which in turn may help the participant to see why the current way of thinking and/or coping is not helpful or effective. It is important that the participant receives information about problem solving immediately [44]. Therefore, the participant immediately receives information about how to recognize, dispute and replace thoughts after becoming aware of his/her 5G-schema, and how to change ineffective coping into effective coping after becoming aware of his/her ineffective coping.

Guided Practice

Guided practice is prompting the participant to rehearse and repeat the desired behavior, discuss the experience and provide feedback [44]. This method is used to increase self-efficacy and behavioral capability. Additionally, it is used to overcome barriers. In this intervention, the participant receives either video-models demonstrating the desired skill (see Figure 4), or comics and digital guides demonstrating and explaining the desired skill, followed by opportunities to practice the skill. Several insight questions are asked in relation to performing the skills, upon which the digital guides give feedback.

Figure 4: Video-model explaining/demonstrating skills. A Dutch actor explains how to recognize, dispute and replace irrational thoughts with rational thoughts, with the help of the 5G-schema.

Providing Information

Providing information is used to increase participant's knowledge, skills, and attitudes, using arguments and persuasive communication [44]. According to the elaboration likelihood model [106], good arguments are effective in reaching stable change in attitudes only when the message is processed through the central route. This happens when the message is personally relevant and not to discrepant from the participant's beliefs [44]. The participant receives general (e.g. what are the dynamics of a bullying situation, what to do and not to do online) and tailored (e.g. questions that aid recognizing irrational thoughts and changing aggressive/passive coping into active and problem solving coping) information. To check whether the participant remembers the correct information, questions are asked interspersed with feedback. Additionally, to prevent the participant from paying attention to information (s)he already knows, at some points in the intervention (s)he can choose which information (s)he wants to read. Furthermore, all important information is summarized on the personal page and sent to the participant's e-mail inbox.

Modeling

In modeling a person serves as an appropriate model for others that is reinforced for the desired behavior assuming that the behavior of the model will be imitated [107]. Modeling is included in this intervention as a method to increase participant's self-efficacy and behavioral capability to carry out the desired behavior change, because it is proven to be an effective teaching tool [108]. For example, previous research indicated that video-counseling - in which a real human speaks and asks questions - can be a promising technique for health interventions [109]. In line with the parameters of modeling, the video-models are coping models (i.e. who previously experienced the health problem, but who learned to deal with it effectively), the participant is able to identify with the models, and the models are being reinforced for positive behavior [44]. The short videos were professionally recorded [110]. In several video-clips, models demonstrate and explain how to perform a behavior (e.g. recognizing, disputing and replacing irrational thoughts, coping behaviors).

Implementation Intentions and Coping Plans

Research indicates that planning is a powerful self-regulatory tool in the process of behavior change [111, 112]. When people plan, they mentally simulate the linking of concrete responses to future situations, replacing spontaneous reactions for pre-planned actions. There are two types of plans: action plans [113], or implementation intentions [114], and coping plans [112]. In action planning, individuals link goal-directed behavior to certain environmental cues by specifying when, where and how to act [112] in if-then statements [115]. As a result, environmental cues should activate - without conscious intent - the initiation of action [112]. In coping planning, individuals anticipate on possible risk situations beforehand by already defining suitable and effective response behavior linked to these potential barriers [112]. Implementation intentions, action and coping plans are found to be effective in translating various intentions into actions [116, 117, 118], and appear to be working synergistically in adolescents [119]. In the intervention, the participant makes a combination of implementation intentions and coping plans. A closed-ended plan setting procedure is used to prevent inadequate goals; from a predefined list, the participant chooses the context *if* (either difficult situations or situations in daily life) and action *then* (applications of learned skills, from a predefined list).

Step 4: Producing Program Components and Materials

Taking the end products of the previous steps into account, we decided to develop one intervention containing three web-based sessions containing tailored pieces of advice addressing mostly personal and psychological determinants. A program plan including the scope, sequence and program materials was developed [44], which is described below. During the process of producing program components and materials, intended program participants and the Linkage group were consulted to determine the preferences for program design by conducting focus group interviews and short voting sessions.

Scope and Sequence

Based on brainstorms and voting sessions with members of the target group, we named the intervention *Online Pestkoppenstoppen* with three web-based tailored pieces of advices named: (1) *Think strong, feel better*; (2) *Stop the bully now!*; and (3) *You are doing great, can you do better?*. Each advice is preceded by several questionnaires – measuring tailoring and effect variables - that take approximately half an hour to complete, and each advice takes approximately 45 minutes to complete. The pieces of advice are offered divided over three months, and e-mails and text messages are used to remind the participant of participation (see Figure 5). The intervention can be found and is accessed on http://www.pestkoppenstoppen.nl.

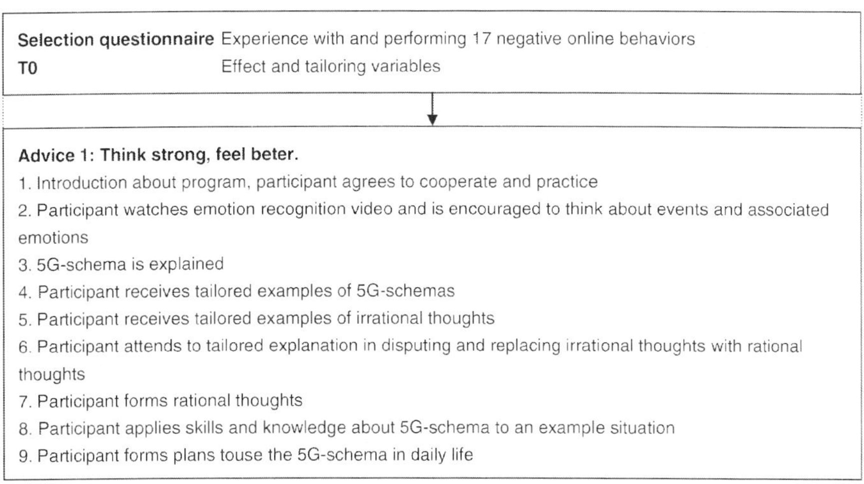

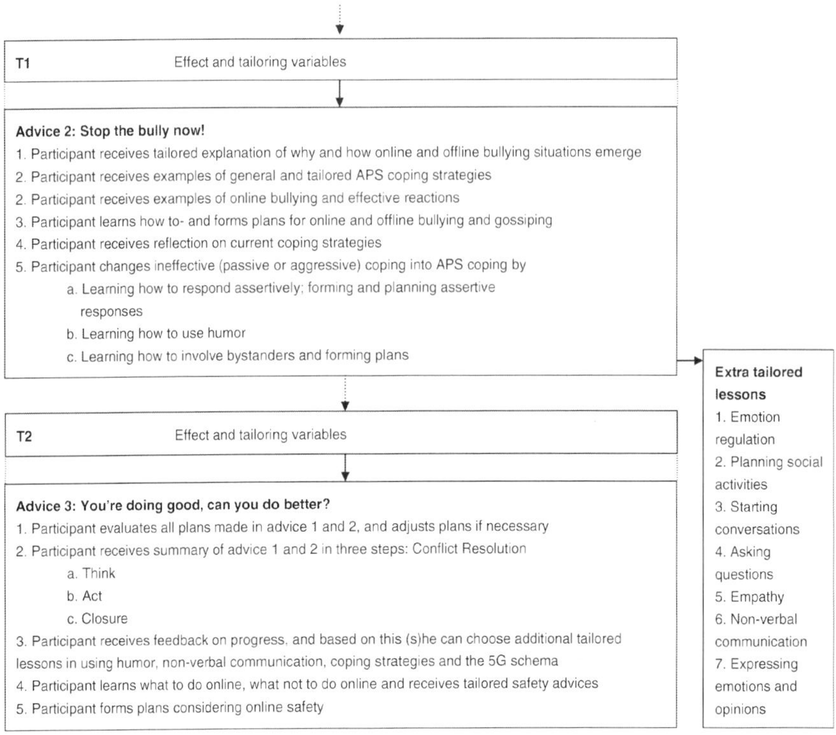

Figure 5: Flowchart of the web-based tailored advices and questionnaires. Questionnaires precede each advice, and are used to tailor the advices to the characteristics of each participant. The questionnaires are also used to do the effect evaluation. Each advice consists out of lessons aimed at teaching different skills.

Selection

Because the literature indicates that an explicit approach (e.g. 'did you experience cyberbullying?') systematically underestimates the problem [47, 58], an implicit approach was used; the individual rates his or her experience with different cyberbullying behaviors. Individuals are included in the intervention if they had experiences with at least one of the cyberbullying behaviors at least 'once a month' during the last half year. Cyberbullies and adolescents who did not experience the 17 deviant cyberbehaviors are excluded from participation. Next, the individual (=participant) fills in his or her (nick)name, age, e-mail address, mobile phone number and a login code that is provided to him/her in an information letter. The e-mail address and mobile phone number will be used to remind participants of participation before the start of each advice, during the process of filling in the questionnaires, and during the process of completing each advice.

Materials

Below, we shortly describe the different materials developed for the intervention.

Personal Page

After selection/logging in, the participant is redirected to the personal page, from which (s)he: (1) can proceed or continue with the questionnaires and/or pieces of advice; (2) can find for each advice pictures, video-clips, comics, summaries, formed helpful thoughts, plans and sentences to use; and (3) has access to the extra tailored social skill lessons of advice 2.

Assessing Tailoring and Effect Measures

Before receiving each web-based tailored advice, the participant answers several questionnaires (T0, T1 and T2) to assess the effect and tailoring variables. Gender of the participant was used to tailor gender of the guides and contexts (e.g. girls will see Noa, Jessica and a girl's bedroom, and boys will see Levi, Mike and a boy's bedroom).

Advice 1. 'Think strong, feel better.'

After the baseline measure (T0), the participant starts with the first advice. The participant learns to: (1) work with the 5G-schema in order to recognize (PO 1), dispute (PO 2) and replace (PO 3) irrational thoughts with rational thoughts; (2) carefully examine emotions in response to certain events (PO 4); and (3) form action plans to use the 5G-schema in daily life (PO 10).

Advice 2 'Stop the bully now!'

A month after the start, the participant begins with the second questionnaire (T1) and advice. The participant: (1) receives knowledge about the dynamics of online and offline bullying situations; (2) receives general APS coping strategies (PO 6); (3) learns and forms implementation intentions for responding towards online and offline bullying (PO 7 and PO 10); (4) becomes aware of ineffective coping style (PO 5); (5) is offered tailored examples of and guidance in APS coping (PO 6 and 7); (6) learns about responding assertively (PO 8 and 9); (7) forms implementation intentions and coping plans regarding assertive responses (PO 10); and (8) receives information about the use and benefits of humor and bystanders (PO 6). Observing victimization on its own can have negative consequences on psychological wellbeing [120]. Therefore, the participant forms implementation intentions and coping plans regarding how to react and involve bystanders in (cyber) bullying situations (PO 10).

Additional Lessons

Additional social skill lessons (PO 7 and 9) were offered to improve specific skills associated with problem behaviors that are tailored to the participant's score on several Youth Self-Report (YSR) scales [121]. The participant can choose if, when and which extra lessons (s)he wants to complete. For several extra lessons implementation intentions and coping plans are formed (PO 10). An overview of all lessons tailored to norm scores (above the 93% clinical range on YSR subscales) can be found in Table 1.

Table 1: Social lessons based on YSR subscales with norm scores for gender

	YSR social problems		**YSR withdrawn/de-pressed**		**YSR aggression**	
	Male > 7	**Female > 7**	**Male > 6**	**Female > 7**	**Male > 12**	**Female > 13**
Starting conversations	X	X	X	X		
Asking questions	X	X	X	X		
Express feelings and opinions	X	X	X	X		
Empathy/social cognition	X	X			X	X
Non-verbal communication	X	X				
Planning to become more socially active			X	X		
Emotional regulation					X	X

Lessons are offered when the participant scores above the 93% clinical range, as can be found in the YSR manual. Norm scores are different for males and females.

Advice 3 'You are doing great, can you do better?'

Two months after the start, the participant starts with the third questionnaire (T2) and follow up advice. The participant evaluates all plans made in advice 1 and 2 on usability, and if necessary adjusts the plans (PO 10). All skills of advice 1 and 2 are summarized into three steps (i.e. 1. Think; 2. Act; 3.Closure). These three steps together form the skill conflict resolution, which is associated with reductions in victimization and fewer internalizing problems [90]. Tailored on progress, the participant receives feedback (on irrational thoughts, coping responses and YSR scores) and if needed additional lessons (5G-schema, coping styles, humor, non-verbal communication and emotion regulation). Finally, the participant learns and plans how to use the Internet and mobile phone in a safe and secure manner (PO 11).

Development

The web-based tailored pieces of advice were developed using special software (Nettailor, Evident, the Netherlands), a program that has been developed specifically for web-based tailored interventions, using digital guides in the delivery of the intervention. Research indicates that the integration of an intervention into a website enhances participants' outcomes and retention [40]. Therefore, the web-based tailored pieces of advice were integrated into a website (http://www.pestkoppenstoppen.nl) (see Figure 6). On this website information about the intervention can be found. After logging in, participants can read general information and watch YouTube video clips about (cyber)bullying, follow the web-based tailored pieces of advice and/or answer the questionnaires.

Figure 6: The website *Online Pestkoppenstoppen.*

Pretest of the Interventions

Parts of the focus group interviews conducted for the development of this intervention were pre- and pilot tests. Members of the target group were instructed to go to the website, complete the questionnaires and follow the pieces of advice. Next, six focus group interviews were held with a total of 41 participants from 4 schools. Based on the results from the pretests, pilot tests and focus group interviews, several adjustments were made: lay-out issues were resolved, bugs were repaired and both the number of questions and the amount of content were reduced.

Step 5: Adoption and Implementation

A plan for the adoption, implementation and continuation of the web-based tailored intervention was developed. To facilitate adoption and implementation, a linkage group was formed [44]. The intervention was developed in such a way that the potential for adoption, implementation and continuation is enhanced. For example, intervention users can find, register and use the intervention online. Therefore, the implementation of the intervention does not need additional human actions. The only actions needed and costs associated with the implementation, adoption and continuation are recruiting participating schools or individuals, hosting the website, preparing the intervention for implementation after the research has been conducted, and keeping the information up-to-date. Hence, the intervention can easily reach a large number of adolescents and at very low costs.

Step 6: Planning for Evaluation

The evaluation of the program - which is described below - was planned. The research on the effectiveness of the intervention *Online Pestkoppenstoppen* has been approved by the Medical Ethics Committee of the Atrium Hospital of Heerlen (NL39072.096.12; METC nr. 12-T-126), and is registered in the Dutch Trial Register (http://NTR3613).

Design and Procedure

A three-group (experimental group, general information group and waiting list control group) randomized control trial (RCT) will be conducted to evaluate the efficacy of the intervention, with self-assessed measures at baseline (T0), before advice two (T1), before advice three (T2), a half-year post start (T3) and 1 year post start (T4) (see Figure 7). Statements about the effectiveness of the three tailored web-based pieces of advice compared to general information can be made by comparing the experimental group with the general information group. The waiting list control group allows for controlling internal validation issues such as aging. However, this group does not receive measurements at T4. After the research, both the waiting list control group and general information group will be allowed to use the intervention.

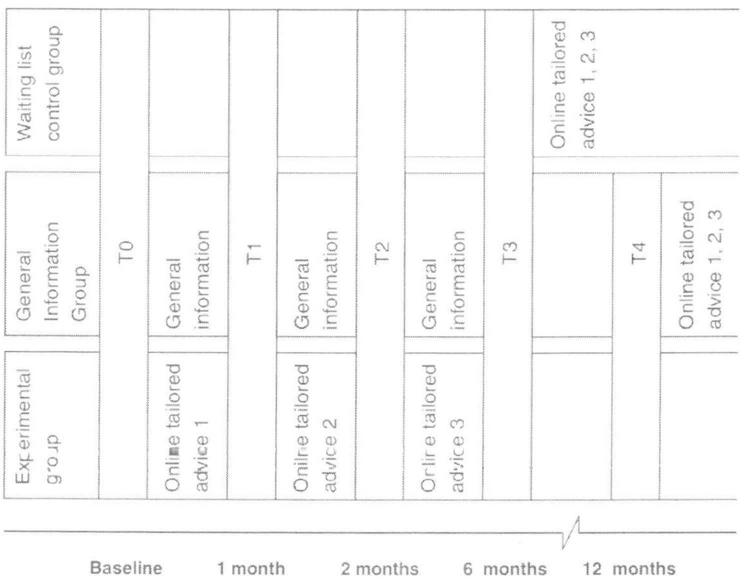

Figure 7: Timing and distribution of the measuring moments between the three conditions.

Participants will be recruited via contacting all secondary vocational education schools in the Netherlands. When schools give their consent to participation, randomization will follow. Schools will be stratified on three categories; a) size (small, medium or large); b) location of school (urban or rural); and c) type of education (theoretical or both theoretical and vocational). Schools will be matched and randomly assigned to one of the three intervention conditions. After randomization, all participants will attend a lesson at school in which the research will be explained. Participants receive a written information letter and informed consent, which has to be signed by both the participant and his or her parent(s). Next, participants have to visit the website and complete the selection questionnaire. When a participant meets the inclusion criteria, registration will follow and the research and intervention procedure will start.

A back-up plan was created in case the above-mentioned method of recruiting did not provide a sufficient number of participants. In case of insufficient participants, adolescents are recruited by placing a message on several popular websites often visited by adolescents and/or their parents. Additionally, recruitment messages are sent via Facebook, LinkedIn and Twitter. In this message individual adolescents are recruited to participate in the research by asking them to send us an e-mail with their name, age, name of school and level of education. Next, they receive instructions (written and on video), a written information letter and informed consent for them and their parents. In case parents read the message, they are asked to let their child participate in the research. Only after the adolescent provides us with the signed informed consents from them and their parents, will a login code be sent to the participant with which (s)he can access the intervention and/or research.

Measurement Instruments

To evaluate the effectiveness of the intervention, several concepts will be measured via self-reported questionnaires. The primary outcomes of this study are frequency of (cyber)bullying, psychological wellbeing, problem behavior, school performance and truancy. These will be assessed at baseline (T0), 6 (T3) and 12 months (T4) follow-up. The secondary outcomes of this study (i.e. moderators or working mechanisms (mediators) of the intervention) are irrational thoughts, self-efficacy, coping with cyberbullying and self-esteem. These will be assessed at baseline (T0), after 1 (T1), 2 (T2), 6 (T3) and 12 months (T4) follow-up. At baseline, several moderators will be measured as well (i.e. demographic characteristics such as gender, age, educational level). In addition, a process evaluation at T3 will be conducted to examine potential moderators.

Power Calculation

The power analysis is based on two important dependencies: decrease in psychosocial problems and the amount of cyberbullying victims after the intervention. The outcomes are based on the PaS training [122]. A power calculation (effect size=.3; power=.80; intracluster correlation coefficient=.1) showed that at baseline about 446 participants were needed (based on a dropout rate of 20%). Based on previous studies we suspect that 25% of the adolescents between 12 and 15 years can be classified as cyberbullying victims, and that 50% of the adolescents are willing to participate. This results in 3570 adolescents, divided over 30 schools, with each school having 4 or 5 classes.

DISCUSSION

The aim of this paper was to provide a detailed description of the systematic development of the three web-based tailored pieces of advice for cyberbully victims that aimed at increasing psychological wellbeing, and decreasing victimization, problem behavior, school problems and truancy. In this intervention, cyberbully victims learn how to recognize, dispute and replace irrational thoughts with rational thoughts. Furthermore, their ineffective coping strategies are replaced with effective coping strategies, and they learn how to use the Internet and mobile phone in a safe and secure manner. The intervention is delivered online, via digital guides in digital environments. Digital guides provide information, ask questions, and show videos, pictures, comics and animations.

This intervention has several strengths. First, in developing, implementing and evaluating a systematic approach [44], the Intervention Mapping approach is used. In the process of developing the intervention, empirical evidence, theories, guidelines and recommendations from the cyberbullying and bullying intervention and prevention literature were used to build a solid framework. Second, the intervention aims to change multiple determinants that were found in a study done by Jacobs et al., [70]. Third, guidelines and recommendations from other, not related to (cyber)bullying, intervention studies and theories were used, combined with results from focus groups interviews with the target groups. Fourth, this intervention is tailored to the specific needs of the target group: cyberbully victims are often unwilling to tell a teacher, parent or other adult that they need help. Therefore, they may feel more comfortable to [33] find help anonymously on the Internet [31]. Furthermore, we tried to incorporate all preferences of the target group as indicated in the pre-tests and pilot tests. Fifth, web-based computer tailored interventions can be used any time [35], can reach a lot of people in a relatively cheap way [36], and allow for tailoring [37], which has the potential for a successful health promotion technique [38, 39]. Sixth, the planned RCT allows several important conclusions to be drawn. Finally, a process evaluation allows us to draw conclusions about several working mechanisms.

This intervention has a number of limitations. First, it was difficult to reduce the number of questions in the questionnaires we used for evaluation purposes. In the focus group interviews, members of the target group clearly stated that too many questions will lead to drop-out, because answering many questions is experienced as boring and fatiguing. Furthermore, too many questions may cause no-saying or yes-saying and response fatigue (for a review, see [123]), leading to less reliable results. Second, the intervention may contain too much information. Based on the literature, it was decided to include the 5G-schema, coping strategies, social skills, planning and safety instructions. In focus group interviews, members of the target-group mentioned the large amount of information making it difficult to remember everything. Third, we cannot exactly check the degree of usage on the experimental and general information. This may hamper the interpretation of the results. Therefore, we have added process evaluation questions, in which we ask the participants if they have read the information.

In conclusion, the *Online Pestkoppenstoppen* program seems to be a promising start in solving current cyberbullying problems. The results of the evaluation studies, which will be reported in other papers, may contribute to the knowledge about how to stop online victimization and how to use tailoring and web-based interventions in this purpose. Additionally, this intervention may also affect offline victimization, because despite the differences, cyberbullying and traditional bullying also have some overlapping characteristics [24, 25, 27]. The results can be used as input for other web-based and computer-tailored interventions aimed at cyberbully victims. If the studies point out that the intervention is effective in its purpose, we have an intervention ready for implementation on a large scale.

DECLARATIONS

Acknowledgements

This work was supported by the Dutch Ministry of Education, Culture and Science [grant number ODB10001]. We would like to thank Peter-Paul Lenssen from the Bernardinuscollege for providing the filming locations and actors, and Jetze Jansma from Kumulus Jeugdtheater for providing actors. Additionally, we would like to thank Pepijn van Halderen, Joelle Canisius, Pim Hovens, Yorn Heijnen, Melissa Vermeulen, Julie Cosemans, Vera Nijssen, Luca Meisters, Benno Geurts, Iris Voogt and Sophie Berg for doing such a great job acting in the movies. We also would like to thank

Sophie Mulder, Jaron Bos, Saskia Wouters, Rick Jacobs and Janneke Duker for providing their voices, and Marcel Maassen for recording and editing the voice recordings. A big thank you goes to Sandra Daems and Annette Bouwels-Hermens for recording and editing several extra movie clips that were used in the recruitment of schools and introducing the participants with the intervention. We would also like to thank Nikki Gerits and Steffi Bekkers for conducting two focus group interviews. Finally, we would like to thank Linda Goossens (research assistant for this project), for all of her hard work and excellent planning and organizing skills.

Authors' Contributions

NJ conceived of the study, developed the online tailored advices, looked for participants, drafted the manuscript and processed all feedback from the other authors. FD and TV helped in brainstorming for- and developing the intervention, looking for participants, helped to draft the manuscript and helped in drafting the final manuscript. LL supervised the whole research and helped with drafting and writing the final manuscript. All authors read and approved the final manuscript.

REFERENCES

1. Gross EF: Adolescent Internet use: What we expect, what teens report. J Appl Dev Psychol. 2004, 25 (6): 633-649. 10.1016/j.appdev.2004.09.005.
2. Smith PK, Mahdavi J, Carvalho M, Fisher S, Russell S, Tippett N: Cyberbullying: its nature and impact in secondary school pupils. J Child Psychol Psychiatry. 2008, 49 (4): 376-385. 10.1111/j.1469-7610.2007.01846.x.
3. Tokunaga RS: Following you home from school: A critical review and synthesis of research on cyberbullying victimization. Comput Hum Behav. 2010, 26 (3): 277-287. 10.1016/j.chb.2009.11.014.
4. Perren S, Dooley J, Shaw T, Cross D: Bullying in school and cyberspace: Associations with depressive symptoms in Swiss and Australian adolescents. Child Adolesc Psychiat Ment Health. 2010, 4 (1): 1-10. 10.1186/1753-2000-4-1.
5. Ybarra ML, Mitchell KJ: Online aggressor/targets, aggressors, and targets: a comparison of associated youth characteristics. J Child Psychol Psychiatry. 2004, 45 (7): 1308-1316. 10.1111/j.1469-7610.2004.00328.x.
6. Campbell M, Spears B, Slee P, Butler D, Kift S: Victims' perceptions of traditional and cyberbullying, and the psychosocial correlates of their victimisation. Emotional Behav Difficulties. 2012, 17 (3–4): 389-401.
7. Hinduja S, Patchin JW: Bullying, cyberbullying, and suicide. Arch Suicide Res. 2010, 14 (3): 206-221. 10.1080/13811118.2010.494133.
8. Schneider SK, O'Donnell L, Stueve A, Coulter RWS: Cyberbullying, school bullying, and psychological distress: A regional census of high school students. Am J Public Health. 2012, 102 (1): 171-177. 10.2105/AJPH.2011.300308.
9. Beran T, Li Q: The relationship between cyberbullying and school bullying. J Stud Wellbeing. 2007, 1 (2): 15-33.
10. Katzer C, Fetchenhauer D, Belschak F: Cyberbullying: who are the victims? a comparison of victimization in internet chatrooms and victimization in school. J Media Psychol. 2009, 21 (1): 25-36. 10.1027/1864-1105.21.1.25.
11. Raskauskas J, Stoltz AD: Involvement in traditional and electronic bullying among adolescents. Dev Psychol. 2007, 43 (3): 564-575.

12. Ybarra ML: Linkages between depressive symptomatology and Internet harassment among young regular internet users. Cyber Psychol Behav. 2004, 7 (2): 247-257. 10.1089/109493104323024500.
13. Ybarra ML, Mitchell KJ, Wolak J, Finkelhor D: Examining characteristics and associated distress related to internet harassment: findings from the second youth internet safety survey. Pediatrics. 2006, 118 (4): e1169-e1177. 10.1542/peds.2006-0815.
14. Ybarra ML, Mitchell KJ, Wolak J, Finkelhor D: Examining characteristics and associated distress related to internet harassment: findings from the second youth internet safety survey. Pediatrics. 2007, 118 (4): 1169-1177.
15. Beran T, Li Q: Cyber-harassment: a study of a new method for an old behavior. J Educ Comput Res. 2005, 32 (3): 265-277. 10.2190/8YQM-B04H-PG4D-BLLH.
16. Lewinsohn PM, Hops H, Roberts RE, Seeley JR, Andrews JA: Adolescent psychopathology: i prevalence and incidence of depression and other dsm-iii-r disorders in high school students. J Abnorm Psychol. 1993, 102 (1): 133-144.
17. Schoffstall CL, Cohen R: Cyber aggression: The relation between online offenders and offline social competence. Soc Dev. 2011, 20 (3): 587-604. 10.1111/j.1467-9507.2011.00609.x.
18. Låftman SB, Modin B, Östberg V: Cyberbullying and subjective health: A large-scale study of students in Stockholm, Sweden. Child Youth Serv Rev. 2013, 35 (1): 112-119. 10.1016/j.childyouth.2012.10.020.
19. Slonje R, Smith PK, Frisén A: The nature of cyberbullying, and strategies for prevention. Comput Hum Behav. 2013, 29 (1): 26-32. 10.1016/j.chb.2012.05.024.
20. Paul S, Smith PK, Blumberg HH: Comparing student perceptions of coping strategies and school interventions in managing bullying and cyberbullying incidents. Pastoral Care in Educ. 2012, 30 (2): 127-146. 10.1080/02643944.2012.679957.
21. Snakenborg J, Van Acker R, Gable RA: Cyberbullying: Prevention and Intervention to Protect Our Children and Youth. Prev Sch Fail. 2011, 55 (2): 88-95. 10.1080/1045988X.2011.539454.
22. Patchin JW, Hinduja S: Traditional and Nontraditional Bullying Among Youth: A Test of General Strain Theory. Youth Soc. 2011, 43 (2): 727-751. 10.1177/0044118X10366951.

23. Tenenbaum LS, Varjas K, Meyers J, Parris L: Coping strategies and perceived effectiveness in fourth through eighth grade victims of bullying. Sch Psychol Int. 2011, 32 (3): 263-287. 10.1177/0143034311402309.
24. Olweus D: Invited expert discussion paper Cyberbullying: An overrated phenomenon?. Eur J Dev Psychol. 2012, 9 (5): 1-19.
25. Hinduja S, Patchin JW: Cyberbullying: An Exploratory Analysis of Factors Related to Offending and Victimization. Deviant Behav. 2008, 29 (2): 129-156. 10.1080/01639620701457816.
26. Hemphill SA, Kotevski A, Tollit M, Smith R, Herrenkohl TI, Toumbourou JW, Catalano RF: Longitudinal Predictors of Cyber and Traditional Bullying Perpetration in Australian Secondary School Students. J Adolesc Health. 2012, 51 (1): 59-65. 10.1016/j.jadohealth.2011.11.019.
27. Casas JA, Del Rey R, Ortega-Ruiz R: Bullying and cyberbullying: Convergent and divergent predictor variables. Comput Hum Behav. 2013, 29 (3): 580-587. 10.1016/j.chb.2012.11.015.
28. Ang RP, Goh DH: Cyberbullying Among Adolescents: The Role of Affective and Cognitive Empathy, and Gender. Child Psychiatry Hum Dev. 2010, 41 (4): 387-397. 10.1007/s10578-010-0176-3.
29. Barlińska J, Szuster A, Winiewski M: Cyberbullying among adolescent bystanders: Role of communication medium, form of violence, and empathy. J Commun Applied Social Psychol. 2013, 23: 37-51. 10.1002/casp.2137.
30. Slonje R, Smith PK: Cyberbullying: Another main type of bullying?. Scand J Psychol. 2008, 49 (2): 147-154. 10.1111/j.1467-9450.2007.00611.x.
31. Ahlfors R: Many Sources, One Theme: Analysis of Cyberbullying Prevention and Intervention Websites. J Soc Sci. 2010, 6 (4): 515-522.
32. Lenhart A, Purcell K, Smith A, Zickuhr K: Social Media & Mobile Internet Use among Teens and Young Adults. 2010, Washington, DC: Pew Research Center, Pew Internet & American Life Project
33. Webb M, Burns J, Collin P: Providing online support for young people with mental health difficulties: challenges and opportunities explored. Early Interv Psychiatry. 2008, 2 (2): 108-113. 10.1111/j.1751-7893.2008.00066.x.
34. Havas J, de Nooijer J, Crutzen R, Feron F: Adolescents' views about an internet platform for adolescents with mental health problems. Health

Educ. 2011, 111 (3): 164-176. 10.1108/09654281111123466.

35. Oenema A, Brug J, Dijkstra A, Weerdt I, Vries H: Efficacy and Use of an Internet-delivered Computer-tailored Lifestyle Intervention, Targeting Saturated Fat Intake, Physical Activity and Smoking Cessation: A Randomized Controlled Trial. Ann Behav Med. 2008, 35 (2): 125-135. 10.1007/s12160-008-9023-1.

36. Cobiac J, Vos T, Barendregt J: Cost-effectiveness of interventions to promote physical activity: a modelling study. PLoS Med. 2009, 6 (7): e1000110-10.1371/journal.pmed.1000110.

37. De Vries H, Brug J: Computer-tailored interventions motivating people to adopt health promoting behaviours: Introduction to a new approach. Patient Educ Couns. 1999, 36 (2): 99-195.

38. Noar SM, Benac CN, Harris MS: Does tailoring matter? Meta-analytic review of tailored print health behavior change interventions. Psychol Bull. 2007, 133 (4): 673-693.

39. Krebs P, Prochaska JO, Rossi JS: A meta-analysis of computer-tailored interventions for health behavior change. Prev Med. 2010, 51 (3–4): 214-221.

40. Brug J, Oenema A, Kroeze W, Raat H: The internet and nutrition education: challenges and opportunities. Eur J Clin Nutr. 2005, 59: S130-S139.

41. Smith PK, Salmivalli C, Cowie H: Effectiveness of school-based programs to reduce bullying: a commentary. J Exp Criminol. 2012, 8 (4): 433-441. 10.1007/s11292-012-9142-3.

42. Michie S, Johnston M, Francis J, Hardeman W, Eccles M: From Theory to Intervention: Mapping Theoretically Derived Behavioural Determinants to Behaviour Change Techniques. Appl Psychol. 2008, 57 (4): 660-680. 10.1111/j.1464-0597.2008.00341.x.

43. Webb TL, Joseph J, Yardley L, Michie S: Using the internet to promote health behavior change: a systematic review and meta-analysis of the impact of theoretical basis, use of behavior change techniques, and mode of delivery on efficacy. J Med Internet Res. 2010, 12 (1): e4-10.2196/jmir.1376. Central

44. Bartholomew LK, Parcel GS, Kok G, Gottlieb NH, Fernández ME: Planning Health Promotion Programs: An Intervention Mapping Approach. 2011, San Francisco: Jossey-Bass

45. Green LW, Kreuter MW: Health Program Planning: An Educational And Ecological Approach. 2005, New York: McGraw-Hill

46. van der Vegt AL, den Blanken M, Jepma I: Nationale scholierenmonitor: meting voorjaar 2007. Onderwijsvernieuwingenrosernl. 2007, http://www.hetccv.nl/dossiers/geweld-op-school/landelijk---nationale-scholierenmonitor-2007

47. Walrave M, Heirman W: Cyberbullying: Predicting Victimisation and Perpetration. Child Soc. 2011, 25 (1): 59-72. 10.1111/j.1099-0860.2009.00260.x.

48. Wade A, Beran T: Cyberbullying: The new era of bullying. Can J Sch Psychol. 2011, 26 (1): 44-61. 10.1177/0829573510396318.

49. Gavin LA, Furman W: Age differences in adolescents' perceptions of their peer groups. Dev Psychol. 1989, 25 (5): 827

50. Faber M, Verkerk G, van Aken M, Lissenburg L, Geerlings M: Plezier op school: sterker naar de brugklas. Kind en Adolescent Praktijk. 2006, 5 (1): 31-39. 10.1007/BF03059577.

51. Lazarus RS, Folkman S: Stress, appraisal, and coping. 1984, New York: Springer

52. Craig W, Pepler D, Blais J: Responding to bullying: what works. Sch Psychol Int. 2007, 28 (4): 465-477. 10.1177/0143034307084136.

53. Kowalski RM, Limber SP, Agatston PW: Cyber Bullying: Bullying in the digital age. 2008, Malden: Blackwell Publishing

54. Mahady Wilton MM, Craig WM, Pepler DJ: Emotional regulation and display in classroom victims of bullying: characteristic expressions of affect, coping styles and relevant contextual factors. Soc Dev. 2000, 9 (2): 226-245.

55. Kristensen SM, Smith PK: The use of coping strategies by Danish children classed as bullies, victims, bully/victims, and not involved, in response to different (hypothetical) types of bullying. Scand J Psychol. 2003, 44: 479-488. 10.1046/j.1467-9450.2003.00369.x.

56. Bijttebier P, Vertommen H: Coping with peer arguments in school-age children with bully/vcitim problems. Br J Educ Psychol. 1998, 68 (3): 387-394. 10.1111/j.2044-8279.1998.tb01299.x.

57. Dooley JJ, Shaw T, Cross D: The association between the mental health and behavioural problems of students and their reactions to cyber-victimization. Eur J Dev Psychol. 2012, 9 (2): 275-289. 10.1080/17405629.2011.648425.

58. Dehue F, Bolman C, Völlink T: Cyberbullying: youngsters' experiences and parental perception. Cyber Psychol Behav. 2008, 11 (2): 217-223. 10.1089/cpb.2007.0008.
59. Acirak OT: Psychiatric symptomatology as predictor of cyberbullying among university students. Eurasian J Educ Res. 2009, 34: 167-184.
60. Riebel JRSJ, Fischer UC: Cyberbullying in Germany – an exploration of prevalence, overlapping with real life bullying and coping strategies. Psychol Sci Q. 2009, 51 (3): 298-314.
61. Perren S, Corcoran L, Cowie H, Dehue F, Garcia D, Mc Guckin C, Sevcikova A, Tsatsou P, Völlink T: Tackling cyberbullying: Review of empirical evidence regarding successful responses by students, parents, and schools. Int J Conflict Violence. 2012, 6 (2): 283-292.
62. Parris L, Varjas K, Meyers J, Cutts H: High School Students' Perceptions of Coping With Cyberbullying. Youth Soc. 2012, 44 (2): 284-306. 10.1177/0044118X11398881.
63. Skrzypiec G, Slee P, Murray-Harvey R, Pereira B: School bullying by one or more ways: Does it matter and how students cope?. Sch Psychol Int. 2011, 32 (3): 288-311. 10.1177/0143034311402308.
64. Andreou E: Bully/Victim Problems and their Association with Coping Behaviour in Conflictual Peer Interactions Among School-age Children. Educ Psychol. 2001, 21 (1): 59-66. 10.1080/01443410125042.
65. Hunter SC, Boyle JME: Appraisal and coping strategy use in victims of school bullying. Br J Educ Psychol. 2004, 74 (1): 83-107. 10.1348/000709904322848833.
66. Perry DG, Hodges EVE, Egan SK, Juvonen J, Graham S: Determinants of Chronic Victimization by Peers: A Review and New Model of Family Influence. Peer Harassment in School: The Plight of the Vulnerable and Victimized. 2001, New York, NY, US: Guilford Press, 73-104.
67. Kanetsuna T, Smith PK, Morita Y: Coping with bullying at school: children's recommended strategies and attitudes to school-based interventions in England and Japan. Aggress Behav. 2006, 32 (6): 570-580. 10.1002/ab.20156.
68. Völlink T, Bolman CAW, Dehue F, Jacobs NCL: Coping with Cyberbullying: Differences Between Victims, Bully-victims and Children not Involved in Bullying. J Commun Applied Soc Psychol. 2013, 23 (1): 7-24. 10.1002/casp.2142.

69. Neary A, Joseph S: Peer victimization and its relationship to self-concept and depression among school girls. Personal Individ Differ. 1994, 16 (1): 183-186. 10.1016/0191-8869(94)90122-8.

70. Jacobs NCL, Dehue F, Völlink T, Lechner L: Determinants of adolescents' ineffective and improved coping with cyberbullying: a Delphi study. J Adolesc. 2014, 37 (4): 373-385. 10.1016/j.adolescence.2014.02.011.

71. Cook CR, Williams KR, Guerra NG, Kim TE, Sadek S: Predictors of bullying and victimization in childhood and adolescence: a meta-analytic investigation. Sch Psychol Q. 2010, 25 (2): 65-83.

72. Bauman S: Cyberbullying in a rural intermediate school: An exploratory study. J Early Adolesc. 2010, 30 (6): 803-833. 10.1177/0272431609350927.

73. Ellis A: The essence of RET. J Ration Emot Cogn Behav Ther. 1984, 2 (1): 19-25. 10.1007/BF02283005.

74. Ellis A: Changing Rational-emotive therapy (RET) to Rational, emotive behavior therapy (REBT). J Ration Emot Cogn Behav Ther. 1995, 13 (2): 85-89. 10.1007/BF02354453.

75. Ringrose HJ, Nijenhuis EH: Bang zijn voor andere kinderen. 1986, Groningen: Wolters-Noordhoff

76. Ellis A: Overcoming Destructive Beliefs, Feelings and Behaviors: New Directions for Rational Emotive Therapy. 2001, New York: Prometheus Books

77. MacInnes D: The theories underpinning rational emotive behaviour therapy: where's the supportive evidence?. Int J Nurs Stud. 2004, 41 (6): 685-695. 10.1016/j.ijnurstu.2004.02.004.

78. Erdur-Baker Ö: Cyberbullying and its correlation to traditional bullying, gender and frequent and risky usage of internet-mediated communication tools. New Media Soc. 2010, 12 (1): 109-125. 10.1177/1461444809341260.

79. Hinduja S, Patchin JW: Offline consequences of online victimization. J Sch Violence. 2007, 6 (3): 89-112. 10.1300/J202v06n03_06.

80. Kim YS, Leventhal BL, Koh Y, Hubbard A, Boyce WT: School Bullying and Youth Violence. Arch Gen Psychiatry. 2006, 63: 1035-1041. 10.1001/archpsyc.63.9.1035.

81. Gonzalez JE, Nelson JR, Gutkin TB, Saunders A, Galloway A, Shwery CS: Rational Emotive Therapy With Children and Adolescents:

A Meta-Analysis. J Emot Behav Disord. 2004, 12 (4): 222-235. 10.1177/10634266040120040301.

82. Banks T, Zionts P: REBT Used with Children and Adolescents who have Emotional and Behavioral Disorders in Educational Settings: A Review of the Literature. J Ration Emot Cogn Behav Ther. 2009, 27 (1): 51-65. 10.1007/s10942-008-0081-x.
83. Woods S, Wolke D, Nowicki S, Hall L: Emotion recognition abilities and empathy of victims of bullying. Child Abuse Negl. 2009, 33 (5): 307-311. 10.1016/j.chiabu.2008.11.002.
84. Nowicki S, Duke MP: Individual differences in the nonverbal communication of affect: The Diagnostic Analysis of Nonverbal Accuracy Scale. J Nonverbal Behav. 1994, 18 (1): 9-35. 10.1007/BF02169077.
85. Kokkinos C, Kipritsi E: The relationship between bullying, victimization, trait emotional intelligence, self-efficacy and empathy among preadolescents. Soc Psychol Educ. 2011, 15 (1): 41-58.
86. Austin EJ, Saklofske DH, Egan V: Personality, well-being and health correlates of trait emotional intelligence. Personal Individ Differ. 2005, 38 (3): 547-558. 10.1016/j.paid.2004.05.009.
87. Mishna F, Cook C, Gadalla T, Daciuk J, Solomon S: Cyber Bullying Behaviors Among Middle and High School Students. Am J Orthopsychiatry. 2010, 80 (3): 362-374.
88. Price M, Dalgleish J: Cyberbullying: experiences, impacts and coping strategies as described by Australian young people. Youth Stud Australia. 2010, 29 (2): 51-59.
89. Fanti KA, Demetriou AG, Hawa VV: A longitudinal study of cyberbullying: Examining riskand protective factors. Eur J Dev Psychol. 2012, 9 (2): 168-181. 10.1080/17405629.2011.643169.
90. Kochenderfer-Ladd B: Peer Victimization: The Role of Emotions in Adaptive and Maladaptive Coping. Soc Dev. 2004, 13 (3): 329-349. 10.1111/j.1467-9507.2004.00271.x.
91. Cross D, Monks H, Campbell MA, Spears B, Slee P: School-based strategies to address cyber bullying. Centre for Strategic Education Occasional Papers. 2011, 119: 1-12.
92. Boulton MJ, Smith PK, Cowie H: Short-Term Longitudinal Relationships Between Children's Peer Victimization/Bullying Experiences and Self-Perceptions Evidence for Reciprocity. Sch

Psychol Int. 2010, 31 (3): 296-311. 10.1177/0143034310362329.

93. Jones SE, Manstead ASR, Livingstone AG: Ganging up or sticking together? Group processes and children's responses to text-message bullying. Br J Psychol. 2011, 102 (1): 71-96.
94. Camodeca M, Goossens FA: Children's opinions on effective strategies to cope with bullying: The importance of bullying role and perspective. Educ Res. 2005, 47 (1): 93-105. 10.1080/0013188042000337587.
95. Vandebosch H, van Cleemput K: Cyberbullying among youngsters: profiles for bullies and victims. New Media Soc. 2009, 11 (8): 1349-1371. 10.1177/1461444809341263.
96. Hinduja S, Patchin JW: Bullying beyond the Schoolyard: Preventing and Responding to Cyberbullying. 2009, California: Corwin press
97. Valcke M, De Wever B, Van Keer H, Schellens T: Long-term study of safe Internet use of young children. Comput Educ. 2011, 57 (1): 1292-1305. 10.1016/j.compedu.2011.01.010.
98. Kok G, Schaalma H, Ruiter RAC, Van Empelen P, Brug J: Intervention Mapping: Protocol for Applying Health Psychology Theory to Prevention Programmes. J Health Psychol. 2004, 9 (1): 85-98. 10.1177/1359105304038379.
99. Bandura A: Social Foundations of Thought and Action: a Social Cognitive Theory. 1986, Englewood Cliffs, NJ: Prentice Hall
100. Bandura A: Perceived Self-Efficacy in Cognitive Development and Functioning. Educ Psychol. 1993, 28 (2): 117-148. 10.1207/s15326985ep2802_3.
101. Kreuter M, Farrell D, Olevitch L, Brennan L: Tailoring Health Messages: Customizing Communication with Computer Technology. 2000, Mahwah, NJ: Erlbaum
102. de Vries H, Kremers SPJ, Smeets T, Brug J, Eijmael K: The Effectiveness of Tailored Feedback and Action Plans in an Intervention Addressing Multiple Health Behaviors. Am J Health Promot. 2008, 22 (6): 417-425. 10.4278/ajhp.22.6.417.
103. Brug J, Oenema A, Campbell M: Past, present, and future of computer-tailored nutrition education. Am J Clin Nutri. 2003, 77 (4): 1028S-1034S.
104. McManus IC, Livingston G, Katona C: The attractions of medicine: the generic motivations of medical school applicants in relation to demography, personality and achievement. BMC Med Educ. 2006, 6:

11-10.1186/1472-6920-6-11.

105. Caspi A, Bem DJ: Personality Continuity and Change across the Life Course. Handbook of Personality: Theory and Research. Edited by: Pervin LA. 1990, New York: Guilford Press, 549-575.
106. Petty RE, Cacioppo JT: The Elaboration Likelihood Model of Persuasion. Communication and Persuasion. 1986, New York: Springer, 1-24.
107. Bandura A: Self-efficacy: The exercise of control. 1997, New York: W.H. Freeman
108. Woolfolk A: Educational Psychology. 2010, Boston: Allyn & Bacon
109. Jackson RA, Stotland NE, Caughey AB, Gerbert B: Improving diet and exercise in pregnancy with Video Doctor counseling: a randomized trial. Patient Educ Couns. 2011, 83 (2): 203-209. 10.1016/j.pec.2010.05.019.
110. Vandelanotte C, Mummery WK: Qualitative and quantitative research into the development and feasibility of a video-tailored physical activity intervention. Int J Behav Nutr Phys Act. 2011, 8 (1): 70-10.1186/1479-5868-8-70.
111. Sniehotta FF, Scholz U, Schwarzer R: Bridging the intention–behaviour gap: Planning, self-efficacy, and action control in the adoption and maintenance of physical exercise. Psychol Health. 2005, 20 (2): 143-160. 10.1080/08870440512331317670.
112. Sniehotta FF, Schwarzer R, Scholz U, Schüz B: Action planning and coping planning for long-term lifestyle change: theory and assessment. Eur J Soc Psychol. 2005, 35 (4): 565-576. 10.1002/ejsp.258.
113. Leventhal H, Singer R, Jones S: Effects of fear and specificity of recommendation upon attitudes and behavior. J Pers Soc Psychol. 1965, 2 (1): 20-29.
114. Gollwitzer PM, Sheeran P: Implementation intentions: Bibliothek der Universität Konstanz. 2008
115. Sheeran P, Webb TL, Gollwitzer PM: The interplay between goal intentions and implementation intentions. Personal Soc Psychol Bull. 2005, 31 (1): 87-98. 10.1177/0146167204271308.
116. Reuter T, Ziegelmann JP, Wiedemann AU, Geiser C, Lippke S, Schüz B, Schwarzer R: Changes in Intentions, Planning, and Self-efficacy Predict Changes in Behaviors: An Application of Latent True Change Modeling. J Health Psychol. 2010, 15 (6): 935-947. 10.1177/1359105309360071.

117. van Osch L, Lechner L, Reubsaet A, Wigger S, de Vries H: Relapse prevention in a national smoking cessation contest: Effects of coping planning. Br J Health Psychol. 2008, 13 (3): 525-535. 10.1348/135910707X224504.
118. Wiedemann AU, Lippke S, Reuter T, Ziegelmann JP, Schwarzer R: How planning facilitates behaviour change: Additive and interactive effects of a randomized controlled trial. Eur J Soc Psychol. 2011, 41 (1): 42-51. 10.1002/ejsp.724.
119. Araújo-Soares V, McIntyre T, Sniehotta FF: Predicting changes in physical activity among adolescents: the role of self-efficacy, intention, action planning and coping planning. Health Educ Res. 2009, 24 (1): 128-139.
120. Rivers I, Poteat PV, Noret N, Ashurst N: Observing bullying at school: The mental health implications of witness status. Sch Psychol Q. 2009, 24 (4): 211-
121. Achenbach TM: Integrative Guide for the 1991 CBCL/4-18, YSR, and TRF Profiles: Department of Psychiatry. 1991, Burlington: Department of Psychiatry, University of Vermont Burlington
122. Geerlings M, Lissenburg L: Evaluatieonderzoek naar de effectiviteit van de cursus 'Plezier op school'. 2005, Utrecht: Universiteit Utrecht
123. Choi BCK, Pak AWP: A catalog of biases in questionnaires. Prev Chronic Dis. 2005, 2 (1): A13

CHAPTER 19

CRIMINOLOGICAL ANALYSIS OF DETERMINANTS OF CYBERCRIME TECHNOLOGIES

Lola F. Tatarinova[a] **, Karimzhan N. Shakirov**[b] **and Danila V. Tatarinov**[b]

[a] "Turan" University, Kazakhstan

[b]Al-Farabi Kazakh National University, Kazakhstan

ABSTRACT

An important task, the government, particularly law enforcement officers and scientists, faces in the rapid development of information technologies, is to prevent crimes committed with their application. Comprehensive analysis of the criminological characteristics of computer crimes, which is the aim of this study, provides an opportunity to identify the motives of these crimes to determine the most effective ways to eliminate them, as well as to work out the best ways and investigation means of criminal cases in this category. One of the fundamental structural elements of the national security of any state in the period of cyberspace development is to protect all information resources and communication networks against criminal assault. A complete

Citation: Tatarinova, Lola F., Karimzhan N. Shakirov and Danila V. Tatarinov (2016). "Criminological Analysis of Determinants of Cybercrime Technologies". IEJME-Mathematics Education 11 (5):1127-1134.

analysis of computer crimes requires the understanding of motivation of illegal intrusion into information systems in order to obtain the information, stored in them, as well as using the opportunities provided by these systems or disabling the whole system or its components. The statement above is confirmed by the global use of computer technologies, information and communication networks.

Keywords: Criminology, cyber security, information technologies, cryptography, criminological methods

INTRODUCTION

Cybersecurity is possible through the methods of criminology.

The innovation of the article is an attempt to adapt the methods of criminological analysis to cyberspace. K. Driscoll (2016) notes, that cyberspace is an integral part of the encrypted system. Thus, the knowledge of cryptography helps to identify and prevent cybercrimes.

An important tool for protection against computer crimes is cyberhygiene – the improvement of the Internet culture, an integral part of which is the possession of the complex procedures applied by cybercriminals. Many works are written on the "phishing" methodology (Murashbekov, 2015, Leukfeldt, 2015a, Leukfeldt, 2015b,

Leukfeldt, Kleemans & Stol, 2016), but much smaller number of works is devoted to the development of an adequate level of cyberculture (Cross, 2016), which should be developed from an early age.

Moreover, the analysis of the situation shows that the growth of computer crime is partly due to the increasing number of professional users (Murashbekov, 2015).

It is important to note that the development of mechanisms for the protection of computer, information and communication networks will be more effective at the international level than at the local, as this type of crime is transnational.

The data results on committing cybercrimes are visualized in diagrams in Figures 1 and 2.

The topicality of this article is due to the expansion tendency of the global network. By the time the Internet covers the entire planet, it will be necessary to master the complex of cybercrime prevention measures.

The practical value of this paper is in the proposed method of reducing the number of cybercrimes by improving the skills of criminology.

This paper makes a significant contribution to the world of science, as it indicates the actual problems, caused by the current globalist tendencies.

Purpose of the Study

The purpose of this study is to identify the criminological specificities of cyberspace crime.

Research Questions

The objectives of the study include:

- establishing the boundaries for cybercrimes;
- transfer of the means of cyberspace protection;
- cybercrime visualization, comparative and quantitative analysis;
- determining the criminological issues in cyberspace.

METHODS

The methodological basis includes complex comparative analysis, statistical data analysis in the field of cybercrime, as well as an interdisciplinary analysis.

In addition, the research specifics are based on the criminological methods, such as studying documents and observation.

RESULTS

The identification of criminological specifics of cyberspace crime helps to prevent crimes in the sphere of information technologies.

Establishing boundaries for cybercrimes bases both on the information space and the nature of the offense, clearly identifiable as such offline. This study determined the basic ways of cyberspace protection, which lie within the area of cryptography, the basics of which are necessary for the IT-specialists, interested in solving cybercrimes.

The study carried out a quantitative and comparative analysis of cybercrimes, the visual results of which are shown in Figures 1 and 2. It should be noted that the motives of financial crimes are easy to determine, while determining the motives of online crimes against human rights and freedoms applies the same principles, as offline. Similar data were obtained based on the materials on Figure 2, which reveals gaps in the criminological knowledge of experts, because a third of cybercrime was found accidentally. In further studies, it is necessary to develop a set of measures to increase the competence of IT-forensics.

Moreover, determining criminological issues in cyberspace was carried out based on the qualitative criteria, such as specific areas in which a civil cybercrime (material or non-material) was committed.

DISCUSSIONS AND CONCLUSION

This part of the study includes the analysis of the cybercrimes, which are divided into the crimes against personal rights (such as harassment and lack of privacy of writing), crimes against financial security (unsafe e-payment) and crimes against the children's morality (bullying).

First of all, there is a list of points that makes the exploitation of the Internet safer, bonded with the cryptography. K. Driscoll (2016) systematically assures that there are some crypto key-management issues:

- (Inter) national cryptography laws – export, import, use, key management
- Two aspects of key-management – trust: whom do you trust? with what? to do what? logistics: Mechanisms to enforce the trust
- Creation of keys and their ownership/association,
- Key distribution and management,
- Allowing only the authorized users for a set time;
- Handling revocations;
- Distribution needs protection for private and secret keys, even if these keys are only used for authentication; popular authentication schemes need secret keys;
- Ordinary use,
- Extraordinary use,
- The need to access the encrypted "plaintext" – the main reason for the easiest and the most common method is to give government access to the keys (but still it can greatly complicate the key distribution and management),
- Just "use the X. SOg-based public key infrastructure (PKI)", but:

full PKI is heavyweight and does not solve all the problems by itself.

- Mitigating most of these issues for avionics – no secrets are stored on aircraft, which simplifies the airborne side of link.

The way in which young people have integrated online and digital technology into their personal relationships and sexual development is an important emerging issue for researchers and policymakers. Over the past few years, news media in Australia, North America and other Western countries have reported their concern on the cases of sexting, where minors have used the digital cameras on mobile phones to take and distribute sexual images of themselves and/or others, in some cases falling foul of child abuse or child pornography laws (Lee, 2013).

S. Hopkins & J. Ostini (2015) rethink the relationships between technology and violence, as it must spread feminist theories in digital cultures and the problems of gender, sex and power online. Cybersafety campaigns tend to locate the problem with the victim rather than the perpetrator, assuming that in cyberspace, as in the physical world, women are responsible for reducing the risk of being attacked (rather than revealing the power relations that create the domestic and sexual violence in the first place).

According to M.K. Musa (2015), the borderless nature of Internet and its easy access to cyberspace has provided a low-cost but high-connectivity ways for criminals to reach victims. This resulted in a rise of crimes which make use of the Internet as a medium, such as frauds, child sexual exploitations and cyber stalking. Cyber stalking has been labelled to be the crime of the nineties, due to its nature, which uses the latest technological telecommunications as a mean to perpetrate such act. Cyber stalking, similarly to stalking, involves threatening or harassing behaviours by one individual against another, with the exception that this particular act makes full use of the Internet. It contradicts the D. Clairmont & K. Waters (2015) search, including Nova Scotia's position that regularly deals with sexual harassment cases.

Thus, lack of cybersecurity intervenes into personal life and has serious consequences. These illegal actions, in turn, can cause the disruption of critical infrastructure elements' work in any state and result in deaths, property damage or other socially dangerous consequences.

Given the current predictions about the increase in computer crime through IT, the degree of their high latency, as a result of which the investigation and solution of crimes in this area is often carried out long after the commission, it is worth noting, that it is necessary to develop the international standards for protecting information about messages, transmitted through the global information and communication networks.

However, there is an example, studied by C. Angus (2016), C. Chalmers et al. (2016), H. Al-Alosi (2016), where Australian police eliminates cyberbullying with the help of a school and its social elements.

Moreover, researches on media-cyberbullying (Arntfield, 2015) have consistently overlooked the role of victims in online offending, as well as the victim behavior. The M. Arntfield's (2015) study provides an interdisciplinary review of existing researches and proposes a new basis for cybervictimology – the traditional victimology in the context of cyber activities. One of the main criteria of "traditional" bullying is its repetition, so the routine activities of victims in social media environments are key facilitators in the bullying process; they serve as advanced indicators of victimization in a space where anti-social behavior is comparatively tolerated by the absence of suitable guardianship. M. Hughes (2015) conceives that the national plan can partly liquidate the cyberbullying.

M. Williams & O. Pearson (2016) note that a national media campaign on legal protection, available to the victims of cyber-hate, should be launched during the hate crime awareness week. This part of battle is also noticed by D. Cross (2016).

E.R. Leukfeldt, E.R. Kleemans & W.P. Stol (2016) assumes that social ties still play an important role in the origin and growth of the majority of networks. Forums, however, also play a significant role in a number of networks, for example, to find suitable co-offenders or to get into contact with enablers. Criminals with access to forums are able to increase criminal capabilities of their network relatively quickly. Forums would seem to make it easier for loners or small groups to find suitable co-offenders and, potentially, to allow such networks to grow quickly. Forums are also used to acquire knowledge and skills. In the digital era, forums are replacing prisons as the 'university for cybercriminals'. Loners experimenting out of curiosity with all sorts of legal or illegal technical tools can end up in criminal networks through forums. More insight is therefore needed into what prompts individual criminals to become active on forums.

Increasing knowledge about these elements will ensure that we are able to better understand what cybercriminal networks are really like, and what countermeasures can be taken. This is not only of academic interest; it also provides law enforcement with an insight into which counter-strategies work best. It goes without saying that an international network of experts will offer different opportunities and challenges for law enforcement agencies than locally rooted networks of criminal all-rounders (Leukfeldt, 2015a).

Researchers (2015b) also compare (low-tech) phishing attacks and (high-tech) malware attacks. Both types of attacks have, for example, almost the same crime script. Furthermore, both groups of criminals are happy with anything they can get and do not discriminate between the rich and poor. There are also differences.

Firstly, regarding the effect of online visibility, almost none of the variables had any effect on phishing victimization.

The victims of malwares, however, tell a different story. There is a clear connection between spending time online and victimization. There are two types of activities, which ensure a higher chance of becoming a victim, namely downloading and online gaming. The second difference can be found within online accessibility. Again, none of the variables mattered when it came to phishing. The malware analysis, however, shows that users with certain (popular and widely used) operating systems and web browsers do have an increased risk of victimization.

M. Alazab & R. Broadhurst (2015) guess that spam pose a global challenge because this remains a major vector for the dissemination of malfare. It can also be the initial contact point for cybercriminals, such as the operators of a fraudulent scheme, who use emails to contact and solicit prospective victims for money (as in advance see frauds) or to commit identity theft by deceiving recipients of such mail into sharing personal, bank, and financial account information.

J. Kerstens and J. Jansen's (2016) findings demonstrate that the overlap between financial cybercrime victimization and perpetration is partially explained by retaliation, low self-control and on-line disinhibition, suggesting that state-dependency and individual heterogeneity explanations should be supplemented by explanations funded in the dynamics of the on-line environment.

Accounting that the above international regulations on cybercrime are rather contradictory including contradictions in determination of cybercrime, it may cause criminal liability avoidance only due to the state where a cybercrime was committed and the state where the guilty person was apprehended are oriented at different international treaties on cybercrime (including growing significance of mobile devices as the main means of Internet access may cause wider use of those devices by criminals), conceives O.B. Murashbekov (2015).

According to R. Taivo (2015), social networking refers to the use of the Internet to connect with people generally and build a network of friends, professional colleagues, business associates, and so forth. Obviously, wideness of communicative elements involves wideness of potential cybervictims. A.C. Moise (2015) lists these spheres as Government information networks, telecommunication networks, navigation systems for maritime and air transport, water control systems, energetic systems, financial systems, or other functions of vital importance for the society.

But the solution to this problem is not so simple, as the development of common standards for new areas is made difficult by technical differences, existing between states with both fundamental and applied nature.

Based on the analysis, authors present a diagram (Figure 1), showing the main types of computer crimes.

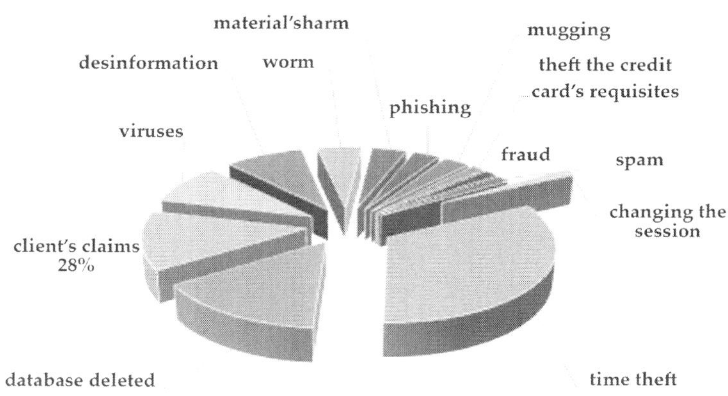

Figure 1. The main computer's crimes.

Another factor, influencing the increase in criminality of the crimes in question, is the existence of legal, legislative and enforcement issues in the field of prevention and fight against crimes in the sphere of computer technologies.

The significant determinants of computer crimes are the gaps in the activities of inquiry and preliminary investigation. This is due to the lack of law enforcement professionals competent in the field of computer technology, as well as the rapid development of the latter, which often are expensive to purchase with the state budget, as opposed to the opportunities of criminal organizations.

However, computer crimes are still recorded, as mostly they are found in the investigation of other crimes. Figure 2 below shows which cases often reveal computer-related crimes.

Thus, the results of this study are quite controversial, as even a society that has come to the legislative regulation of cybercrime, according to D. Clairmont & K. Waters (2015), tends to excuse certain types of civil rights violation (as harassment and sexting), due to the inability to determine them in cyberspace. Perhaps this is partly due to the complexity of determining of the fact of the crime.

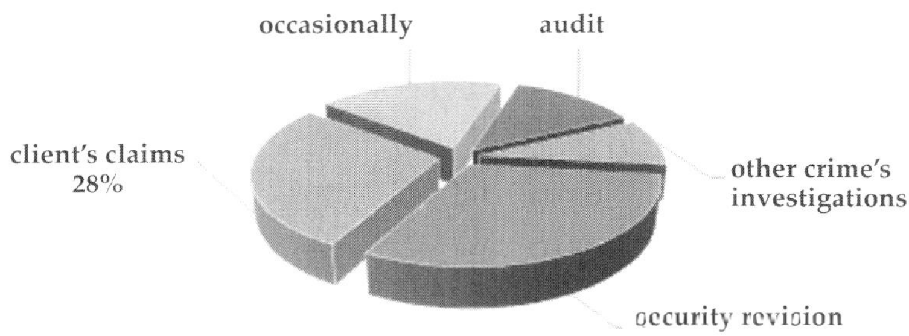

Figure 2. Computer crimes' revealing.

This study takes an important place in the structure of human knowledge, as it contains the results of a multidisciplinary analysis, at the moment not conducted thoroughly in any related disciplines.

IMPLICATIONS AND RECOMMENDATIONS

The scientific value of the article is a comprehensive analysis of possible cooperation between criminology and cybersecurity.

This study opens up the possibility of studying the multidimensional issues of cybersecurity and further liability for committing cybercrime. Practical application of the article may be implemented in the revision of the liability as a result of the cybercrime commission or and implementation into legislation.

The analysis of the causes for the emergence and development of crime in the field of computer technology and computer information leads to the following conclusion: the cross-border nature of the global information and communication networks allows computer criminals to bypass existing state borders, increasing the activity of international organized criminal groups.

Therefore, it is necessary to reinforce in the consciousness of the whole society the existing aspects of computer crime (improving cyberculture), as well as the rapid personnel policy expansion of law enforcement bodies, aimed at improving the level of expertise among employees, involved in the investigation of cases, related to computer crimes.

The stated complex of measures to be implemented at the state level will not only consider the causes and conditions of committing computer crimes, but also take conceptual measures for their prevention and elimination.

The benefits of the proposed investigation method are based on combining methods of one sphere (Criminology) with other spheres (cyberspace), allowing to accurately describe the surrounding reality and to prevent the appearance of crimes in cyberspace.

REFERENCES

1. Al-Alosi, H. (2016) The role of bystanders in cyberbullying. *Precedent NSW Conference in the Sydney, 132,* 20-24.
2. Alazab, M. & Broadhurst, R. (2015) The Role of Spam in Cybercrime: Data from the Australian Cybercrime Pilot Observatory. *Cybercrime Risks and Responses. Palgrave Macmillan*, 103-120.
3. Angus, C. (2016) Cyberbullying of children. *Parliament of NSW Government,* 1-22.
4. Arntfield, M. (2015) Toward a Cybervictimology: Cyberbullying, Routine Activities Theory, and the Anti-Sociality of Social Media. *Canadian Journal of Communication, 40(3),* 138-144.
5. Chalmers, C., Campbell, M., Spears, B., Butler, D., Cross, D., Slee, P. & Kift, S. (2016) School policies on bullying and cyberbullying: perspectives across three Australian states. *Educational Research, 58,* 91-92.
6. Clairmont, D., & Waters, K. (2015*) The Nova Scotia Restorative Justice Program*. Dalhousie: Dalhousie University. 104p.
7. Cross, D. (2016) Longitudinal impact of the Cyber Friendly Schools program on adolescents' cyberbullying behavior. *Aggressive behavior, 42(2),* 166-180.
8. Driscoll, K. (2016) Cyber safety and security for Reduced Crew Operations. *Integrated Communications Navigation and Surveillance*, 1-21. .
9. Hopkins S. & Ostini J. (2015) Digitized Domestic Violence: Technology Abuse is a Feminist Issue. *Media, Technology*, 23-25.
10. Hughes, M. (2015) Facing Cyberbullying: *A National Implementation Plan*. The London Anti-Bullying Coalition, 1-28.
11. Kerstens J. & Jansen J. (2016) The Victim–Perpetrator Overlap in Financial Cybercrime: Evidence and Reflection on the Overlap of Youth's On-Line Victimization and Perpetration. *Deviant Behavior, 37(5),* 585-600.
12. Lee, M. (2015) Sexting among young people: Perceptions and practices. *Trends & Issues in Crime and Criminal Justice, 508*, 1-35.
13. Leukfeldt, E .R. (2015a) Organised Cybercrime and Social Opportunity Structures. A Proposal for Future Research Directions. *European Review of Organised Crime, 2*, 91-103.

14. Leukfeldt, E. R. (2015b) Comparing victims of phishing and malware attacks: Unraveling risk factors and possibilities for situational crime prevention. *arXiv preprint arXiv,* 1506.00769
15. Leukfeldt, E. R., Kleemans, E. R. & Stol, W. P. (2016) Cybercriminal Networks, Social Ties and Online Forums. *British Journal of Criminology, 9*, 35-44.
16. Moise, A. C. (2015) Some Considerations on the Phenomenon of Cyberterrorism. *Law Annals Titu Maiorescu, 5,* 146.
17. Murashbekov, O. B. (2015) Methods for Cybercrime Fighting Improvement in Developed Countries. *The Journal of Internet Banking and Commerce, 5*, 24-29.
18. Musa, M. K. (2015) *Cyber Stalking: Social Issues of Harassment on Internet.* Direct access: idosi.org/aejaes/jaes15(tesms)15/2.pdf
19. Taivo, R. (2015) Cyber Behavior. *Encyclopedia of Information Science and Technology, 3rd Edition, Hershey*, 638-646.
20. Williams M., & Pearson O. (2016) Hate Crime and Bullying in the Age of Social Media. Current Perspectives. *Hate Crime Awareness Week, 35,* 25-26

INDEX

C

R

S

T